A2

ENGLISH LANGUAGE AND LITERATURE

for AQA B

Alison Ross
Jen Greatrex

Heinemann

Published by Heinemann Educational Publishers, Halley Court, Jordan Hill, Oxford OX2 8EJ
A division of Reed Educational and Professional Publishing Ltd

OXFORD MELBOURNE AUCKLAND
JOHANNESBURG BLANTYRE GABORONE
IBADAN PORTSMOUTH (NH) USA CHICAGO

First published 2001

05 04 03 02
10 9 8 7 6 5 4

ISBN 0435 109804

Acknowledgements

The Publishers would like to thank the following for permission to use copyright material:

Extract from *Textual Intervention* by Bob Pope, published by Routledge 1995. Reprinted with permission of ITPS; Extract from 'Connection between reading and writing' by Susan Sontag, published in The Guardian, 22nd January, 2001; 'Musee des Beaux Arts' by W. H. Auden from *Collected Poems* by W. H. Auden, published by Faber and Faber Limited. Reprinted by permission of the publishers; 'Mrs. Icarus' by Carol Ann Duffy, from *The World's Wife* by Carol Ann Duffy published by Picador 2000. (c) Carol Ann Duffy 2000. Reprinted by permission of Macmillan UK; Blurb from the cover of *Island* by Jane Rogers published by Abacus 1999. Reprinted by permission of Little Brown & Co. Ltd, London; Extract from 'digested read' from The Guardian, 25th February, 2000 . Copyright (c) The Guardian, 25th February, 2000. Reprinted with permission; Extract from *Wuthering Heights according to Spike Milligan* by Spike Milligan, published by Penguin. Reprinted by permission of Spike Milligan Productions; 'Pike' by Ted Hughes, from *Lupercal* by Ted Hughes published by Faber and Faber Limited. Reprinted by permission of the publishers; 'You Fit into me' by Margaret Atwood. Reproduced with permission of Curtis Brown Limited, London on behalf of Margaret Atwood, Copyright (c) Margaret Atwood 1971; 'Slavewoman's Song' by David Dabydeen, from 'New Statesman and Society' Jan 1990. Copyright (c) David Dabydeen, reprinted by permission of the author; 'Man to Man' by U. A. Fanthorpe, Copyright U. A. Fanthorpe. Reprinted by permission of the author; Extract from *The Collector* by John Fowles, published by Vintage 1998. Copyright (c) John Fowles 1998. Reprinted by permission of Sheil Land Associates Limited on behalf of the author; 'The Answer' by Frederic Brown, from *Angels and Spaceships*. Copyright (c) 1954 by Frederic Brown, Copyright renewed 1982, by the Estate of Frederic Brown. Reprinted by permission of the author's Estate and its agents, Scott Meredith Literary Agency, LP; 'Dr. Chevalier's Lie' by Kate Chopin (1851-1904); Extracts from 'Business Before Pleasure' by Daphne Glazer from *Last Oasis* by Daphne Glazer, published by Sumach Press. Copyright (c) Daphne Glazer. Reprinted by permission of A. M. Heath & Co. Ltd; Extract from *Road* by Jim Cartwright, published by Methuen. Reprinted by permission of Methuen Publishing Limited; Extract from *Nefertiti and Cleopatra* by Julia Sansom, published by Rubicon 1985; Extract from *Translations* by Brian Friel, published by Faber and Faber Limited. Reprinted by permission of the publishers; Extract 'The use of creole poetry' by David Dabydeen, from 'The State of the Language' edited by Ricks and Michaels and published by Faber and Faber 1990. Copyright (c) David Dabydeen. Reprinted by permission of the author; Extract from *Blood Brothers* by Willy Russell, published by Methuen Drama 1986. Reprinted by permission of Methuen Publishing Limited; Extract from *Big Brother: The Unseen Story* by Jean Ritchie, published by Channel 4 Books, 2000. Reprinted by permission of Macmillan UK; Extract from *Light Shining in Buckinghamshire* by Caryl Churchill, published by Nick Hern Books Limited. Copyright (c) Caryl Churchill. Reprinted by permission of Nick Hern Books Limited; Extract from *Chunky* by Victoria Wood, published by Methuen 1996. Reprinted by permission of Methuen Publishing Limited; Extract from *Educating Rita* by Willy Russell, published by Methuen Drama 1986. Reprinted by permission of Methuen Publishing Limited; Extract from *Cloud Nine* by Caryl Churchill, published by Nick Hern Books Limited. Copyright (c) Caryl Churchill. Reprinted by permission of Nick Hern Books Limited; Extracts from *A phenomenology of working class experience* by Simon J. Charlesworth, published by Cambridge University Press 2001. Reprinted by permission of the publishers; Extract from *White Teeth* by Zadie Smith (Hamish Hamilton 2000) copyright (c) Zadie Smith, 2000. Reprinted by permission of Penguin Books UK; Extract from *Abigail's Party* by Mike Leigh, published by Samuel French, 1979. Copyright (c) Mike Leigh 1979. Reprinted by permission of Peters Fraser & Dunlop on behalf of Mike Leigh; Extract from *Oleanna* by David Mamet, published by Methuen Drama, 1993. Reprinted by permission of Methuen Publishing Limited; Extract from 'Prime Minister's Question Time' transcript of Tony Blair and William Hague, found in The Guardian, January 25th 2001; Extract from *Pinter, The Playwright* by Martin Esslin published by Methuen, 1970. Reprinted by permission of Methuen Publishing Limited; Extract from *The Caretaker* by Harold Pinter, published by Faber and Faber Limited. Reprinted by permission of the publishers; Extract from *Waiting for Godot* by Samuel Beckett , published by Faber and Faber Limited. Reprinted by permission of the publishers; Extract from *In Love and Trouble: Stories of Black Women* by Alice Walker, published by The Women's Press. Reprinted by permission of David Higham Associates Limited; Extract 'Are Britains to become the dunces of the Western World?' By Daniel Johnson, from Daily Telegraph February 8, 2001. (c) Telegraph Group Limited 8 February, 2001. Reprinted with permission; Extract from *Wild Swans* by Jung Chan, published by HarperCollins Publishers 1991. (c) Jung Chan. Reprinted by permission of the publishers; Extract from http://pup.princeton.edu.titles/7024.html Reprinted by permission of Princeton University Press. All rights reserved; 'Review of Chocolat' by Jonathan Romney, first published in The Independent, Sunday 4 March, 2001, and 'Article of Chocolat' by Michele Roberts, first published in The Independent, 24 February, 2001. Reprinted by permission of The Independent, Syndication; Extracts 'Article on Barcelona' by Will Storr, from *Loaded* January 2001, and 'Article on Anthea Turner' by Will Storr, from *Loaded* January 2001, published by IPC Magazines. Reprinted by permission of IPC Syndication; Extract an 'Article on Hunter Davies' by Julie Burchill, in The Guardian Weekend, April 7th, 2001. (c) Julie Burchill. Reprinted by permission of Capel & Co; Extract from 'Interview with Quentin Tarantino, with Laurence Bender, Robert Forster, and Pam Grier. Interviewed by Adrian Wootton, Monday 5th January 1998 about film 'Jackie Brown' transcribed by Harry Counsell and Co, Cliffords Inn, Fetter Lane, London EC4. Used with permission; Extract from *Riding The Rap* by Elmore Leonard (Viking 1995) Copyright (c) Elmore Leonard 1995. Reprinted by permission of Penguin UK; Blurb from the back cover of *The Wasp Factory* by Iain Banks, published by Abacus 1990. Reprinted by permission of Little Brown & Co. Limited, London; Reviews from the back cover of *The Wasp Factory* by Iain Banks, reprinted by permission of Punch; Extract from *Complicity* by Iain Banks, published by Little Brown and Co. 1993. Reprinted by permission of Little Brown & Co. Limited, London; 'Text message poem' by Hetty Hughes, winner of Guardian text message poetry competition, found at www.guardian.co.uk/books May 7 2001 (c) Guardian 2001. Reprinted with permission; Comments on text message poem made by U. A. Fanthorpe, (c) U. A. Fanthorpe. Found at www.guardian.co.uk/books May 7 2001. Reprinted by permission of The Guardian; Extract from *Written on the Body* by Jeanette Winterson, published by Jonathan Cape . Used by permission of The Random House Group Limited; Extracts from 'Some Things to do with English Language Vol 2' and 'some more things to do with Language' published by Sheffield Hallam University Publications. Reprinted by permission of Dr. Dave Hurry, Sheffield Hallam University Press; 'On Receiving a Jamaican Postcard' by Grace Nichols, from *Lazy Thoughts of a Lazy Woman* Copyright (c) Grace Nichols 1989. Reprinted by permission of Curtis Brown Ltd, London on behalf of Grace Nichols; Extract from *Trainspotting* by Irvine Welsh, published by Secker & Warburg. Reprinted by permission of The Random House Group Limited; Extract from *Psychology for A Level* by Mike Cardwell, Liz Clark and Claire Meldrum, published by HarperCollins Publishers. Reprinted by permission of the publishers; *Sweet Dreams Are Made of this* words and music by David A. Stewart and Annie Lennox. Copyright (c) BMG Music Publishing Limited. Reprinted with permission; Extract from *The Undiscovered Chekhov* translated by Peter Constantine, published by Duckworth. Reprinted by permission of the publishers; Extract from *Martin Luther King* by Harry Harmer, published by Sutton Publishers. Reprinted by permission of Haynes Publishing; Extract from *A Man on the Moon* by Andrew Chalkin (Michael Joseph 1994) Copyright (c) Andrew Chalkin, 1994. Reprinted by permission of Penguin UK; Extract 'In Your Dreams' by David Newnham, in The Weekend Guardian February 17 2001 Copyright (c) David Newnham 2001. Reprinted with permission of The Guardian; Extract from *The Blind Assassin* by Margaret Atwood, published by Bloombury Publishing, 2000. Reprinted by permission of the publishers

Thanks also to Stephanie Bishop, for granting permission to reproduce a transcript recorded as part of her A Level work.
The Publishers have made every effort to trace the copyright holders, but if they have inadvertently overlooked any, they will be pleased to make the necessary arrangements at the first opportunity.

Typeset by TechType, Abingdon, Oxon
Printed and bound by Bath Press in the UK

Contents

Examples of key websites are suggested. Although these were up to date at the time of writing, it is essential for teachers to preview these sites before using them with pupils. This will ensure that the URL is still accurate and the content is suitable for your needs. We suggest that you bookmark useful sites and consider enabling pupils to access them through the school intranet. We are bringing this to your attention as we are aware of legitimate sites being appropriated illegally by people wanting to distribute unsuitable or offensive material. We strongly advise you to purchase screening software so that pupils are protected from unsuitable sites and their material.

Introduction

This book offers a structured approach to the study of the three A2 (second year of the A level) modules of the English Language and Literature course. These modules build on the knowledge and skills developed over the AS course.

Continuity and change

Skills and knowledge carried over from AS modules

AO1 communicate clearly the knowledge, understanding and insights gained from the combination of literary and linguistic study, using appropriate terminology and accurate written expression

In Modules 1 and 2, you gained insights into linguistic and literary approaches to poetry, prose and a variety of non-literary texts. Some of these texts were pre-twentieth century, where an understanding of language change was an important element.

AO2 in responding to literary and non-literary texts, distinguish, describe and interpret variation in meaning and form

At AS level you responded to poetry and prose and to a variety of non-literary texts. At A Level, you will concentrate on spoken dialogue both in transcripts of conversation and in literary forms, particularly drama. The final synoptic module will focus on an anthology, which will include texts from a wide variety of genres.

AO3 respond to and analyse texts, using literary and linguistic concepts and approaches

Module 1 introduced you to the use of literary and linguistic concepts at a basic level. Module 2 required focus on language change and development.

AO4 show understanding of the ways contextual variation and choices of form, style and vocabulary shape the meaning of texts

This objective is central and is assessed in every module at both AS and A Level. Context refers not only to the historical perspective but also the psychological, sociological and cultural contexts which shape meaning and form.

AO5 identify and consider the ways attitudes and values are created and conveyed in speech and writing

This objective is also central and assessed in every module at both AS and A Level.

AO6 demonstrate expertise and accuracy in writing for a variety of specific purposes and audiences, drawing on knowledge of literary texts and features of language to explain and comment on the choices made

Assessment of this objective was concentrated on the coursework Module 3, where you produced a folder of your own writing for both readers and listeners. A commentary reflecting on the choices made in *your* texts was given equal weighting to the final drafts of the texts themselves.

New skills and knowledge for A2

The assessment objectives for A2 remain broadly the same as AS, but there are two significant additions:

AO2ii respond with knowledge and understanding of texts of different types and from different periods, exploring and commenting on relationships and comparisons between them

At A Level your response to texts will be deepened. The relationships between texts of different types and from different periods are examined. In Module 5 you will focus on the effects of imposing a literary form on spoken dialogue. In Module 6 you will find a range of texts on a common theme, Dreams. You will be asked to explain and interpret them by applying a range of different critical approaches.

AO3ii use and evaluate different literary and linguistic approaches to the study of written and spoken language, showing how these approaches inform their readings

This objective is tested only at A Level. As well as being able to use a variety of approaches in your analysis of texts, you will need to stand back and explicitly evaluate the appropriateness of the framework you have chosen.

The order of the modules in this book

You may be studying the three A2 modules simultaneously for assessment in May and June. Or you may be preparing to take the Module 5 examination in January, present the Module 4 coursework in May, and take the synoptic Module 6 in June. This book presents the modules in numerical order, beginning with 'Text transformation' (Module 4). You are strongly advised to begin studying this section first, as the skills developed in Module 4 lay an important foundation for the study of texts in the Module 5 and introduce some of the critical approaches needed for Module 6.

MODULE ④ Text Transformation

This module counts for 15% of the total A Level marks.

ASSESSMENT OBJECTIVES

The skills and knowledge that you develop in this module, and that will be assessed in your coursework, are defined by the examination board's Assessment Objectives. These require that you:

AO1 communicate clearly the knowledge, understanding and insights gained from the combination of literary and linguistic study, using appropriate terminology and accurate written expression (2.5%)

AO4 show understanding of the ways contextual variation and choices of form, style and vocabulary shape the meaning of texts (2.5%)

AO5 identify and consider the ways attitudes and values are created and conveyed in speech and writing (2.5%)

AO6 demonstrate expertise and accuracy in writing for a variety of specific purposes and audiences, drawing on knowledge of literary texts and features of language to explain and comment on the choices made (7.5%)

Content of folder

You will notice similarities between this module and the coursework folder you produced for Production of Texts at AS: the folder for this module, Text Transformation, will also contain one or two pieces of your own writing, together with an accompanying commentary. However, the basis for your own writing is different here: you are now required to take a literary work of any genre and transform this original, or 'base' text, into a different genre. You may choose to produce one long piece or two shorter pieces of work, your total being 1,500 to 2,000 words. If you choose two pieces of work, these can be either:

- transformations of two separate literary texts, or

- two different transformations of a single text.

The folder of work is worth 50% of the marks for the module and will be assessed under the following Assessment Objectives:

- AO1 assesses your ability to communicate clearly and accurately in writing

- AO6 assesses your ability to write in a specific genre for your chosen purpose and audience

Your *commentary* will discuss your transformation(s) of the original text(s). This should be approximately 1,500 words and is worth 50% of the marks for the module. The commentary will be assessed under the following assessment objectives:

- AO4 assesses your understanding of the ways in which your new text has altered the form and therefore the meanings of the original

- AO5 assesses your understanding of the ways that values and attitudes were created in the original and your transformed version

- AO6 assesses your ability to explain and comment on relevant aspects of literary texts and features of language in the choices you made

What texts can you choose?

The Specification states that you should use a 'literary text'. You will have seen from your study of the Anthology in Module 1 that there is no clear-cut distinction between 'literary' and 'non-literary' texts. In its broadest sense, 'literature' refers to anything written down and read. However, the word is often used with a capital letter as an evaluative term identifying written works of 'beauty or emotional effect'. This value judgement about what counts as literature is the subject of much debate and you should continue to consider such issues, particularly when you focus on the Anthology in Module 6. The Specification for the present module bypasses the debate, however, and offers a more straightforward approach to a literary work by specifying the three genres that have been traditionally accepted as literature:

- poetry

- drama

- prose fiction (including written versions of myths and legends).

You must choose a text, or texts, from these three genres. Ideally, it will be a text that you know well; it may be one that you particularly like, but it might also be a text with which you take issue in some way. You can choose a text that you have already studied as part of this course or your English GCSE, or one that you have read independently; you may even decide to start looking for a suitable text. Collections of poetry and short stories have the advantage of providing short texts that can be dealt with as a whole. If you choose a play or novel, you will probably focus on a part of the work. The activities in this module tend to focus on short, complete texts, but there will also be suggestions for work with longer texts.

Developing skills

Although Module 4 is not assessed until May, it's important to begin work on it from the beginning of your A2 course, as it provides a valuable link between the skills developed in the AS modules and the skills that need to be developed for A Level modules.

Text transformation clearly builds on the skills developed in Module 3, Production of Texts. The aim now is to create your own text using the stimulus of an existing literary work. Before you start, however, it's important for you to recognise that you are being offered approaches to text transformation that have been generated by contemporary ways of looking at language, literature and thought. The notion of different critical approaches will be explored further in Module 6, where we will discuss more explicitly the range of tools, both linguistic and literary, that are available to analyse texts. Your work as an active reader and creative re-writer for the present module will provide a valuable basis for your application of key critical approaches later.

The three literary genres of poetry, drama, and prose fiction provide the focus for three modules of the Language and Literature course. The genre of poetry was studied in Module 1, prose in Module 2, and drama will be the focus of Module 5. Your study of these modules is meant to develop your skills in responding to and analysing these three genres. Your understanding of the chosen genre will be *implicit* in your transformation of the text and *explicit* in your commentary.

What's the point of transforming texts?

The principle of using transformation as a way of studying literature was established by Rob Pope, Principal Lecturer in English Studies at Oxford Brookes University. In *Textual Intervention* (1995) he describes the rationale of text transformation as follows:

> The best way to understand how a text works . . . is to change it: to play around with it, to intervene in it in some way (large or small), and then to try to account for the exact effect of what you have done.

The assumption behind this practice is that it is both possible and valuable to 're-centre' and 're-construct' texts. In Module 6 you will have the opportunity to set this 're-construction approach' – a relatively new way of studying literature – alongside other approaches.

Text transformation, therefore, will not only improve your writing skills, it will increase your reading skills, and will also act as an introduction to a number of contemporary critical approaches to literature.

Writing skills

Creating a new work based on an existing text is not in fact a new practice. Indeed, some people would claim that no work is truly 'original'; this is one reason for using the term 'base' text in this module.

Shakespeare reworked existing story lines in all of his plays. *Romeo and Juliet*, for example, is based on a popular Italian story; *Antony and Cleopatra* on well-known events in Roman history as described by a Greek historian; and *Hamlet* on an obscure incident in Scandinavian history as retold by a French writer in 1570. Shakespeare's plays have been transformed in their turn by other writers. The play *Rosencrantz and Guildenstern are Dead* by Tom Stoppard is based on a reading of *Hamlet* that gives prominence to two minor characters, with the events of the royal court being seen from this perspective. There have been cartoon versions of Shakespeare plays, and in the nineteenth century the essayist Charles Lamb and his sister, Mary, produced a simplified narrative version of some of the plays in *Tales from Shakespeare*.

Sometimes the purpose is to bring the work to a wider audience; there are, for example, many TV and film adaptations of novels, notably those of Jane Austen. Such adaptations usually aim to be faithful to the original, though the scriptwriters inevitably bring their own interpretation to the story; Alan Bleasdale's television version of *Oliver Twist*, for instance, added an imaginative prelude that reconstructs the circumstances of Oliver's birth and his mother's situation.

But not all readings aim to be 'faithful' to the original; some seek to highlight a *missing* perspective. The literary theorist Pierre Macherey has suggested a method of reading the 'gaps and silences' within a text – in other words, what it *would* not or *could* not say. The novel *Wide Sargasso Sea* by Jean Rhys, for example, is based on a reading of Charlotte Brontë's novel *Jane Eyre*. In the new version, the character called Bertha in *Jane Eyre*, where she is referred to as 'the madwoman in the attic', becomes the central character and is now given her real name, Antoinette.

This 'reading across the grain' makes the reader aware of the partial view of *any* narrative. Traditional stories from mythology and folklore have been transformed in many ways, one of the effects being to make us aware of the 'gaps and silences' in these narratives, which tend to deal with the heroic exploits of nobles. One collection of traditional stories, *The Woman in the Moon and Other Tales of Forgotten Heroines* (1984) by James Riordan, brings together stories that feature females as positive protagonists to offset the common role of women as passive creatures waiting to snare a prince as husband. The novel *Troy* by Adele Geras is a version of the Trojan War told from the point of view of children living in the servants' quarters. In Carol Ann Duffy's collection *The World's Wife*, each poem is told from the perspective of a woman, real or imaginary, so there is Queen Kong, Mrs Faust, and Elvis' Twin Sister, among others. And Angela Carter has explored the preconceptions of a range of traditional stories: her short story *The Company of Wolves*, which was made into a film, derives from the tale of Little Red Riding Hood. These are only a few examples of the many transformations of myths and legends.

ACTIVITY 1

You will need cards of two different colours for this activity.

- As a group, list examples of poetry, drama, and prose fiction (including traditional narratives). Each piece of card should have the title (and author) of a literary work written on it.

- Now list as many examples of genres as possible. These need not be literary, so you can include articles, letters, adverts, chat shows, and so on. Write each of these on a card of a different colour from those on which the titles are written.

- Each person should take one card of each colour and say how and why the literary work might be transformed into that genre.

Now read the commentary on page 52.

Reading skills

One of the main aims of the Language and Literature course is to 'encourage students to develop as independent, confident and reflective readers'. This module may seem, primarily, to develop writing skills, but it should be clear from the examples above that the writers have produced new *readings* of the base texts.

The American author Susan Sontag explained the connection between reading and writing for her in the following terms:

Reading novels seems to me such a normal activity, while writing them is such an odd thing to do . . . At least so I think, until I remind myself how firmly the two are related.

First, to write is to practice [sic], with intensity and attentiveness, the art of reading. You write in order to read what you've written and see if it's OK and, since of course it never is, to rewrite it: once, twice, as many times as it takes. You are your own first, maybe severest reader. 'To write is to sit in judgement on oneself,' wrote Ibsen. Hard to imagine writing without rereading.

(The *Guardian*, 22 Jan 2001)

The hypothetical question 'What if the text were different in some way?' produces some interesting readings of literary works. William Golding's novel *Lord of the Flies*, which is about a group of schoolboys marooned on an island, offers a pessimistic view of human nature reverting to the savage. What if the characters were girls? *John Dollar* by Marianne Wiggins places schoolgirls and their teacher on an island. Baz Lurman's film version of *Romeo and Juliet* imagines: What if this love story happened in Los Angeles in the twentieth century?

This module offers ideas for 'playing around with texts' that will develop your reading skills, as well as your skills in writing for this particular module. There are many transformations you can employ – simply change the title, alter the perspective, modernise the setting, change the ending, and so on. The next activity asks you to think of possible transformations for a single text.

ACTIVITY 2

Take one of the literary texts listed in Activity 1 and pose a question beginning, 'What if. . . .?'

- What if . . . it had a contemporary setting?

- What if . . . a minor character became the main focus?

- What if . . . the ending was changed?

- What if . . . [add several questions of your own]?

Discuss the suggestions in small groups and report back to the full group.

Now read the commentary on page 52.

Understanding critical approaches

Your explorations of 'What if . . .?' questions about texts are closely linked to some key literary theories and critical approaches. The German dramatist Berthold Brecht, for example, felt that it was important for audiences and readers to think of a story as a series of events and interaction that *might have been otherwise*. In this way, he believed, they can make their own critical judgements about the implications of the story *as it was told*.

In his essay *The Critic as Artist* (1891), Oscar Wilde suggested that 'The highest Criticism, then, is more creative . . . and the primary aim of the critic is to see the object as in itself it really is not'. This seems a paradox: to see something as 'it really is not'. But asking yourself the question 'What if . . . ' is a way of exploring the things not said or shown, the 'gaps and silences' in literary texts. This does not mean that the writers should have written them in a different way: considering precisely *why* they wrote their stories in the way they did is one of the key elements of a critical response to a text. But an awareness of what is not said acknowledges the fact that the particular work is just *one* view or version of the story. This helps us to see any text as rooted in a particular 'social, cultural and historical context', which is one of the aims of the A Level course.

Example

The next activity looks at transformations of a story from Greek mythology, which is briefly summarised here.

Icarus and his father, Daedalus, were held captive on the island of Crete by King Minos. Daedalus, a great architect and inventor, had designed a complex labyrinth to house the terrible Minotaur, and it was here that father and son were now imprisoned. Determined to escape, Daedalus set his skills to making pairs of wings from feathers stuck together with wax. Finally, father and son were able to fly to freedom. Nervous at first, Icarus soon became intoxicated with the thrill of flying and gradually got nearer and nearer the sun, until its heat melted the wax and he fell to his death in the sea.

This story has been transformed many times, once in a painting by the Flemish artist Jan Brueghel (1568–1625), which shows a broad landscape in which people are busily carrying on their daily routine. In the right foreground you can just make out a tiny splash and the legs of a figure sinking into the sea. The tragedy of Icarus has been reduced to an event no one even notices.

This painting inspired the following poem by W. H. Auden, 'Musée des Beaux Arts' (the title refers to Auden's fictional variant of the museum in Brussels where Brueghel's painting is on display).

About suffering they were never wrong,
The Old Masters: how well they understood
Its human position; how it takes place
While someone else is eating or opening a window or just walking dully along;
How when the aged are reverently, passionately waiting
For the miraculous birth, there must always be
Children who did not specially want it to happen, skating
On a pond at the edge of a wood:
They never forgot
That even the dreadful martyrdom must run its course
Anyhow in a corner, some untidy spot
Where the dogs go on with their doggy life and the torturer's horse
Scratches its innocent behind on a tree.

In Brueghel's *Icarus* for instance: how everything turns away
Quite leisurely from the disaster; the ploughman may
Have heard the splash, the forsaken cry,
But for him it was not an important failure; the sun shone
As it had to on the white legs disappearing into the green
Water; and the expensive delicate ship that must have seen
Something amazing, a boy falling out of the sky,
Had somewhere to get to and sailed calmly on.

ACTIVITY 3

Read the following two poems based on the Icarus story, the second inspired by the first.

- What does each writer imagine might have been 'otherwise' in the base text?

- What does this say about the implications of the story as told in the base text?

Mrs Icarus

I'm not the first or last
to stand on a hillock,
watching the man she married
prove to the world
he's a total, utter, absolute, Grade A pillock.

(Carol Ann Duffy)

The Sister of Icarus

I am the sister of Icarus.
My father never gave me wings
to fly and stray too close to the sun.

He fastened those great white feathers
to the bony arms of his boy
and whispering in his ear, 'Be a man, my son,'
pushed him into flight.

From the small window I watched
his fearful flapping
and saw him grow smaller.

He became a bird rising on warm swells
until my eyes were dazzled
and lost my brother from sight.

Each morning when the sun rises I cast
a small feather out on a puff of wind
and hold my breath for its looping rise
its spiralling fall.

(Alison Ross)

Now read the commentary on page 53.

Working with short texts

The activities in this section are often based not on literary texts, but on very short texts that will allow you to explore some ways of transforming texts.

Short propositions

A fascinating example of the transformation of a short text is given by Rob Pope in *Textual Intervention* and it's worth repeating here. The works of the French philosopher René Descartes (1596–1650) may not be very well known, but most people have heard one of his propositions:

I think, therefore I am.

About one hundred years later, this statement was transformed by another French philosopher, Jean-Jacques Rousseau (1712–78):

I feel, therefore I am.

By keeping to the same structure, Rousseau alludes to the original proposition and so highlights the significant change. As readers we are aware of the contrast, or the contradiction – for Rousseau it is not *thinking* but *feeling* that is an essential factor of human identity. But this was just one possible transformation. What if the pronoun was changed?

> *We think, therefore we are.*

The practice of graffiti often involves transforming texts. There have been various versions of this statement, usually scribbled on walls; this one was used to caption a cartoon showing a very puzzled philosopher:

> *I think I think, therefore I think I am . . . I think.*

The original proposition was also transformed in an advert slogan:

> *I think, therefore IBM.*

ACTIVITY 4

- Take a short text and change it. Some suggestions follow (you can add your own examples):

  All you need is *love*. (The Beatles)

  Beauty is truth, truth *beauty*, – that is all ye know on earth, and all ye need to know. (Keats, 'Ode on a Grecian Urn')

  All the world's a *stage*, And all the men and women merely players. (Shakespeare, *As You Like It*)

- First change the words in italics, and then compare the transformations made by other members of your group.

- Try making other changes, such as adding a few words.

- In small groups, discuss the effects of the changes made.

No commentary.

Nursery rhymes

Moving to slightly longer, more familiar texts, a reading of many traditional stories and nursery rhymes suggests a world where stepmothers are evil, youngest brothers succeed in their quests for gold, the wicked are finally defeated, and orphan girls marry squires or princes. The world of nursery rhymes is a strange and unpredictable one. Experts may be able to explain that a particular rhyme is really an allegory referring to such and such a king or political situation. But how do we read them today?

ACTIVITY 5

- Take a familiar nursery rhyme and transform it in some way.

Suggestions follow for the rhymes and possible transformations, but you need not stick to these.

A.
Jack and Jill went up the hill
To fetch a pail of water.
Jack fell down and broke his crown
And Jill came tumbling after.

B.
There was a little girl
And she had a little curl
Right in the middle of her forehead.
When she was good, she was very, very good
But when she was bad, she was horrid.

Possible transformations:

Change the context:

- Turn A into a public service advert with a message. Describe the visuals and add the slogan.

- Turn B into a caption for a news photo or political cartoon.

Change the audience:

- Modernise the rhyme, and make the references contemporary.

Add to the story:

- Write the prelude for Jack and Jill. Why were they fetching water? What made them fall?

- Write the aftermath: in other words their separate versions of what happened.

Change the perspective:

- Give the little girl in B a name. Let her tell her own story. What does she do that's 'good' and what is 'horrid'?

- Perhaps her brother or sister can give their account.

Now read the commentary on page 53.

Fables

A fable is a tale that has a moral; among the best known are Aesop's fables, in which the characters are animals. In Module 2 of the AS book, there was a short Zen Buddhist fable given as an example of external narration. It is told in the third-person from an apparently detached, objective perspective. At first reading, you might think that the 'facts are being allowed to speak for themselves'. However, the Russian literary theorist Mikhail Bakhtin suggests that novelists (any storytellers) renegotiate the meanings and values of words by placing them in the mouths and minds of different people. In this version of the story, Tanzin is presented favourably, Ekido less so, and the girl remains silent. The purpose of the original is to present a moral about following the spirit rather than the letter of the law, but this is only one possible interpretation of the actions of the men.

ACTIVITY 6

Here is the fable again. You could choose another fable instead.

- Keep the *events* the same, but transform the words spoken by the characters so that it has a different *message*.

- In order to change the perspective, give more prominence to Ekido or the girl by saying more from their point of view.

Two monks, Tanzan and Ekido, were once travelling together down a muddy road. A heavy rain was falling. Coming around a bend, they met a young girl in a silk kimono and sash, unable to cross the intersection.

'Come on, girl,' said Tanzan at once. Lifting her in his arms, he carried her over the mud.

Ekido did not speak again until that night when they reached a lodging temple. Then he could no longer restrain himself. 'We monks don't go near females,' he told Tanzan, 'especially not young and lovely ones. It is dangerous. Why did you do that?'

'I left the girl there,' said Tanzan. 'Are you still carrying her?'

Now read the commentary on page 53.

Summaries of novels

One way in which the reader's interpretation of the text is made explicit is in reviews, trailers and blurbs (on the cover of a book). The purpose of trailers and blurbs is to 'puff' the film or book in order to persuade the target audience to spend their money. Reviews, on the other hand, are written by critics and may be negative rather than positive.

The example of a review given in the following activity is an unusual way of presenting an opinion on a novel: it parodies the style of the base text and leaves the evaluative comment implicit (parody usually signals mockery of the original).

ACTIVITY 7

Read the following blurb for a novel and the review that parodies the style of another novel.

- Are you encouraged to read the first novel and dissuaded from reading the second?

- Why? Is any publicity good publicity?

The blurb on the cover of *Island* (1999), a novel by Jane Rogers:

The island is a place where things are not as they appear; a magical place where the murder of a reclusive woman is not a cut-and-dried case.

Nikki Black, intent on punishing the mother who abandoned her at birth, goes to the island with only one aim in mind: revenge. But her plans are confounded by the discovery that she has a brother. Not just any old brother, but a brother strangely possessed by their mother; a brother with a terrifyingly violent streak; a brother whose dangerous love and strange way of seeing the world transform Nikki's life.

From the *Guardian*, 25 February 2000:

The Digested Read. Too busy to read the hot books? Let us read them for you. *Love Hexagon*, William Sutcliffe, Hamish Hamilton, digested in the style of the original.

Like Guy and Lisa are an item, right. They do commitment, not one-night stands. They're so comfortable together, right, that Lisa wanders round the flat in her BRA AND KNICKERS. Wow.

Guy is emotionally remote and a bit dull; Lisa is, like, out there. Guy is working on a Phd; Lisa works for a TV production company. Cool. Lisa works with Josh. Josh is VERY good-looking but insecure. He says he gets laid a lot but Lisa knows he doesn't. That's why she fancies him. Lisa pairs Josh off with her best friend, Keri, a MEGABABE and MEGABITCH. They spend the night together. Josh hears wedding bells; Keri doesn't. Josh is very upset.

- Choose a novel or play that you know well.

- Write a blurb for it, or a summary parodying the original.

- Read and comment in groups. What is the blurb or summary saying about the base text?

No commentary.

Types of text transformation

This module requires you to take a literary text and transform it into a different **genre**. As you have seen from Activity 1, there are many possibilities for the new genre, but you can also explore other aspects of the transformed text.

Adaptation: the new text can have a slightly – or radically – different **audience** and **purpose** because of the changes you made. Although your transformed text may be 'faithful' to the themes, attitudes and values of the base text, you may produce a new text that challenges these. A change of **perspective** is likely to have this effect. You may decide to adapt the text for a new audience – simplified for younger readers, for example, or modernised for a contemporary audience.

The technique of **collage** refers to the inclusion of material from various sources, perhaps factual as well as literary. Your aim may be to enhance the base text or to offer a new slant on it. This is related to the technique of 'sampling' in music, where elements from different sources are juxtaposed to create a new work.

If you decide to **parody** the original text, by exaggerating certain features, or by introducing incongruous elements, you will suggest a new reading. Spike Milligan, for example, has written parodies of several novels, such as *Wuthering Heights* by Emily Brontë. As you read the parody, ask yourself what has been changed.

From *Wuthering Heights* (1847):

> 1801. – I have just returned from a visit to my landlord – the solitary neighbour that I shall be troubled with. This is certainly, a beautiful country! In all England, I do not believe that I could have fixed on a situation so completely removed from the stir of society. A perfect misanthropist's Heaven – and Mr. Heathcliff and I are such a suitable pair to divide the desolation between us. A capital fellow! He little imagined how my heart warmed towards him when I beheld his black eyes withdraw so suspiciously under their brows, as I rode up, and when his fingers sheltered themselves, with a jealous resolution, still further in his waistcoat, as I announced my name.
>
> 'Mr. Heathcliff?' I said.
>
> A nod was the answer.

From *Wuthering Heights according to Spike Milligan* (1994):

> 1801 year of our Lord and a nit called Lockwood – i.e. me, the narrator. I have just returned from a visit to my landlord, whereby, killing him has stopped any increase in the rent. In all England, I do not believe I could have fixed on a situation so completely removed from the stir of society; indeed there are societies that do nothing but stir all day. They are porridge brotherhoods, a perfect misanthrope's Heaven: I myself was an imperfect misanthrope as I had piles, and Mr Heathcliff and I are such a suitable pair to divide life's desolation between us, we had half each. A capital fellow, it came to about

£40,000. Imagine how my heart warmed to him along with my liver, kidneys and bacon.

'Mr Heathcliff,' I said.

A nod was the answer, but not very loud.

Summary

For convenience, the points raised above can be summarised as follows.

Required transformation:

Genre: using a different genre

Other possible changes:

Adaptation: changing audience or purpose
Perspective: switching the focus of interest/point of view
Collage: combining various texts
Parody: using exaggeration or incongruity

Suggested approach:

1. Take a text and ask: What if the text were different in some way?

2. Transform the text genre, and any other aspect you choose.

3. For your commentary, ask the following questions:

   - Why did I make that change?

   - What is the effect?

   - What does it reveal about the original?

The following sections in this module will deal with each literary genre in turn: poetry, prose fiction, and then drama. Wherever possible, whole texts are used, so short stories have been used instead of novels. For the drama section, extracts have been because of limitations of space. The activities will explore various types of transformation for each base text, with the points summarised above acting as a focus for your commentary. A full list of relevant questions will be given later (Activity 31, page 49).

Poetry as the base text

The following activities use poems as the base text with which you can experiment when trying various types of transformation. There is a section on perspective and suggestions for genre changes, collage, and adaptation.

Perspective

An interesting place to start when reading a poem with a view to transformation is perspective. Some poems do not mention the eye that is seeing or the voice that is speaking as 'I'. Their pronouns are confined to third-person (it, they, he, she). An example is the poem 'Pike' by Ted Hughes, the first two stanzas of which read:

Pike, three inches long, perfect
Pike in all parts, green tigering the gold.
Killers from the egg: the malevolent aged grin.
They dance on the surface among the flies.

Or move, stunned by their own grandeur,
Over a bed of emerald, silhouette
Of submarine delicacy and horror.
A hundred feet long in their world.

However, the reader may have a sense of an observing 'I' – an awestruck angler on the riverbank, perhaps? This could be made more explicit in a transformation. Alternatively the focus could fall on object of the poem. Magazines devoted to angling are amongst the best-selling magazines in Britain, so an article about pike fishing could use lines from the poem juxtaposed with factual material about pike.

ACTIVITY 8

Read the following anonymous poem dating from the 1980s. Although it has no 'I', there is a clear perspective shown on the state of Britain at the time.

- How do you visualise the 'I' observer?

- What view of society is created?

- Collect images and phrases that represent *your* view of today's Britain.

- Work in small groups to create a short poem.

- Comment on the particular view of contemporary Britain that the new texts convey.

Contemporary Britain

a pools win, sin bin,
wimpy bar, two car,
first name, loose dame,
rolling stone, ansaphone,
loud sound, sleep around,
disco scenes, tight jeans,
colour telly, slingawelly,
page threes, deep freeze,
opt out, be a lout,
dull void, unemployed
type of society.

Now read the commentary on page 54.

Love poems, on the other hand, use the first- and second-person singular pronouns (I, me, you) to capture the sense of a direct address to the loved one from the lover. This is the case for end-of-love poems also, as in the following by Margaret Atwood, 'You fit into me':

> you fit into me
> like a hook in an eye
> a fish hook
> an open eye

The *silent* voice in such poems is the 'you' persona, the person addressed. A transformation could be a form of reply, changing the perspective of the 'you' into 'I'.

Whose voice tells the story?

Are all literary texts written in Standard British English regardless of their perspective? As you will have noticed from your study of narrative in Module 2, the perspective may be that of a particular character, but the style may not be in their voice. If you have studied fiction with a young person as the main character – for example *Huckleberry Finn*, *The Secret Diary of Adrian Mole*, *Alice's Adventures in Wonderland*, or *The BFG* – you may have noticed that the first two adopt the voice of the protagonists, whereas the latter two novels use a standard narrative style.

The novel *Trainspotting* by Irving Welsh is notable for its use of Scots vernacular, which some publishers thought made it unsuitable for a mainstream audience. Yet the notion of a Glasgow character like Sick Boy speaking like an English newsreader is inconceivable. Ken Loach's film of the novel *Kes* (by Barry Hines) had to be subtitled for audiences in the USA, but the Barnsley voices were not dubbed with a mainstream dialect and accent.

Yet such 'dubbing' of voices happens in literary representations. The poet and academic David Dabydeen left Guyana as a child, attended English schools and then studied English at Cambridge University. There was no Caribbean literature studied, and he noticed not only 'gaps and silences', but also distortions. If black experience was portrayed, it was in elegant language: 'the wrapping of stark experiences in a napkin of poetic diction'. In the poem 'The Sugar Cane', for example, by the eighteenth-century poet James Grainger, slaves are called 'assistant planters' or 'Africa's sable progeny'. Dabydeen realised that 'London is supposed to provide the models of standard English, and we in the Caribbean our dialect versions'.

ACTIVITY 9

- Read the poem following poem, 'Slavewoman's Song', by David Dabydeen. It is written in **creole** – or the 'Nation Language', as the poet Edward Braithwaite terms it – so it needs to be heard, rather than looked at on the page. (A pickni is a child.)

- What is the effect of using the voice of the slavewoman?

- Can you imagine it wrapped 'in a napkin of poetic diction'?

Slavewoman's Song

Ya howl–
Hear how ya howl–
Tell me what ya howl foh
Tell me noh?
Pickni?
Dem tek pickni way?
Wha dem do wid pickni
Mek yu knaack yu head wid stone
Bite yu haan like daag-bone?

Is husban mek yu halla gal?
Wha dem do wid maan
Mek yu daub yu face wid cow dung
Juk yu eye an chap yu tongue?
Dem trow am Demerara, feed am alligita?

Muma? Pupa? Africa?
Belly big wid Massa?

Ya howl–
Hear how ya howl–
Tell me wha ya howl foh
Tell me noh?

Now read the commentary on page 54.

So far in this section we have looked at changes to perspective. In the following Activities we will look again at perspective (Activity 10), and then at changing genre (Activity 11) and the use of collage (Activity 12).

ACTIVITY 10

The poem 'Man to Man' by U. A. Fanthorpe is about the shipwrecked *Mary Rose*. Your task is to organise an oral presentation of this poem.

- Read the poem 'Man to Man' silently, before deciding what voice or voices you would use.

- Re-read the poem a second time, noting all the personal pronouns used.

- What does this suggest about the perspective? Who might the words be addressed to?

- Work in small groups to discuss your ideas for reading this poem aloud.

- Feedback your ideas to the full group.

Man to Man

Your divers' bubbling summons has roused
Us at our mooring, where we lay
Waiting for Gabriel.

We are the men who foundered, who plunged
Smartly to our stations, under
The eyes of the bright king

In July weather, in a flat calm,
In home waters, among the fleet,
Without giving reasons.

The long wait spliced us. Artificers,
Officers, gunmen and bowmen,
Old salts, surgeons, sea-cooks,

Captain, Vice-Admiral, all of us
Lay together in our common
Catafalque like lovers.

Tides passed. The mild fish consumed our flesh,
Bones dropped neat and nice as rope coils,
Jaws fell, grinning welcome

To the certain resurrection, when
The lovely rigging of the bone
Leaps to the last whistle

Of Bo'sun Christ. But the next coming
Was yours, who harrowed our petty
Harvest of every day –

Boots, bricks, barrels, baskets, rigging-blocks,
Dice, daggers, dead-eyes, pipe-and-drum,
A bell, books, candlesticks,

Hairs of the ship's dog, bones of the rat
He might have caught, bones of the men
Embalmed in Solent mud.

What will you do with us, you to whom
The sea yields its secrets, who plumbed
Our permanent instant?

Museums will house our chattels. Even
Degraded wood has its uses.
Only our nameless bones

Remain dully unadaptable,
Impossible to show or sell,
Being the same as yours.

Now read the commentary on page 55.

Changing genre

There are opportunities for Key Skills in the following activities that suggest ways of changing genre or using collage. You may use technology for research, or find and use images in a spoken presentation.

ACTIVITY 11

1. Find out more about the *Mary Rose* from the Internet or an encyclopaedia, for example:

   • What type of ship was it?

   • Where was it sailing to?

   • Where did it sink?

   • When?

   • What caused it to sink?

2. Choose a way of transforming the poem, for example:

- It is said that the wife of one of the senior officers stood in King Henry VIII's party on the land as the ship went down. Write a short story based upon this scene, choosing the point of view from which to tell the story.

3. Collect a range of images relating to the *Mary Rose*, and then write the soundtrack for a Power Point presentation, interspersing lines from the poem with historical/factual narrative.

No commentary.

Collage

For the following activities, three texts have been juxtaposed to form a collage: an extract from a novel, a complete poem, and a T-shirt slogan. In a sense, these texts have already been *transformed* by being placed in a context that suggests relationships between them. You should notice the ways in which your reading is steered towards certain aspects of the texts by this context and by the accompanying activities. You might have read and responded to them differently, if they had been presented singly or in another context.

ACTIVITY 12

Read the following extract from *The Collector*, a novel by John Fowles.

- What do you infer about the narrator, the 'I' of the text (age, occupation, personality, and so on)?

- How does he perceive the girl? Pick out the descriptive phrases or group them into **semantic fields**. What are the **connotations** of these words?

- What is his relationship with her? Pick out all the phrases that give an indication.

- How does the title of the novel guide your interpretation?

When she was home from her boarding-school I used to see her almost every day sometimes, because their house was right opposite the Town Hall Annexe. She and her younger sister used to go in and out a lot, often with young men, which of course I didn't like. When I had a free moment from the files and ledgers I stood by the window and used to look down over the road over the frosting and sometimes I'd see her. In the evening I marked it in my observation diary, at first with X, and then when I knew her name with M. I saw her several times outside too. I stood right behind her once in a queue at the public library down Crossfield Street. She didn't look once at me, but I watched the back of her head and her hair in a long pigtail. It was very pale, silky, like burnet cocoons. All in one pigtail coming down almost to her waist, sometimes in front, sometimes at the back. Sometimes she wore it up. Only once, before she came to be my guest here, did I have the privilege to see her with it loose, and it took my breath away it was so beautiful, like a mermaid.

Another time one Saturday off when I went up to the Natural History Museum I came back on the same train. She sat three seats down and sideways to me, and read a book, so I could watch her for thirty-five minutes. Seeing her always made me feel like I was catching a rarity, going up to it very careful, heart-in-mouth as they say. A Pale Clouded Yellow, for instance. I always thought of her like that, I mean words like elusive and sporadic, and very refined – not like the other ones, even the pretty ones. More for the real connoisseur.

Now read the commentary on page 55.

The second text is a dramatic monologue by the Victorian poet Robert Browning.

ACTIVITY 13

1. The poem's title is 'Porphyria's Lover'.

   • List your expectations of a poem with such a title.

   • Read the opening few lines and discuss the following in small groups.

      What is the effect of the description of the setting on you?

      How is the 'I' narrator first presented?

      How does he respond to Porphyria's arrival?

Porphyria's Lover

The rain set early in to-night,
    The sullen wind was soon awake,
It tore the elm-tops down for spite,
    And did its worst to vex the lake,
I listened with heart fit to break;
When glided in Porphyria: straight
    She shut the cold out and the storm,
And kneeled and made the cheerless grate
    Blaze up, and all the cottage warm;

2. Read the next section of the poem and then answer the following questions.

   • Who speaks? Who moves? Who watches?

   • What effect does this action/inaction have/suggest?

   • Is a third person suggested in this relationship?

   • The narrator debates what to do – what possibilities occur to the reader?

Which done, she rose, and from her form
Withdrew the dripping cloak and shawl,
    And laid her soiled gloves by, untied
Her hat and let the damp hair fall,
    And, last, she sate down by my side
And called me. When no voice replied,
She put my arm about her waist,
    And made her smooth white shoulder bare,
And all her yellow hair displaced,
    And, stooping, made my cheek lie there,
And spread o'er all her yellow hair,
Murmuring how she loved me; she
    Too weak, for all her heart's endeavour,
To set its struggling passion free
    From pride, and vainer ties dissever,
And give herself to me for ever:
But passion sometimes would prevail,
    Nor could to-night's gay feast restrain
A sudden thought of one so pale
    For love of her, and all in vain;
So, she was come through wind and rain.
Be sure I looked up at her eyes
    Proud, very proud; at last I knew
Porphyria worshipped me; surprise
    Made my heart swell, and still it grew
While I debated what to do.

3. Read the final section of the poem.

- Is the outcome a shock or were you prepared for it? Why?

- Are there similar images in *The Collector* and this poem? List them.

That moment she was mine, mine, fair,
    Perfectly pure and good: I found
A thing to do, and all her hair
    In one long yellow string I wound
Three times her little throat around,
And strangled her. No pain felt she;
    I am quite sure she felt no pain.
As a shut bud that holds a bee
    I warily oped her lids; again
Laughed the blue eyes without a stain.
And I untightened next the tress

> About her neck; her cheek once more
> Blushed bright beneath my burning kiss:
>   I propped her head up as before,
> Only, this time *my* shoulder bore
> Her head, which droops upon it still:
>   The smiling rosy little head,
> So glad it has its utmost will,
>   That all it scorned at once is fled,
> And I, its love, am gained instead!
> Porphyria's love: she guessed not how
>   Her darling one wish would be heard.
> And thus we sit together now,
>   And all night long we have not stirred,
> And yet God has not said a word!

Now read the commentary on page 56.

Both of these literary texts – Fowles' *The Collector* and Browning's 'Porphyria's Lover' – are studied in schools and have been on reading lists for English Literature exams. Although the subject matter is the murder of women, they are not deemed offensive. In contrast, the lyrics of the American singer Eminem have caused outrage because they feature violence and might be seen to incite hatred of women and homosexuals. But some commentators draw comparisons between his song lyrics and other literary works, asking whether the portrayal of violent acts necessarily means that the writer is advocating them. Supporters of Eminem claim that the characters in his songs are imaginative persona and should not be taken as his voice and ideas, just as Shakespeare is not accused of promoting wife-murder in *Othello*.

The final activity in this section introduces a text that may upset or offend. It is included so that you can consider the boundaries between art and pornography, and between imaginative portrayal of violence and actual incitement to violence.

ACTIVITY 14

The final text is a slogan seen on the back of a T-shirt:

> DEAD GIRLS CAN'T SAY NO

Discuss the following questions in groups.

- What does it 'mean'? Can you make the underlying assumptions explicit?

- How do you respond to this slogan? Is it shocking? Funny? Ironic? Threatening? Dangerous?

- What if this was the title of either the novel or the poem, how would that transform your reading of the texts?

- It could be the title of a violent/pornographic movie. What distinguishes *The Collector* and 'Porphyria's Lover' from pornography?

- Do you think it is an unfair distortion to juxtapose these three texts?

- If so, what other texts might have been chosen?

Now read the commentary on page 56.

ACTIVITY 15

Use these three juxtaposed texts – Fowles' *The Collector*, Browning's 'Porphyria's Lover', and the slogan – as the basis for a collage transformation.

- Decide on your purpose and audience.

- Decide on the genre (this could include developing words and images for a poster, a soundtrack to moving images, and so on).

- In groups, provide feedback comments on the transformations of the base texts.

No commentary.

Prose fiction as the base text

The choice of short stories, rather than novels, as material for transformations might seem the sensible decision, given the restraints of both time and word count on the work for your folder. You could look for collections of short stories by writers you already know, or try anthologies of stories by various writers. However, you could also work with a novel as your base text, as you can transform a part of the text, rather than the entire work. Being clearly episodic, fiction in the form of diaries might lend itself to short transformations. The humorous novel *The Diary of a Nobody* (1892) by George and Weedon Grossmith, for example, has been transformed in various forms: one version, for example, used a contemporary protagonist to amusing effect, and there has also been a version written from the perspective of the central character's wife, Mrs Pooter.

The following activities work with complete short stories. There are many anthologies of stories from genres such as science fiction, horror, fantasy, romance. The first short story is from the genre of science fiction. These occasionally seem strangely prophetic when read many years later; alternatively they can seem very dated.

ACTIVITY 16

Read the following short story by Fredric Brown. It was published in 1968, so some details might seem dated in this age of sophisticated computers. The activity that follows suggests ways of approaching a science fiction story by making small changes and then discussing the effects. Remember that your coursework transformation *must* involve a change of genre.

- What details help establish the futuristic context: names, dialogue, setting, semantic fields?

- In *The Handmaid's Tale* by Margaret Atwood, the women are named Offred, Ofglen and so on to denote that the woman is the possession of the favoured male and has no personal identity unique to herself. What do you think is the function of the first name, Dwar?

- If this story was a fable, what moral would you add after the story?

- Where are the women? The children?

- What question would you ask such a machine? Would there be an answer? In groups, list other possible questions (and answers).

- How does this transformation change the effect of the story?

Answer

Dwar Ev ceremoniously soldered the final connection with gold. The eyes of a dozen television cameras watched him and the subether bore throughout the universe a dozen pictures of what he was doing.

He straightened and nodded to Dwar Reyn, then moved to a position beside the switch that would connect, all at once, all of the populated planets in the universe – ninety-six billion planets – into the supercircuit that would connect them all into one cybernetics machine that would combine all the knowledge of all the galaxies.

Dwar Reyn spoke briefly to the watching and listening trillions. Then after a moment's silence he said, 'Now, Dwar Ev.'

Dwar Ev threw the switch. There was a mighty hum, the surge of power from ninety-six billion planets. Lights flashed and quieted along the miles-long panel.

Dwar Ev stepped back and drew a deep breath. 'The honour of asking the first question is yours, Dwar Reyn.'

'Thank you,' said Dwar Reyn. 'It shall be a question which no single cybernetics machine has been able to answer'.

He turned to face the machine. 'Is there a God?'

The mighty voice answered without hesitation, without the clicking of a single relay.

'Yes, NOW there is a God.'

Sudden fear flashed on the face of Dwar Ev. He leaped to grab the switch.

A bolt of lightning from a cloudless sky struck him down and fused the switch shut.

Before choosing one of the following writing tasks, read the commentary on page 57.

Suggested writing tasks

Choose a piece of today's modern technology, for example a mobile phone with Internet connection. Or think of other means whereby we expect big questions to be answered – crystal balls, tea leaves, the I Ching, Tarot cards.

- Write a story with a similar ending, where someone's hopes for a means to answer the 'big questions' are dashed.

- Write the script for an imagined scene where all the possible questions are discussed before the final one is chosen. Some characters at this meeting should be female.

- Write a newspaper report or a chapter in a history text about the incident and its aftermath.

The following complete short story, *Doctor Chevalier's Lie*, by the American writer Kate Chopin, is set in New Orleans in the second half of the nineteenth century. The activities explore the perspective, chronology and narrative structure of the story by posing the question: 'What if such features were different, how would that alter the effect?' The notion of 'gaps and silences' in the text is used to introduce one of the critical approaches (Deconstruction) that will be studied in Module 6. Suggestions for your own transformations of the text can be used as short exercises, or you may decide to work on a similar transformation of a story of your own choice, which can be assessed in the coursework folder.

ACTIVITY 17

Doctor Chevalier's Lie

The quick report of a pistol rang through the quiet autumn night. It was no unusual sound in the unsavory quarter where Dr. Chevalier had his office. Screams commonly went with it. This time there had been none.

Midnight had already rung in the old cathedral tower.

The doctor closed the book over which he had lingered so late, and awaited the summons that was almost sure to come.

As he entered the house to which he had been called he could not but note the ghastly sameness of detail that accompanied these oft-recurring events. The same scurrying; the same groups of tawdry, frightened women bending over the banisters – hysterical, some of them; morbidly curious, others; and not a few shedding womanly tears; with a dead girl stretched somewhere, as this one was.

And yet it was not the same. Certainly she was dead: there was the hole in the temple where she had sent the bullet through. Yet it was different. Other such faces had been unfamiliar to him, except so far as they bore the common stamp of death. This one was not.

Like a flash he saw it again amid other surroundings. The time was little more than a year ago. The place, a homely cabin down in Arkansas, in which he and a friend had found shelter and hospitality during a hunting expedition.

There were others beside. A little sister or two; a father and mother – coarse, and bent with toil, but proud as archangels of their handsome girl, who was too clever to stay in an Arkansas cabin, and who was going away to seek her fortune in the big city.

'The girl is dead,' said Doctor Chevalier. 'I knew her well, and charge myself with her remains and decent burial.'

The following day he wrote a letter. One, doubtless, to carry sorrow, but no shame to the cabin down there in the forest.

It told that the girl had sickened and died. A lock of hair was sent and other trifles with it. Tender last words were even invented.

Of course it was noised about that Doctor Chevalier had cared for the remains of a woman of doubtful repute.

Shoulders were shrugged. Society thought of cutting him. Society did not, for some reason or other, so the affair blew over.

Perspective:
- How does the title affect your reading of the story?

- Supply other titles that suggest a different perspective, for example that of the dead woman, her companions, her family, the gossiping people of the city.

Narrative structure:
- The reader is not immediately aware that the story is being told from the viewpoint of the doctor. What clues are there in the first five sentences?

- What details are given about the female character? What is omitted? What is suggested?

- Notice the use of 'girl' meaning woman; later she is described as a 'woman of doubtful repute'. What different effects do these ways of referring to her achieve?

Now read the commentary on page 57.

Chronology and narrative structure

The chronology of this story is significant to the perspective. It has a short time span, from midnight to the following day; there is a brief comment about the aftermath of rumours and the reader is left imagining the impact of the letter to the family. The focus of this time span is Dr Chevalier, as the story opens at the moment of the young woman's death. There is a flashback to one year before, when the doctor first encountered her, but the intervening months are missing from the story and hidden from her family. They are guessed at by the doctor and assumed by gossips in the city's 'society'.

Actual time line	Story chronology	Gaps
One year before	[brief flashback later in narrative]	Girl plans to leave for city
		Her experiences in the city
Midnight and the following hours	Story begins just after Dr C. deals with body	She kills herself
Next day	He writes a letter to her family	
Following days	Rumours mentioned	Effect of suicide on family

Presumably the missing year involves the crucial changes in the young woman's life that led her to suicide. The reader can guess in general terms, so the details do not need to be told, but a different version of the story might choose to tell them. Film versions of stories, for example, tend to fill in a lot of gaps and make things that were left to the imagination explicit. Silent characters in the base text might speak: the woman herself; her companions in the city; her parents and little sisters, perhaps as she prepared to leave and when the letter arrives; the gossiping people in the city. The city would have to become specific in a film version, but could remain an **archetypal** city in a stage drama.

ACTIVITY 18

1. Choose a short story and chart the time span and chronology, indicating intriguing gaps.

2. Make notes filling in the gaps. In the case of *Doctor Chevalier's Lie*, for example, you could answer these questions, based on clues in the text:

   - What is the young woman's name?

   - How old is she?

   - Which city does she head for?

   - What are her dreams of life in the city?

   - What happens on her arrival?

   - Where does she spend the first night?

- Who does she meet/befriend first?

- How does she become involved in prostitution, or drugs, or crime?

- What succession of events brings her to her final desperate act?

3. Choose a short scene to write, for example:

- the night with her family before she leaves

- her first encounter(s) in the city

- a key episode in her downfall.

4. Other suggestions for *Doctor Chevalier's Lie*:

- Write the letter that Dr Chevalier might have written to the parents.

- Write a dialogue between Dr Chevalier and the (hunting) friend who is mentioned in the story. You can choose at which point the dialogue takes place – it can be after the action of the story is complete, for example.

Now read the commentary on page 57.

Narrative to drama

A common transformation of genre involves creating a film or play script from a narrative. The conventions of a play script are to represent dialogue on separate lines preceded by the speaker's name; stage directions are given in italics (and brackets) to distinguish them clearly from the words spoken.

A film or TV script has slightly different conventions, but the purpose is the same, to distinguish dialogue from other information or directions. (The director's shooting script would include details of camera angles, and so on.) You can use upper-case for directions and lower-case for speech, lighting or use italics and brackets. Examples follow of three possible openings for a filmscript based on *Doctor Chevalier's Lie*.

ACTIVITY 19

Read the following three openings to film scripts.

- Which do you prefer as the opening to a film and why?

- What does each suggest is the focus of interest in the film's story?

SCRIPT 1

INTERIOR. A CLOCK CHIMES MIDNIGHT. A MAN IS WORKING AT HIS DESK. THE SOUND OF A PISTOL SHOT. THE MAN LOOKS STARTLED FOR A MOMENT, THEN CLOSES HIS BOOK AND GATHERS TOGETHER MEDICAL EQUIPMENT IN A LEATHER HOLDALL. THE SOUND OF FOOTSTEPS AND A KNOCK AT THE DOOR. HE OPENS IT TO SEE A DISTRAUGHT WOMAN.

WOMAN   Doctor, please. You must come quickly.

HE QUICKLY FOLLOWS HER OUT OF HIS OFFICE.

SCRIPT 2

EXTERIOR. A SMALL RAILWAY STATION IN THE MIDDLE OF NOWHERE. A FAMILY GROUP – MAN, WOMAN, DAUGHTER AND TWO YOUNG GIRLS – ARE SITTING BY A LARGE SHABBY SUITCASE.

YOUNG GIRL 1   How long will you stay in Chicago, Edie?

YOUNG GIRL 2   I want to come with you.

EDITH HUGS HER SISTERS.

EDITH   Just as soon as I get my first pay check, I'll send you both some beautiful ribbons. Promise.

THE SOUND OF A TRAIN APPROACHING. THE MOTHER STARTS TO SOB.

SCRIPT 3

INTERIOR. THE LANDING OF A SHABBY LODGING HOUSE. A MAN IS OPENING THE DOOR TO SHOW THE YOUNG WOMAN WITH A SUITCASE A SMALL ROOM. OTHER WOMEN LOOK ON CURIOUSLY.

WOMAN   Best room for her, is it? (*Laughs*) We're not good enough for you any more?

MAN   Take no notice of them. It's ten dollars down and then the rent up front each week, no excuses.

YOUNG WOMAN   Ten dollars! I don't have that sort of money.

Now read the commentary on page 58.

Critical approach I: Deconstruction

In the last few Activities you have considered the perspective and narrative structure of *Doctor Chevalier's Lie*, exploring the potential for alternative ways of telling the story. At this point it is worth introducing the critical approach of Deconstruction.

Deconstruction

Key person: Jacques Derrida – French philosopher and critic

Key text: Derrida, *Structure, Sign and Play in the Discourse of Human Science* (1966)

Key ideas: Western thought has generally divided the world of human experience into pairs of opposites in order to make sense of it, and then *privileged* one side of the oppositions over the other. For example:

> Day – Night
> White – Black
> Good – Evil
> Hot – Cold
> Man – Woman
> Head – Heart
> Objective – Subjective
> Fact – Fiction
> Dominant – Subordinate

Deconstruction does not mean taking the text apart by looking at its devices and levels of language. It means identifying what 'binary assumptions' (pairing) are implicit in a text. Derrida argues that one side of the binary opposition is usually seen as positive (consider the first terms in the pairs listed above) and the second as negative or undesirable. As this is an over-simplified way of describing the world and the relations found in it, the text itself (not the writer consciously) will present contradictions. If we explore what these are, then we will begin to establish other (hidden) meanings in the text.

You may never have questioned how, in using language, we automatically use such pairings. The approach has major implications for the way we go about organising our responses to the world and all we find in it.

ACTIVITY 20

- Read *Doctor Chevalier's Lie* again (page 26).

- Work in small groups to deconstruct the binary assumptions in the text.

Now read the commentary on page 58.

Predicting the ending

The final activities in this section on prose fiction use a longer short story as the base text. It is taken from *Last Oasis,* a collection of short stories by Daphne Glazer. You will be asked to provide the ending for the story. Your decisions about the outcome will be influenced by the writer's construction of the story up to the point what it is interrupted. In other words, you will notice how the writer creates certain expectations. Even though endings may to some extent be a 'surprise', they should seem inevitable in retrospect. The writer is, of course, writing the story with the end in view, preparing for the outcome in the construction of the beginning. The reader would feel cheated by an ending that seemed completely random. This is particularly true of detective stories, which are constructed as a puzzle with clues, but it is also the case with other genres. A romance could not end with the main character marrying someone s/he met out of the blue: the potential suitors are present throughout the story. The genre of tragedy often involves an inevitable outcome that is signalled to the audience from the beginning. The tragic death is never simply an unfortunate accident – as often in life – but a direct consequence of the protagonist's own actions or 'fatal flaw'. Even when telling stories and anecdotes to friends, we craft them with the ending 'in sight' so that the listener is prepared.

ACTIVITY 21

Read the title and opening lines to the short story below.

- What does the protagonist, Joanne, believe will happen?

- What do you as the reader think will happen?

- Find out whether this expectation is shared by others in the group.

- How is this expectation created?

Business Before Pleasure

It was winning the 'Dream Holiday for Two' that did it. Like the forbidden fruit in the Garden of Eden it changed things for ever.

Me and Jason'll be able to go, she'd told her mother. Eh, think about it . . . Bermuda . . . . It'll be like that Bacardi Coke ad . . . rafts and palm trees and surf! Beautiful people, she'd thought, and cut-away swimsuits.

Now read the commentary on page 59.

This is a summary of the next few paragraphs of the story: Joanne imagines her fantasy of 'a sort of honeymoon' with 'a white satin négligé' and 'frangipani blossoms' all day until she has the chance to phone Jason. She is excited as the news 'bubbled' inside her.

ACTIVITY 22

Read the following section, where Jason's mother answers the phone to Joanne.

- How does the phone conversation damage Joanne's bubbling excitement?

- Pick out phrases or images that suggest problems to come.

- In groups, try to agree on one *significant detail* about each of the three characters: Joanne, Jason and Mrs Brennan.

. . . Please could I have a little word with Jason?

Just a minute, we're very busy.

Joanne had pictured Mrs Brennan with her auburn blow-waved hair that had an acrylic gleam and her scarlet nails and knuckle-duster rings. They made her hands into claws that patted and counted.

Joanne, what's up?

Jay, fantastic news . . . I've just won a holiday for two . . .

Silence . . . and then Oh . . . Just, oh, like that, and Got to go, very busy . . . see you later.

The next paragraphs of the narrative focus on Joanne's disturbed feelings for the rest of the day. She thinks about the Brennan's superior status – they are wealthy farmers and butchers and Jason is their only son, while Joanne's dad is a tenant farmer. She recalls how Mrs Brennan often patronises her. When she meets Jason in a pub that evening, she decides not to have her usual half of lager: 'I'd like something a bit different for a change – a Bacardi Coke, please.' She notices how smart Jason always looks, as his mother and father do, and she remembers the first time she had noticed him and they had started to go out together and, not long afterwards, got engaged. However 'She hadn't liked the idea of her ruby and diamond ring coming from Mrs Brennan'. He responds to her talk about the holiday 'chance of a lifetime' with a flat response: 'I don't think I'll be able to get.' She is upset; they argue; the next day he tells her it's impossible for him to leave his parents' business for two weeks. Joanne doesn't bother to go out with him that Saturday and decides to move into a flat with her friend. When she tells Jason, he tells her: 'If you go . . . that's it.' Joanne's feelings are mixed. Everything hangs in the balance at this point in the narrative.

It's all over, she thought, all over – but somehow she couldn't bear the idea of never seeing him again. Inside her churned anger and despair and still the old attraction, because she couldn't escape it. She liked his deep blue eyes and black lashes and his shiny black hair. His butcher's hands charmed and revolted her. But there was this other side: the obsessive worker, the one who lived for business, who had a scrubbed smartness – a Mrs Brennan smartness.

Here there is a sort of false climax: 'He'd gone . . . It was all over.' But the narrative continues. Now read the commentary on page 59, and then turn to Activity 23.

ACTIVITY 23

Read the rest of the story and answer the questions that follow.

She moved into the flat on a Saturday. Her flatmate, Tricia, was away at the time, gone home for the weekend. So there she was, alone for the first time in her entire life. It was a strange feeling.

After she'd closed the curtains, turned on the telly and settled herself with a mug of coffee and a plate of biscuits some of the oddness seemed to disappear. It was all slightly unreal, as though she had now assumed responsibility for herself: she would have to turn out the lights, snap off the gas fire, decide when it was bedtime – she would have to be the one who listened for prowlers and unusual sounds . . . she must act. There was nothing to protect her from what would come . . . no comfortable buffer between her and the Bermuda breakers . . .

Little shivers of panic prickled down her back and shoulders but she sipped her coffee and gazed resolutely at the screen. Then the doorbell pinged. All of a sudden she was terrified. There seemed to be acres of room and the silence was deeper because the doorbell had broken it. Should she pretend she hadn't heard? She got up and went into the corridor, her heart blundering and bounding with fear.

She eased the door open on the chain. Jason was standing there, his cheeks red, his eyes bright.

'Jo,' he said, 'I've come to see you.'

'Oh, right . . .'

'You don't mind?'

'Of course not . . . come in.'

She unchained the door and went through all the motions in a dream. He took off his leather jacket and draped it on the back of a chair and sat there in his white shirt, which was open at the neck so that she glimpsed the dark hair which lay like fur on his chest. The hair seemed impossibly erotic – animal and male . . . she thought of bulls with chocolate-brown curly hair; of shaggy Highland cattle with long fringes trailing in their eyes; pelts . . . foxes . . . Under the thin cotton she could make out the dark pips of his small hard nipples and that too caused the excitement to flutter in her throat. They had never been alone like this before – there had always been his mother hovering, or his parents watching telly or at least never far away. And now, here they were in this room on a Saturday evening . . . everything was pending . . .

'Do you want a coffee?'

He said yes and she went through into the kitchenette. She felt she was different in that place . . . and he was too. It was like playing at house . . . she'd done that as a little girl. Now I'm the Mummy and I'm making the dinner and you . . .

If she'd met him for the first time now, she wouldn't have known anything about the butchering or Mrs Brennan and her copper waves and her rings and her bright red nails. He'd just have been a man with red cheeks and blue eyes and glassy black hair. They were out drifting on a raft under a melon moon and the air was filled with the drone of cicadas . . .

'Thanks,' he said as she handed him the coffee, and he sat there on the sofa with his thighs spread wide and his hands braced round the mug, and she gave a secret shudder which started in her stomach like pins and needles and became a thrill.

'Flat looks all right.'

'Yes, it's real comfortable . . . won't be hard to clean either. Tricia's at her mum and dad's this weekend – back tomorrow night. How've you been?'

'All right. Got a lot on.'

He talked, she listened. She stared at his hands and avoided prolonged eye-contact.

It got to eleven o'clock, midnight . . .

'I'd best push off.'

'Yes,' she said. 'does your mother know where you are?'

'No.'

'Well then . . .'

She waited. The evening had drawn into that moment. She studied her fingernails.

'It's a pity . . .' he began, and was staring at her.

'Yes?'

'That we live far away.'

'You could stay the night.' She felt the blood whoosh into her cheeks.

- In groups, discuss 'What happens next?', exploring at least two possibilities.

- Choose the one you think the most likely and justify your decision by reference to the way the narrative has been handled up to that point

Now read the commentary on page 59.

Genre endings

The three short stories we have looked at – *Answer*, *Doctor Chevalier's Lie*, and *Business Before Pleasure* – all ended with dashed hopes. You could consider whether this, rather than a neatly resolved happy ending, is a common feature of modern short stories. The conventions of romance genres such as Mills and Boon novels, however, require a happy ending with the pretty young heroine beating off her more sophisticated rivals to win the heart of the aloof, powerful male and rejecting the affable, younger man as 'just a good friend'. If you are interested in a particular genre of story, try to identify its conventions. If you choose to transform an example of such a genre, you could subvert the usual expectations by writing an ending that is unconventional. Thus, the female protagonist of a Mills and Boon story could have a fling with Mr Powerful, but choose qualities of kindness and sincerity for her life's partner. Though unexpected in the 'world' of the literary genre, it poses another, equally logical, 'world' of love. Or you could have her marrying no one. Or . . . ? Your choice of ending would implicitly reveal something about the usual conventions of the genre. Your commentary should make this explicit.

Drama as the base text

The following activities use drama as the base text from which you can experiment with types of transformations.

Monologue

A **dialogue** is a conversation between two or more people. A **monologue** is a soliloquy or speech by one person. The term **soliloquy** is used if the person is apparently speaking to her/himself. This is a dramatic device in plays whereby the audience hears a character give voice to thoughts. There are some examples of drama scripts that are all one voice: Alan Bennett's *Talking Heads* is a series of monologues written for TV performance. The speech of the single character usually suggests or reports other voices. Willy Russell's stage play *Shirley Valentine* is all monologue, but the film version developed the other characters and gave them dialogue, perhaps because the genre of film is conventionally more life-like than stage drama. Because dialogue is the norm for talk, this tends to highlight the occurrence of monologues in drama scripts.

ACTIVITY 24

- Read the following monologue extract from *Road* (1986) by Jim Cartwright. (A brief summary of the play: in the course of one wild night, the drunken guide, Scullery, conducts a tour of Road, his derelict Lancashire street. The following monologue is by his wife, Valerie.)

- Then do one or more of the tasks that follow.

The lights come up on a woman waiting, smoking. She is in her mid-thirties, sitting on a hard kitchen chair. She has a scruffy dressing-gown on, a bit of sad nightie showing.

VALERIE: I'm fed up of sitting here waiting for him, he'll be another hundred years at his rate. What a life, get up, feed every baby in the house. Do everything else I can, without cash. While he drinks, drinks it, drinks it, and shoves nothing my way except his fat hard hands in bed at night. Rough dog he is. Big rough heavy dog. Dog with sick in its fur. He has me pulling my hair out. Look at my hair, it's so dry. So sadly dried. I'd cry but I don't think tears would come. And there's nothing worse than an empty cry. It's like choking. Why do we do it? Why do I stay? Why the why why? You can cover yourself in questions and you're none the wiser 'cause you're too tired to answer. Always scrimping and scraping. He just takes the Giro and does what he wants with it. Leaves a few pounds on the table corner sometimes, sometimes. But you never know when and if you ask him he chops you one. That's why I have to borrow, borrow off everyone. I am like a bony rat going here, going there, trying to sniffle something out. They help me, though I'll bet you they hate me really. Despise me really. Because I'm always there an' keep asking, asking and they can't say no. They just open their purses, and I says, thank you, thank you a thousand times till we all feel sick. God I can't wait till the kids are older then I can send them. He'll come in soon. Pissied drunk through. Telling me I should do more about the place. Eating whatever's in the house. Pissing and missing the bog. Squeezing the kids too hard. Shouting then sulking. Then sleeping all deep and smelly, wrapped over and over in the blankets. Drink's a bastard. Drink's a swilly brown bastard. A smelling stench sea. And he's the captain with his bristles wet through. Swallowing and throwing, swallowing and throwing white brown water all over me. Oh what am I saying, it's a nightmare all this. I blame him then I don't blame him. It's not his fault there's no work. He's such a big man, he's nowhere to put himself. He looks so awkward and sad at the sink, the vacuum's like a toy in his hand. When he's in all day he fills up the room. Like a big wounded animal, moving about, trying to find his slippers, clumsy with the small things of the house, bewildered. I see this. I see the poor beast in the wrong world. I see his eyes sad and low. I see him as the days go on, old damp sacks one on top of another. I see him, the waste. The human waste of the land. But I can't forgive him. I can't forgive the cruel of the big fucking heap. The big fucking clumsy heap. [*She startles herself with what she's saying, nearly cries.*] He's so big and hunched and ugly. [*Holding back.*] Oh my man. [*She chokes.*] I hate him now, and I didn't used to. I hate him now, and I don't want to. [*She cries.*] Can we not have before again, can we not? [*She cries.*] Can we not have before again? [*She looks out manic and abrupt.*] Can we not?

Blackout.

Valerie says at one point: 'I blame him then I don't blame him.' Near the end of her monologue she says: 'I hate him now, and I didn't used to.'

- Working in pairs, re-read her monologue, one of you finding her reasons for blaming and hating her husband, the other finding her reasons for not blaming him.

- Prepare a reading for two voices, alternating between phrases of hate and blame, and phrases of understanding and affection.

- Work in small groups to listen to and comment on each others' readings.

No commentary.

In the monologue, Valerie voices thoughts and feelings that she may not share with her family or friends. It is an inside view of her life and marriage from Valerie's perspective. The following activity suggests changes of perspective. You can continue to work with this extract from *Road* or choose another monologue or another play.

ACTIVITY 25

Work in groups of four, five or six. Each choose a different perspective and write a short monologue or dialogue based on *Road*.

Possible transformations of perspective:

- The husband speaks (scene in the pub with friends).

- The neighbours talk (just before Valerie comes round to borrow, or just after).

- As teenagers, her children reminisce about their childhood.

- The young Valerie speaks (flashback to Valerie's wedding day or hen night).

- Create a collage of these different perspectives. Decide which is to be read first and which last.

- As a full class, give each other feedback.

Possible changes of genre:

The following tasks suggest changes to this monologue from *Road*. You could choose one of these as an exercise in transformation, or select your own drama text and produce a transformation for your coursework folder.

- A third-person prose narrative (A narrative could focus on Valerie, or a character from your chosen drama text. Narratives often imply the thoughts and feelings of characters, rather than express them explicitly in an internal monologue. Your task would be to suggest thoughts and feelings in your description of the character's movements, actions, and conversation with others. In the case of Valerie, you could choose an episode, for example a meal with the children while waiting for her husband to come home.)

- A radio play (develop Valerie's story without reliance on visuals).

- A musical (transform the monologue into song lyrics).

- A diary.

- A newspaper feature article about unemployment in inner-city areas (with Valerie's family as the case-study).

- A collage (facts and figures, opinions about unemployment, drink, and so on, mixed with lines from Valerie).

- A biography.

The commentary on page 61 provides an example of song lyrics from Willie Russell's musical *Blood Brothers*, in which the main female character charts the hopes and disappointments of her married life.

Shakespeare plays

Shakespeare's *Antony and Cleopatra* is used for the next Activities, but you may choose another Shakespeare play.

First, a reminder of the historical context: Antony was a Roman general and Cleopatra was the ruler of Egypt, one of the last of the Ptolemy dynasty. Whilst there is evidence of a strong physical attraction between the pair, there was also a more pragmatic reason on both sides for a liaison to occur. Cleopatra wanted to protect her empire against incursions by Rome and to reduce the debt to Rome her father had amassed, while Antony wanted to use Egypt as a gateway to the East to extend his control over Asia.

Next, let's consider a synopsis of *Antony and Cleopatra*:

Cleopatra is depicted by Shakespeare as engrossed in a passion for Antony. Antony (Marcus Antonius) is portrayed as being torn between his desire for Cleopatra and his need to maintain his position as part of the ruling triumvirate (Octavius Caesar, Antony and Lepidus). In a tactical move, Antony agrees to marry Octavius Caesar's sister Octavia. (It is after this scene that Enobarbus describes how Cleopatra first appeared to Antony on a barge.) It is important that Antony demonstrates loyalty to Octavius and, for a while, all is well. However he returns to Cleopatra and makes an enemy of Octavius. In a challenge at sea, an error of tactics or a change in the weather leaves Antony defeated. He fails to negotiate a truce and Octavius refuses his challenge of a duel. In the ensuing battle, although he gains a temporary advantage, Antony is later defeated and blames Cleopatra, believing she is capable of betraying him. He threatens to kill her. She pretends she is dead. Full of remorse, and believing the news that she is dead, he attempts to kill himself and is then taken to her and dies in her arms. Caesar quickly plays matters to his advantage and forces Cleopatra to be captured. Unable to face the humiliation of defeat, Cleopatra kills herself by allowing a poisonous snake (an asp) to bite her.

In all there are forty scenes in the play. Cleopatra appears in ten of these.

You need to be aware that even this seemingly neutral task of writing a summary is in itself a transformation of the text. Reworking a text into a synopsis generates a new text in which certain details are emphasised. Remember that it is someone's version and that s/he will have *interpreted* the action and characters, not merely described them.

ACTIVITY 26

Find out the title of the Shakespeare play that you are studying in Module 5.

- Download a synopsis of the play from the Internet. The most helpful example would be one that includes a synopsis of the play scene by scene.

- Highlight the bits that interest you.

- Put your comments on a poster and display it in the classroom.

- After studying the play, see whether your interests have changed and consider what led to the change.

Now read the commentary on page 62.

Shakespeare would have been aware of a translation of Plutarch's *The Life of Marcus Antonius*, translated into French by Jacques Amyot and then from French into English by Thomas North. Plutarch, a Greek historian born 76 years after the death of Cleopatra, is said to have listened to his grandfather's accounts of her life. Yet again a text – this time an oral text – has been transformed.

ACTIVITY 27

What does Shakespeare do with North's version of Jacques Amyot's version of Plutarch's version of his grandfather's version of a particular detail?

- Identify the details which are the same.

- What common elements do you find? What is different?

- What view of Cleopatra are we offered in Shakespeare's version?

- When you read between the lines, what view is Enobarbus taking of Cleopatra?

Plutarch: *The Life of Marcus Antonius* (translated by Thomas North, 1579). Plutarch is describing Cleopatra's barge.

' ... the sails of purple, and the oars of silver, which kept stroke in rowing after the sound of the music of flutes, howboys, citherns, viols, and such other instruments as they played upon in the barge. And now for the person of herself: she was laid under a pavilion of cloth of gold of tissue, apparelled and attired like the goddess Venus commonly drawn in picture, and hard by her, on either hand of her, pretty fair boys apparelled as painters do set forth god Cupid, with little fans in their hands, with the which they fanned wind upon her. Her ladies and gentlewomen also, the fairest of them were apparelled like the nymphs Nereides (of which are the mermaids of the waters) and like the Graces, some steering the helm, others tending the tackle and ropes of the barge, out of the which there came a wonderful passing sweet savour of perfumes, that perfumed the wharf's side, pestered with innumerable multitudes of people. Some of them followed the barge all alongst the river's side; others also ran out of the city to see her coming in; so that in the end there ran such multitudes of people one after another to see her that Antonius [Antony] was left post-alone in the market-place in his imperial seat to give audience.'

Shakespeare: *Antony and Cleopatra*

DOMITIUS ENOBARBUS
I will tell you.
The barge she sat in, like a burnish'd throne
Burn'd on the water: the poop was beaten gold;
Purple the sails, and so perfumed that
The winds were love-sick with them; the oars were silver,
Which to the tune of flutes kept stroke, and made
The water which they beat to follow faster,
As amorous of their strokes. For her own person,
It beggar'd all description: she did lie
In her pavilion – cloth of gold, of tissue –
O'er-picturing that Venus where we see
The fancy outwork nature. On each side her
Stood pretty dimpled boys, like smiling Cupids,
With divers-colour'd fans, whose wind did seem
To glow the delicate cheeks which they did cool,
And what they undid did.

AGRIPPA
                    O, rare for Antony!
DOMITIUS ENOBARBUS
Her gentlewomen, like the Nereides,
So many mermaids, tended her i' the eyes,
And made their bends adornings. At the helm
A seeming mermaid steers: the silken tackle
Swell with the touches of those flower-soft hands,
That yarely frame the office. From the barge
A strange invisible perfume hits the sense
Of the adjacent wharfs. The city cast
Her people out upon her; and Antony,
Enthron'd i' the market-place, did sit alone,
Whistling to the air; which, but for vacancy,
Had gone to gaze on Cleopatra too,
And made a gap in nature.

AGRIPPA
                    Rare Egyptian!

DOMITIUS ENOBARBUS
Upon her landing, Antony sent to her,
Invited her to supper: she replied,
It should be better he became her guest,

Which she entreated: our courteous Antony,
Whom ne'er the word of 'No' woman heard speak,
Being barber'd ten times o'er, goes to the feast;
And for his ordinary, pays his heart,
For what his eyes eat only,

(Act 2, Scene 2)

Find out the sources Shakespeare used for the play you are studying in Module 5. (Usually the introduction to the play will identify these.)

Now read the commentary on page 62.

Types of transformations

Text transformations of a Shakespeare play may be something you encountered at GCSE. For example, newspaper accounts of key events in *Macbeth*, or Friar Lawrence's version of why he officiated at the wedding ceremony of Romeo and Juliet told at an inquest, make useful exercises in demonstrating knowledge of the text and characterisation. Here is an opportunity to explore how writers can present attitudes and values through their texts with varying degrees of subtlety.

ACTIVITY 28

Decide which of the following activities would give you the scope to present a *negative* view of Cleopatra's arrival for a fashion show preview.

- A gossip column in a classy women's magazine.

- A BBC court correspondent reporting on the royal visit for BBC News.

- A Roman politician's memoir.

- The soap-style dialogue of two of the maids who participated in the event.

- The Royle Family dad who, by mistake, has switched to a channel showing a performance of the play at the moment when Cleopatra's famous arrival is being enacted.

No commentary.

The notion of 'translation'

The following activities focus on the play *Translations* by Brian Friel. It makes explicit some of the issues with which modern readers and critics of literature have been concerned. As the title suggests, it is dangerous to assume that there is only one version of 'reality' – the title is plural, suggesting that there can be many 'versions'. You may know from your own studies of another language that when you translate, something is lost – often there is no exact equivalent for a word or phrase, which is one reason why English makes use of foreign borrowings: for example the French *ennui*, for a type of boredom, and the German *Vorsprung durch Technik* for 'advancement through technology'. Similarly, if you have ever written a report of the minutes for a meeting, you will have noticed that what you represent as having taken place has shades of meaning you put into the text. Who controls the translation or version, and what they seek to emphasise, often tell us a great deal about their point of view.

Brian Friel set the action of *Translations* in Ireland in the early 1830s and it was first performed in Northern Ireland in the early 1980s, before there were any moves by the British government to broker a power-sharing agreement with representatives of the Protestant and Catholic communities. Friel presents the effect of the English occupation of Ireland. Halfway through the first act the audience realise that a *translation* has occurred even to bring the play to English audiences: the characters are speaking in Irish Gaelic, *translated* into English. Ironically, this is shown because they refer to their lack of English and discuss whether they need to learn it. The audience begins to realise that the Irish people were robbed of their language, and to understand what has happened in Ireland between the period when the play is set and the present. Friel takes care to set the play very much in the domain of the Irish. They are introduced first, and are shown in their hedge school (schools run by Irish-speaking teachers who received small payments from their students). We see the close-knit community that they represent, gain insights into the central importance they place on superstition and learning, and enjoy their humour and banter. They are not portrayed as uneducated: Jimmy Jack Cassie knows Greek, Latin and Gaelic; Manus knows all of these languages and English.

The following extract occurs in Act 1. Owen, the son of the schoolmaster, Hugh, and brother to Manus, has returned from Dublin with English sappers (army engineers). He is now paid by them to assist in the mapping of Donegal. Lancey is an English captain in charge of the expedition. Yolland (George) is the lieutenant who will make changes to place-names based upon anglicising them into recognisable English sounds and spellings or by translating them into their English equivalents.

ACTIVITY 29

Read the following extract out in class together, and then do the tasks that follow.

OWEN: And I'll translate as you go along.

LANCEY: I see. Yes. Very well. Perhaps you're right. Well. What we are doing is this. [*He looks at* OWEN. OWEN *nods reassuringly.*] His Majesty's government has ordered the first ever comprehensive survey of this entire country – a general triangulation which will embrace detailed hydrographic and topographic information and which will be executed to a scale of six inches to the English mile.

HUGH   [*Pouring a drink*] Excellent – excellent.

          [LANCEY *looks at* OWEN]

OWEN: A new map is being made of the whole country.

[LANCEY *looks to* OWEN: *Is that all?* OWEN *smiles reassuringly and indicates to proceed.*]

LANCEY: This enormous task has been embarked on so that the military authorities will be equipped with up-to-date and accurate information on every corner of this part of the Empire.

OWEN: The job is being done by soldiers because they are skilled in this work.

LANCEY: And also so that the entire basis of land valuation can be reassessed for the purposes of more equitable taxation.

OWEN: This new map will take the place of the estate agent's map so that from now on you will know exactly what is yours in law.

LANCEY: In conclusion I wish to quote two brief extracts from the white paper which is our governing charter [*Reads*] 'All former surveys of Ireland originated in forfeiture and violent transfer of property; the present survey has for its object the relief which can be afforded to the proprietors and occupiers of land from unequal taxation.'

OWEN: The captain hopes that the public will cooperate with the sappers and that the new map will mean that taxes are reduced.

HUGH: A worthy enterprise – *opus honestum*! And Extract B?

LANCEY: 'Ireland is privileged. No such survey is being undertaken in England. So that this survey cannot be but received as proof of the disposition of this government to advance the interests of Ireland'. My sentiments too.

OWEN: This survey demonstrates the government's interest in Ireland and the captain thanks you for listening so attentively to him.

HUGH: Our pleasure, Captain.

LANCEY: Lieutenant Yolland?

YOLLAND: I – I – I've nothing to say – really–

OWEN: The captain is the man who actually makes the new map. George's task is to see that the place-names on this map are . . . correct. [*To* YOLLAND] Just a few words – they'd like to hear you. [*To* CLASS] Don't you want to hear George too?

MAIRE: Has he anything to say?

YOLLAND: [*To* MAIRE] Sorry – sorry?

OWEN: She says she's dying to hear you.

YOLLAND: [*To* MAIRE] Very kind of you – thank you . . . [*To class*] I can only say that I feel – I feel very foolish to – to – to be working here and not to speak your language. But I intend to rectify that – with Roland's help – indeed I do.

OWEN: He wants me to teach him Irish!

HUGH: You are doubly welcome, sir.

YOLLAND: I think your countryside is – is – is very beautiful. I've fallen in love with it already. I hope we're not too – too crude an intrusion on your lives. And I know that I'm going to be happy, very happy, here.

OWEN: He's already a committed Hibernophile –

JIMMY: He loves –

OWEN: Alright Jimmy – we know – he loves Baile Beag; and he loves you all.

HUGH: Please . . . May I . . . ?

[HUGH *is now drunk. He holds on to the edge of the table.*]

OWEN: Go ahead, Father. [*Hands up for quiet*] Please – please.

HUGH: And we, gentlemen, we in turn are happy to offer you our friendship, our hospitality, and every assistance that you may require. Gentlemen – welcome!

[*A few desultory claps. The formalities are over. General conversation. The soldiers meet the locals.* MANUS *and* OWEN *down stage.*]

OWEN: Lancey's a bloody ramrod but George's alright. How are you anyway?

MANUS: What sort of translation was that, Owen?

OWEN: Did I make a mess of it?

MANUS: You weren't saying what Lancey was saying!

OWEN: 'Uncertainty in meaning is incipient poetry' – who said that?

MANUS: There was nothing uncertain about what Lancey said: it's a bloody military operation, Owen! And what's Yolland's function? What's 'incorrect' about the place-names we have here?

OWEN: Nothing at all. They are just going to be standardised.

MANUS: You mean changed into English?

OWEN: Where there is ambiguity, they'll be Anglicised.

- Make a list of the reasons why the English would want a map of the whole area.

- Look up any of the English words which are not familiar (they probably have Greek or Latin roots).

- Divide your page in two and then closely match what Captain Lancey says to Owen's translation.

- Using as a prompt Manus's claim that, 'it's a bloody military occupation', rewrite the piece as a speech giving (a) Manus's version of the translation, and (b) a version based upon what you understand to be the English government's original intention.

Now read the commentary on page 62.

Critical approach II: Structuralism

The second extract from *Translations* will explore the interaction of the Irish and English in terms of the ways in which we interpret signs. In order to do this, we can look briefly at a critical approach known as Structuralism.

Structuralism

Key person: Ferdinand de Saussure – Swiss linguist

Key texts: Saussure, *Course in General Linguistics* (1915)

Key ideas: Deriving from linguistics, Structuralism has had a profound impact on the study of literature. You may have already come across structuralist narratology, the study of the underlying structures common to narratives regardless of their subject. The Russian theorist Vladimir Propp, for example, drew up a list of 31 'functions' or main actions he'd identified in Russian fairy stories; you may have applied them to your own oral narrative when you worked on Original Writing in Module 3.

In exploring the relationship between words and things, Ferdinand de Saussure drew a distinction between a language system (for example the English language, with all its rules of grammar) and individual utterance in that language — our own utterances, for example. Saussure called the language system *langue* and the individual use of language *parole*. For Saussure words are not symbols which simply correspond to referents (objects) but signs made up of two things: a *signifier* (a mark on the page or a spoken word) and a *signified* (the meaning, what is thought when the mark is made or the word is spoken). If we apply this distinction to human communication in general — to sign systems of any kind — then we can, for example, see an act by someone as a signifier that can be 'read' by someone else — as long as they share a common recognition of the relationship between the two (the signifier and the signified) that makes understanding possible.

You may already have looked at how advertisers subtly exploit this relationship between signifier and signified in their use of images and words. In literature, this distinction allows us to explore, among other things, how *mis*readings of a signifier occur when someone wrongly assumes what the signified is.

To see this in action, read the following extract from *Translations* (Act 2, Scene 2) and consider the comments that follow:

YOLLAND: Thank you for – I – I'm very grateful to you for –

DOALTY: Wasting your time. I don't know a word you're saying. Hi, Manus, there's two bucks down the road there asking for you.

MANUS: [*descending*] Who are they?

DOALTY: Never clapped eyes on them. They want to talk to you.

MANUS: What about?

DOALTY: They wouldn't say. Come on. The bloody beasts'll end up in Loch an Iubhair if they're not capped. Good luck, boys!

    [DOALTY *rushes off.* MANUS *follows him*]

OWEN: Good luck! What were you thanking Doalty for?

YOLLAND: I was washing outside my tent this morning and he was passing with a scythe across his shoulder and he came up to me and pointed to the long grass and then cut a pathway round my tent and from the tent down to the road – so that my feet won't get wet with the dew. Wasn't that kind of him? And I have no words to thank him . . . .

Yolland has interpreted an act in a particular way. It may well be that cutting the grass around the tent area was intended as a gesture of good will, but, given that long grass rustles and gives you away if you or your confederates try to approach a tent unannounced, there could be a more sinister meaning to Doalty's act; the audience do not forget whose side Doalty is on. Later in the play he states that however much he would like to be a part of Irish culture, he will never completely be assimilated into it. It is of course a utopian dream on his part, since the Ireland which attracts him is being changed.

ACTIVITY 30

Create a first-person account in which Doalty reflects upon the attitudes he and others may have had towards the English, and include any events or actions which would illustrate these. You can choose to locate the writing at whatever time and in whatever circumstances you choose to invent for Doalty.

Now read the commentary on page 63.

Writing your commentary

Your commentary on your text transformation is worth 50% of the marks. The total word count is 1,500 words. If you have produced two linked texts, you may choose to write either a single commentary or two shorter ones. If you have used two separate base texts and produced two distinct transformations, you will need to write separate commentaries of about 750 words each. In this case, your commentary will have to be concise and focused on the most significant factors in order to meet the criteria for the higher mark bands.

The top band descriptor for AO6, for example, requires that a commentary 'comments effectively and *in detail* on *a range* of features of own choices and language use'. These comments will be based on your linguistic knowledge, so it is important to remind yourself of the systematic framework for language analysis. The following diagram is based on a suggested distinction between the areas of syntax, semantics, and pragmatics. The term 'discourse' will be discussed further to show how it spans these three areas.

DISCOURSE

SYNTAX	SEMANTICS	PRAGMATICS

grammar
lexis
morphology
phonology
graphology

Syntax: words and the relationship between words

Semantics: the relationship between words and meaning

Pragmatics: the relationship between words and their users and interpreters

Comments based on linguistic knowledge

Some people have a narrow view of what 'linguistic knowledge' involves, believing that it is simply the identification of word classes, such as nouns and verbs, or sentence structures. These two levels of lexis and grammar may well be significant, but it is important to remember that you could also look at the 'lower' levels of morphology (word formation), phonology (sounds), or graphology (the visual marks on the page). It's better, however, to start with the broad picture and consider the semantics (meanings), pragmatics (implied meanings), and discourse. In the AS book, a definition of discourse was provided, which needs to be extended now.

What does 'discourse' refer to?

The term 'discourse' is difficcult to define for it is used in different ways by different writers. However complex this concept is, it is important that you understand it, for it underpins the Assessment Objectives for your commentary.

1. The basic definition is 'text type or structure'. You can see that this definition already suggests two aspects.

   - 'Text type' is similar to 'genre' – the way we classify texts not only as poetry, prose, drama, but also as speeches, advertisements, articles, essays, letters, emails, conversations, and so on.

   - However, 'structure' suggests a further analysis of each text type, perhaps looking at the way it begins, develops and ends. In drama, a play may be structured into three or five acts, which stand in a significant relationship to each other. In poetry, a sonnet has a tight structure of an octet (eight lines) followed by a sestet (six lines), with the rhyme scheme changing from alternate lines to a final rhyming couplet. In prose fiction, there have been various accounts of narrative structure developing the simple notion of a beginning, middle, and end; for example aim–problem–climax–resolution. The structures of oral narratives have been studies by a number of literary theorists; William Labov's framework was provided in Module 1 (page 11 of the AS book).

   As AO4 assesses your ability to describe form and style and explain how they shape meaning, this aspect of discourse will be an important focus.

There are two further meanings of the term 'discourse'.

2. In Module 5, you will study aspects of 'discourse analysis', where the term 'discourse' refers to spoken conversations.

3. The term has also been used in a wider sense, one that is important in the study of language and literature. In *Textual Intervention*, Rob Pope describes discourse as: 'communicative practices expressing the interests and characteristic "ways of seeing and saying" of a particular socio-historical group or institution; these are always definable in terms of relative power or powerlessness.'

   As AO5 assesses your ability to discuss ways in which attitudes and values are created and conveyed, this third sense of 'discourse' will be particularly important.

The first draft of your commentary

Although you will submit only the final version of your commentary, you should be preparing notes for it throughout your work on the transformation of a literary text. The following activities suggest questions and headings that you can use to formulate relevant comments about your own transformation. When you write up the final draft of your commentary, you will need to select the most revealing points.

ACTIVITY 31

Use these points and questions as the basis for your notes.

1. **Your choice of text and genre:**

   - What is the base text?

   - How did you arrive at the text: did you know it already? If not, then how did you hear about it?

   - When was it written?

- Note any points about the context (historical, cultural, social, political) that the reader needs to be aware of.

- Note any insights into the author, works, outlook and viewpoint that might be useful.

- What interest did the text have for you?

- What form did your studies take: original version, film or stage version, discussion in group?

2. **Your choice of transformation:**

- Did you ask a *What if . . . ?* question of the base text?

- Why did you choose this particular genre for your transformation?

- What other texts did you know/use to focus on the genre?

- What are the conventions of the genre of your piece?

- What other changes did you make – audience, purpose, perspective, style, etc?

- What further ideas or questions were you hoping to plant in the reader's mind?

3. **Your selection/reworking of material from the base text:**

- What did you notice which gave rise to an idea for transformation?

- What attitudes and values are created/conveyed in the base text?

- Note some of the ways attitudes and values are created (through plot, characterisation, viewpoint, chronology, style, and so on).

- What aspects did you retain? What did you change?

- Were your thoughts based on any approach you have learnt about during the course?

4. **The effect/meanings created in your transformation:**

- How do you think a reader will respond to your text?

- Is it important that the reader is familiar with the base text, or can your text stand alone?

- What attitudes and values are created in your text?

- Were you attempting to remain faithful to the base text, or provide a counter-interpretation?

5. **The linguistic choices in your transformation:**

- What are the relevant and significant features of your text? Begin at the level of discourse, before moving to the 'lower' levels of lexis, grammar, graphology, or phonology.

- What is significant about the overall structure of your text?

- What style/tone/voice is created? Why?

- What attitudes and values are created and how?

No commentary.

The second draft of your commentary

As you write the final draft of your commentary, consider the following questions:

- What transformation did you make, how, and why? (Consider genre, structure, style.)

- What is the effect? What does it reveal about the original? (Consider attitudes and values.)

Remember to include detailed comment on language use throughout.

Putting the coursework folder together

You should include the following in your folder:

1. **one** or **two** transformations totalling 1,500 to 2,500 words

2. a commentary of approximately 1,500 words.

Remember that your text transformation *must* be based on literary texts. If you submit two pieces of work, these may be transformations of a single text or two different texts. Indicate the title and author of the base text(s) clearly. If the texts are relatively short, you may append a copy for the assessor to read.

Your transformation *must* involve a change of genre. It may also involve a clearly different purpose and/or audience.

Your transformed texts and commentary carry equal marks. However, they are assessed under different objectives.

Your *text(s)* will be assessed under:

AO1: *communicate clearly* the knowledge, understanding and insights gained from the combination of literary and linguistic study, *using appropriate terminology and accurate written expression*

AO6: *demonstrate expertise and accuracy in writing for a variety of specific purposes and audiences,* drawing on knowledge of literary texts and features of language to explain and comment on the choices made

Your *commentary* will be assessed under:

AO4: show understanding of the ways contextual variation and choices of form, style and vocabulary shape the meanings of texts (2.5%)

AO5: identify and consider the ways attitudes and values are created and conveyed in speech and writing (2.5%)

AO6: demonstrate expertise and accuracy in writing for a variety of specific purposes and audiences, *drawing on knowledge of literary texts and features of language to explain and comment on the choices made* (2.5%)

Commentaries

Activity 1

This commentary provides a list of genres. You may be able to suggest interesting examples of base text combinations.

Base texts	Genres
	Trailer for film version/blurb for novel
	Review
	Obituary/funeral speeches
	Film script
	Documentary (soundtrack)
	Power Point presentation
	Fable
	Letters
	Public service advertisement
	Oral testimony
	'Theatre in Education' drama

Activity 2

These are some examples of literary works that have been transformed into new texts, and often different genres. You may be familiar with some of these and be able to supply other examples.

Pride and Prejudice, Jane Austen	Ad for Thompson Holidays
Jean de Florette, Marcel Pagnol	Ad for Stella Artois beer
The Bible	*The Poisonwood Bible*, Barbara Kingsolver
The Bible	*Pangs of Love*, Jane Gardam
King Lear, Shakespeare	Poems, U. A. Fanthorpe
King Lear, Shakespeare	Poems, Margaret Atwood
King Lear, Shakespeare	*A Thousand Acres*, Jane Smiley film
Romeo and Juliet, Shakespeare	*West Side Story* musical
Macbeth, Shakespeare	*Wyrd Sisters*, Terry Pratchett
All sorts of texts	The Simpsons cartoons
Nursery rhymes	*Revolting Rhymes*, Roald Dahl
Pygmalion, G. B. Shaw	*My Fair Lady* musical
King Arthur, legend	*Dream Damsel*, Hunter Davies

Activity 3

Did Icarus have a wife, mother, sister? No females feature in the story.

The poem by Carol Ann Duffy imagines that Icarus had a wife, who has suffered his foolish tendency to show off for so long that she feels embarrassment and irritation at his plight. The language of the poem clearly shows that the story has been modernised – the concept of 'pillock' is modern. Just as we no longer have the concept of 'the vapours', for example, to describe a type of nervous state, so 'pillock' and even 'Grade A' are anachronisms for the context of Greek mythology. 'Heroic' exploits can be viewed in different ways: the British mountaineer, Alison Hargreaves, who died in her attempt on the mountain K2, was criticised implicitly in the media for embarking on such a risky enterprise when she had young children. Male adventurers – such as Scott of the Antarctic – are rarely blamed for neglecting their family responsibilities. This poem fills in that 'gap'.

The second poem, 'The Sister of Icarus', is a reading of the myth inspired by some classroom versions that highlighted the young boy's nervousness at the exploit his father is asking him to perform. Though made to feel ashamed of his lack of courage, once he has taken to the air Icarus loses all caution in the excitement of the venture. Although the poem suggests that any sister he had would be 'invisible' in the dominant male world of myths, it retains a sense of regret for the pressures put on young males.

Activity 5

A Water Board advert:

Voiceover soundtrack of Jack and Jill nursery rhyme. Simple cartoon visuals. Cut to shots of modern water-processing plant, then a hand turning on a tap. 'Nowadays fetching water is at your fingertips. It's safe, it's simple. Thanks to North Western Water, Jack and Jill can . . . ' Shot of boy washing mud off forehead and girl downing a glass of water.

> Mayday 2000
>
> This little girl has a little stud
> Right in the middle of her tongue
> When she hears about child labour in sweat shops
> She knows what her voice is good for
> And if everyone joins in the protest
> The world might change for the better.

Activity 6

A dramatised version:

The fable of the two monks is read aloud by a narrator in a softly significant tone that signals its purpose as a moral message. The actions of the three people are shown in simple mime, except that the two men do not move far away from the girl after she has been carried across the road. There is a short pause after the two lines of dialogue between Tanzan and Ekido at the end of the fable. Then the girl calls to the two men: 'Can I say something? Sorry to interrupt your spiritual discussion, but did either of you wonder whether I wanted to cross that road in the first place?' Then she lifts up her skirts and walks back across the muddy road.

Activity 8

The implied 'I' commentator has a jaded, critical viewpoint on Britain in the 1980s. The final lines are completely negative: opt out, be a lout, dull void, unemployed. Many of the images chosen suggest a materialistic way of life full of possessions and gadgets: two car, ansaphone, colour telly, deep freeze. Other images suggest there is a lack of morality: loose dame, sleep around, tight jeans, 'page threes'. This overriding negative context suggests that the following should also be read as unfavourable aspects of society: first name, disco scenes, slingawelly. If these items were included in a more favourable context, they might acquire more positive connotations, as might the reference to tight jeans and ansaphone. Perhaps your short poems take a positive view of modern technology and disco culture. Equally, you may want to suggest unfavourable connotations for other aspects of modern life that are regarded as positive by other people.

Activity 9

This is an extract from an essay David Dabydeen contributed to the book *The State of the Language* (edited by Ricks and Michaels, 1990), in which he talks about the use of creole in poetry and the use of sounds in the reciting of poetry.

In the preface to Slave Song I speak of the brokenness of the language which reflects the suffering of its original users. Its potential as a naturally tragic language is there in its brokenness and rawness, which is like the rawness of a wound. If one has learnt and used the Queen's English for some years, the return to creole is painful, almost nauseous, for the language is uncomfortably raw. One has to shed one's protective sheath of abstracts and let the tongue move freely in blood again.

... [Linton Kwesi] Johnson's poetry is recited to music from a reggae band. The paraphernalia of sound systems, amplifiers, speakers, microphones, electric guitars, and the rest which dominates the stage and accompanies what one music critic has dismissed as 'jungle-talk' is a deliberate 'misuse' of white technology. 'Sound systems', essential to 'dub-poetry', are often home-made contraptions, cannibalised parts of diverse machines reordered for black expression. This de/reconstruction is in itself an assertive statement, a denial of the charge of black incapacity to understand technology. The mass-produced technology is remade for self-use in the way that the patois is a 'private' reordering of 'standard English. The deliberate exploitation of high-tech to serve black 'jungle-talk' is a reversal of colonial history. Caliban [in Shakespeare's *The Tempest*] is tearing up the pages of Prospero's magic book and repasting it in his own order, by his own method, and for his own purpose.

Activity 10

Pronouns: we our us / you your yours

This suggests a group perspective: the imagined voices of all the men who drowned, from the cooks to the sailors, possibly including the captain? The second-person pronoun (you) is ambiguous in English, as it can refer to a single person or a group. The words could be addressed to the individual reader, but suggest another collective group: the people who discovered and recovered the wreck, or perhaps all those who are looking at the wreck as a museum spectacle. The very first word is 'your' so the person addressed is immediately foregrounded. The last word is 'yours'. The direct question 'What will you do with us . . .?' is left hanging, without a response. Is this a challenge, or perhaps a plea?

If you have planned to use multiple voices for the reading, there would be a different effect if it were read as a chorus, or one by one. The words might be addressed to a visible representation of the 'you', possibly a singular representative or crowd.

Activity 12

The narrator works in the Town Hall Annexe and is older than the girl. His job allows him plenty of time to stare out of the window. He seems obsessive, as he keeps an observation diary. Although very interested in her, he never speaks, only watches. His attention to detail is so precise, he notices that he watches for thirty-five minutes (rather than 'about half an hour'). His hobbies are solitary and academic – the public library and Natural History Museum – and he is knowledgeable about species of butterflies. He may describe himself as a 'connoisseur', but he seems insane and dangerous.

He perceives the girl in an impersonal way, referring to her as 'she' or 'her' or even 'X' in his diary. Once he knows her name, she remains an initial, 'M'. He notices both her and her younger sister and is jealous of the young men they are with. When he describes her, it is her physical appearance he notices, concentrating on the back of her head and hair. Phrases referring to her hair are repeated: 'a long pigtail', 'very pale, silky, like burnet cocoons. All in one pigtail'; 'so beautiful, like a mermaid'. He sums up her attraction for him as 'rarity . . . elusive . . . refined'. She is better than 'the pretty ones'. Although the connotations of the words are positive, they suggest the sort of praise one might use for a zoological specimen. Words like 'silky' and 'cocoons' would occur in descriptions of butterflies, as the proper name 'Pale Clouded Yellow' makes clear.

His relationship with her is that of a stalker, watching and following. The statement 'before she came to be my guest here' is a shock, as it's hard to imagine any reason why she would visit him. In the following paragraph he describes his relationship with her as 'catching a rarity, going up to it very careful', which sounds as if she is like a butterfly to him. The title, *The Collector*, makes the reader suspect that his motives are, in fact, sinister: she is just another beautiful specimen, so the phrase 'not like the other ones' has a chilling reference.

Activity 13

The title suggests a love poem, except that it focuses on the 'lover' rather than the woman herself. The bleak weather described is unsettling. In a film, the audience might expect something dreadful is about to happen. However, the warmth inside is a comforting contrast and it is associated with the arrival of Porphyria, so this might be the setting for a love story, particularly the image 'blaze'. The 'I' narrator's heart was 'fit to break' before she came in, so he seems besotted with her.

The narrator of the poem is strangely silent and passive. Porphyria moves about doing domestic things; he watches her. She calls to him; he doesn't reply. He notices her hair fall loose when she takes off her hat. Because of the juxtaposition of the previous text, this strikes a worrying note. Might it do so anyway? The image of a woman 'letting her hair down' is often given sexual overtones, if the watcher is male. Her hair is 'yellow'; the previous girl's was 'pale', and blondeness is a familiar image of sexual attractiveness in our culture. The length and colour of her hair is noted by the narrator repeatedly. Like the 'collector', he notices other physical attributes in a coldly detached way – 'smooth white shoulder'. A third person is suggested, a rival perhaps. The narrator feels surprise and pride that she loves him and wants her to 'give herself to me for ever'. Perhaps he is going to ask her to marry him?

The outcome is shocking, but perhaps not unexpected. Apart from the juxtaposition of a text with a similar attitude, you might have been made uneasy by a coldness in his comments about her. The matter-of-fact way he describes the murder is shocking, but not surprising. Like the collector, he also perceives the woman as a botanical specimen: 'a shut bud that holds a bee' and 'rosy little head.' The poem itself suggests a pathological detachment in the narrator. As readers, we have already been prepared for it by reading *The Collector*.

Activity 14

The juxtaposition of these three texts may encourage a critical look at the subject matter of the novel and the poem. Placing them in the context of the T-shirt slogan may be considered a distortion. Both literary texts are well-known, popular, and often studied in literature courses. They are not a representative sample, however; I could have chosen two optimistic and loving texts about male-female relationships.

Perhaps an important difference between the novel and poem and the slogan is the irony in allowing the narrator to reveal unwittingly their own pathology. But is it offered to the reader for a similar frisson to the excitement of watching portrayals of violence against women in pornographic films?

The selection of these three texts in juxtaposition is an important aspect of the *context* of reading them. We could have chosen, instead, two texts portraying a woman's desire to possess a man leading her to cold-blooded murder. Yet, few examples spring to mind. Is this one of the gaps and silences in literature? The novel *Dirty Weekend* by Helen Zahavi, which outraged some readers, is a surprising transformation of the genre in which a man kills women violently. In *Dirty Weekend* a woman goes on a killing spree of all the men who have crossed her. On the other hand, it would be relatively simple to supply titles of other literary works about the killing of women.

Activity 16

There are details that suggest an imagined future world, such as references to populated planets and subether, but possibly supercircuits and a cybernetics machine still seem possible today.

The name Dwar is shared by the two men, so might be a title. The moral of the story is that it is presumptuous to question the existence of God, so they have been struck down by his (or her?) wrath. The genre of science fiction is often populated by men, perhaps because it is assumed that adventure is a male domain, more so at the time the story was written. Changes to the questions (and answers) may add humour or suggest a different moral.

Activity 17

The opening sentences mention details that suggest the perspective of someone who has experienced this before: 'no unusual sound . . . commonly . . . this time.'

The details given about the female character emphasise the doctor's observations that, like others before her, she is stretched out, dead, that she has a hole in the temple where she had shot herself. Unlike the others, she is familiar to the doctor. He recalls her as part of a family, handsome and clever and about to leave to seek her fortune in the city. As the story is told from his perspective, the reader is given no other details about her. She is referred to as 'a dead girl' and remembered as the family's 'handsome girl'. This choice of term suggests her youth and innocence in the eyes of the doctor and contrasts with the reference to her as 'a woman of doubtful repute' by gossips. To them, she deserves no compassion. Her profession labels her, as did newspaper headlines in May 2001 when they referred to a woman who had died in a car crash as 'the prostitute in the Jeffrey Archer case'.

Activity 18

When we tell a story, it can never be the truth, the whole truth and nothing but the truth. Writers and speakers choose where to begin, where to end, what to include and what to leave out. Kate Chopin's story has a very compressed timespan and restricts the details to Dr Chevalier's perspective, even though the focus of interest would usually be the young woman. Who was she? How did she die? Why did she die? You may have noticed the tone and style of the final sentences of the story: 'Shoulders were shrugged . . . the affair blew over.' This emphasises the view of it as a minor event; no one cared very much. Her family would grieve, but they would never know the full story 'down there in the forest'.

Activity 19

The first opening scene is faithful to the original story, placing the focus of interest on the doctor, his role and later his dilemma.

The second opening shifts the focus to the situation of a poor rural family whose daughter's best hope of improving her life is to leave for the city. Presumably the film will later show the family's response to the letter from the doctor.

The third opening skips over the young woman's previous life and begins with her arrival in the city, introducing potential dangers and potential friends. The film will presumably focus in detail on this part of her life as the cause of her suicide. The role of the doctor may become minor and the family she left behind may remain largely unseen.

The third storyline may have the strongest popular appeal, though many Hollywood films have a strong male character in a lead role, so the doctor's dilemma may need to be interwoven.

Activity 20

In *Doctor Chevalier's Lie*, you may have noted the following binary assumptions:

- Male – female.

- Narrative viewpoint – subject of the narration; in other words: voice – lack of voice. This is carried through in the narration: Dr Chevalier is not the narrator, but the story is narrated from his point of view.

- Recognised profession – prostitution, which is said to be the 'oldest profession' yet lacks status.

- City – countryside. The contrasts between city and countryside are represented by Dr Chevalier and his friend's hunting expedition for leisure, as opposed to the family's need to gain a living out of the countryside.

- Prosperity – poverty.

- Scientific – emotional. A further dichotomy can be seen in the women's emotional and helpless response to the death and *Dr* Chevalier's scientific and dispassionate approach.

- Named – anonymous. 'Dr Chevalier' and 'the young woman', who is never given a name.

- Powerful – powerless. Dr Chevalier lies, so the parents remain uninformed.

The narrative presents a male's world in which woman is *other* – unnamed and invisible up to the moment of her death. Her *otherness* is emphasised. She has no access to a respectable life. She arrived in a city unable to use her intelligence because she was seen by others to be a young, attractive and naive country woman. Her gender has led to her destruction. In this story there are no woodcutters or princes to rescue her from the wolf. Her father has surrendered her to her own destruction. Chevalier arrives too late to play the role of gallant, fairy-tale deliverer from all evil. He protects the corrupt city way of life by lying and thus maintains the established order.

Activity 21

Candice Bushnell, author of *Sex in the City* (novel and Channel 4 series), commented on the need for thwarted hopes in narratives. An interviewer said: 'Your characters are all searching for men. But they never seem to find one.' She replied: 'Thank God. Or I'd have nothing to write about!' (Breakfast News, 29 Jan 2001)

Obviously Jason and Joanne do not become beautiful people in Bermuda. That wouldn't make the sort of ending we expect when the story is introduced by mentioning something the character 'had' hoped for and expected. The use of the past perfect tense immediately sets up the expectation that later events were different. We are told that the winning of a prize 'changed things for ever', but we guess it is not the desired happy outcome, that they will not live 'happily ever after'.

Activity 22

For Joanne, you may have noticed how tentatively she behaves, asking 'please' for 'a little word'. Mrs Brennan is seen by Joanne in hostile imagery, such as 'knuckle-duster rings' and 'claws'. Claws in this sort of context might suggest 'getting your claws into someone'. Jason's response of 'Silence' and then 'Oh' is infuriatingly passive. His use of the adjective 'busy' reminds us of the title: *Business Before Pleasure.*

Activity 23

Possible resolutions:

1. Jason stays the night and decides to defy his parents and go on holiday with Joanne.

2. His mother arrives and he meekly returns home with her.

3. Joanne spends the night with him, but decides to go to Bermuda alone or with Tricia.

Unlikely:

4. Joanne gives the prize holiday to her future in-laws.

You may have decided that the narrative had been signalling number 2, rather than the more positive 1 or 3. Outcome 4 would probably be a complete defeat for Joanne. Can you imagine a context in which it would be acceptable – dutiful younger generation deferring to family?

This is how the original narrative ends:

He hesitated for the merest moment.

'Right,' he said, 'right . . . yer . . .'

They stood up at the same time. She kept glancing at the fur in the neck of his shirt and she seemed to feel inside her the awful glancing of the cleaver striking through flesh and bone. . . . there was something blunted, yet powerful, about him; things she couldn't understand. He kissed her then.

'You go and get into bed,' he said, 'I'll just use your loo.'

'Right.'

This was some strange dream; something she hadn't expected; she'd never dreamt he'd come. His mother wouldn't have allowed it. Brennans didn't let go like that.

She took off her sweater and skirt and sprayed a mist of Poison (his last Christmas present to her) over her neck and at her armpits. Naked she lay under the duvet and waited.

She didn't look at him as he slipped off his clothes. Just as he was about to slide in beside her, she heard the phone start ringing.

'I'd better answer it . . . oh God!'

She felt stupid, winding herself into her towelling dressing gown and racing into the sitting room.

A man's voice spoke to her. 'Is that you, Joanne?'

'Yes,' she said, and the icy goose-pimples rose on her back.

'It's Mr Brennan here. Is our Jason with you?'

'Yes,' she said.

'Mrs Brennan's been took ill— we've had to get the doctor . . . Get him, will you!'

'Yes.'

She returned to the bedroom. 'Jason, it's your dad.'

Something changed in his face. It went hard and different. She hovered near him as he talked into the mouthpiece.

'Yes,' he kept repeating, 'yes.'

'Well?'

'I'll have to go home,' he said, 'she's ill . . . very bad, my dad said.'

'Never mind,' Joanne said, 'perhaps another time . . .' But she knew that Mrs Brennan would see there never was another time.

Activity 25

At the beginning of the musical *Blood Brothers* the character Mrs Johnstone has a song that provides some background to her life:

Once I had a husband,
You know the sort of chap,
I met him at a dance and how he came on with the chat.

He said my eyes were deep blue pools,
My skin as soft as snow,
He told me I was sexier than Marilyn Monroe.

And we went dancing,
We went dancing.

Then, of course, I found
That I was six weeks overdue.
We got married at the registry an' then we had a 'do'.
We all had curly salmon sandwiches,
An' how the ale did flow,
They said the bride was lovelier than Marilyn Monroe.

And we went dancing,
Yes, we went dancing.

Then the baby came along,
We called him Darren Wayne,
Then three months on I found that I was in the club again.
An' though I still fancied dancing,
My husband wouldn't go,
With a wife he said was twice the size of Marilyn Monroe.

No more dancing
No more dancing.

By the time I was twenty-five,
I looked like forty-two,
With seven hungry mouths to feed and one more nearly due.
Me husband, he'd walked out on me,
A month or two ago,
For a girl they say who looks a bit like Marilyn Monroe.

And they go dancing
They go dancing
Yes they go dancing.

Activity 26

When students carried out this task on Shakespeare's *Antony and Cleopatra,* they all found a range of different things to interest them, for example:

- the military strategy of a battle at sea and how Shakespeare could present such a battle on stage

- the moment when Pompey forbids Menas to kill the triumvirs (even though he would then have had all their power and lands)

- Antony and the decisions he takes

- Cleopatra and her motives

- the suicides at the end.

The important point here is to try to ensure that the reading you give is your own.

Activity 27

Plutarch: Much of the language is used to elevate Cleopatra to the status of a goddess. Similes are set alongside extravagant detail (purple sails . . . silver oars) and we are not sure how far to believe any of this. The rhythmic beating of oars in time to music transforms real sounds into art. The peculiar use of *she was laid* to imply passivity or today's vernacular use of the verb to lie ('she was sat', for example, meaning 'she was sitting'). Reference by the tale teller to a tableau effect describes Cleopatra imitating art (her maids are similarly transformed into creatures of fancy: mermaids do not exist). The males present are merely boys and what is offered is a female world. The practical aspect of sailing the barge is not forgotten and the groups of busy women are a contrast to Cleopatra's inactivity. If you have ever been to a wharf or quayside you will understand how difficult it would be to hide the pungent natural smells of water, mud, weed or fish, yet here they are masked by perfume wafting from the barge.

Shakespeare: Just before this scene, Antony has agreed to a marriage of convenience with Octavius Caesar's sister, Octavia. This signals to Caesar that Antony wishes to be reconciled to him and will no longer work with Cleopatra for mutual benefit, wealth and empire. Domitius Enobarbus is a character invented by Shakespeare. He offers the audience a perspective on Antony and (as here) on Cleopatra. In the imagery there is extreme wealth – gold – but also excess. The sexual imagery builds with the love-sick winds, the interplay of flutes, beating oars and the effect on the water. We are told she outdoes Venus, the goddess of love! When fanned, her cheeks, though cooled, glow gently. A man is describing a woman to a man. Throughout the play Shakespeare presents Cleopatra as a sexually manipulative woman.

Activity 29

The English would need an accurate map that depicted the features of the terrain – where there were hills, valleys, forests, streams and bogs – to ensure that should military force be needed they could plan their strategy. We use Ordnance Survey maps today without giving a second thought to their military origins and function. Place names that could not be recognised and pronounced accurately would lead to poor communication and possible confusion for the English. There is also the issue of removing from the language words that are identified with the old culture. It is said that 85% of a local population needs to be using a language for it to survive. Language is an emotive issue because it is at the heart of communication, cultural values, identity, and our link with the past.

Terms such as *hydrographic* and *topographic* derive from Greek words for *water* and *place*.

If you have put Lancey's original speech alongside Owen's translation you will see that not only does Owen simplify, he also puts a positive version forward to persuade the Irish that there is no need to worry about the motives of the English.

You will have noticed that Manus sees through the English; he knows what their true motives are. They regard Ireland as just another part of the Empire – something they own. They want to be able to calculate accurately how much tax is due. The map and the translation of place names is for their benefit.

Activity 30

From whatever perspective you explored, you will have found the opportunity to persuade the reader of a particular view. For example, you may have decided that an interesting perspective to explore would be that of Doalty describing his attempts to challenge the English. A perspective that looked back on his life and gave his version of 'events' would have obvious interest. How you accomplished this in your writing would be explored in your commentary.

This module counts for 15% of the total A Level marks.

ASSESSMENT OBJECTIVES

The skills and knowledge that you develop in this module, and that will be assessed in the examination, are defined by the Examination Board's Assessment Objectives. These require you to:

AO1 communicate clearly the knowledge, understanding and insights gained from the combination of literary and linguistic study, using appropriate terminology and accurate written expression (2.5%)

AO2ii respond with knowledge and understanding of texts of different types and from different periods, exploring and commenting on relationships and comparisons between them (2.5%)

AO3ii use and evaluate different literary and linguistic approaches to the study of written and spoken language, showing how these approaches inform their readings (5%)

AO4 show understanding of the ways contextual variation and choices of form, style and vocabulary shape the meaning of texts (2.5%)

AO5 identify and consider the ways attitudes and values are created and conveyed in speech and writing (2.5%)

Introduction

As Module 6 forms the synoptic module that is intended to assess all the knowledge, skills and understanding gained over the AS and A2 course, you can see Module 5 as the penultimate step in your A Level study of Language and Literature. In taking this course you study a range of texts spanning various genres and historical contexts. Although there is a certain amount of choice and flexibility, there are some compulsory elements: the set texts *must* include (a) the three main literary genres of poetry, prose and drama; (b) non-literary genres; (c) spoken as well as written language; and (d) texts from earlier periods. In your analysis of the texts you should use terms and concepts from the fields of both literary and linguistic studies.

This module gives particular emphasis to the literary genre of drama. The genre of poetry is included as part of the Anthology in Module 1, where you were introduced to some basic language and literary terms and concepts. In Module 2 you focus on prose fiction as the set texts, using awareness of language change and narrative techniques for your analysis. The non-literary texts in this module are transcripts of conversations, which you first studied in the Module 1 Anthology; you are now given further theories, concepts and terms to use in analysis. In preparation for Module 6, keep a note of the approaches that you use and evaluate the effectiveness of each.

Content

This module includes a Shakespeare play as a set text for one of the two examination questions, but you should also study representations of dialogue in other literary texts: modern drama, prose fiction or poetry. Apart from these written texts from literature, you will study transcripts of talk from a range of contexts. The activities in this section will provide extracts of dialogue from drama and prose fiction and transcripts of conversations; the focus of an activity can then be applied to a relevant extract from the Shakespeare play you are studying.

The title of the module, 'Talk in Life and Literature', refers to one approach to the analysis of literary dialogue. In this approach you will be asked to compare literary representations of dialogue with examples of everyday conversation. Transcripts of conversations are not set, so they need to be selected to represent a variety of contexts in order to avoid stereotyping the notion of 'life' as opposed to 'literature'.

As well as comparing literary dialogue with everyday conversation, you should also employ approaches to the ways in which the dialogue functions in the literary work. Thus you will be using a combination of linguistic and literary approaches in your analysis.

In the two-hour examination, you will answer two questions of equal weighting:

- one comparing two unseen extracts: a transcript of a conversation and a literary dialogue

- one based on two extracts from your chosen Shakespeare play.

Your focus in both questions is on the *ways* in which writers transform the strategies and forms of everyday conversation in their representations of dialogue. You should also comment on the *effects* of such representations in the literary work; in the Shakespeare question, you should refer to the function of that specific piece of dialogue in the play as a whole.

Unseen question

In this question, you will have two unseen texts: a transcript of a conversation and a literary representation of a conversation from poetry, prose fiction, or a drama script. The sample task, which will remain broadly similar, is to:

> identify some essential differences and similarities between conversations in life and literature. You are asked to make reference to variation in forms and meanings; how attitudes and values are conveyed; the contexts of the texts.

Shakespeare question

In this question, you will be given two extracts from your chosen Shakespeare play. The sample task provided in the Specimen Units and Mark Scheme booklet, which will remain broadly similar, reads:

> referring to knowledge of some of the characteristics of everyday talk, show how Shakespeare turns these to dramatic effect.

As in Modules 1 and 2, you have to study not only set texts, but also a framework of concepts and terminology drawn from literary and linguistic approaches. This section of the book will introduce some useful frameworks and show how they can be applied both to transcripts of everyday conversation and also literary representations of dialogue. You should then apply these frameworks to your chosen Shakespeare play, extracts from play scripts, prose fiction, poetry, and transcripts of everyday conversation.

It would be useful to have access to a dictaphone or tape-recorder, so that you can collect your own examples of conversation for analysis. Data supplied in textbooks tends to reflect the social situations that the writers have access to, such as classroom talk, dinner-party conversations, talk with colleagues. You may be able to supply data that demonstrates the variety of social contexts that you are familiar with. It would also be helpful to make recordings of both scripted and unscripted conversations on the radio or TV: soap operas, documentaries, chat shows, interviews, and so on. Alternatively, you may be able to find a collection of such data, for example in *Talk on the Box* (National Association for Teachers of English).

Concepts and terminology

Linguistic concepts and approaches

The Specification sets out the following four frameworks to be used in your analysis of the ways in which meanings are constructed and interpreted in conversations and dramatic dialogue. This is an approach that you may want to employ in your analysis of texts in Module 6 and later evaluate in the second part of the examination. Some of the activities in this section will ask you to reflect on the usefulness of certain approaches to the analysis of texts. Although an explicit evaluation is not required in Module 5, you will do this implicitly by choosing relevant aspects in your analysis.

These four headings can provide a helpful way of organising your notes and planning your answer in the examination, but do not try to use them as a checklist. You should certainly begin with the 'larger' issues of context and then consider which aspects of the other three groupings are significant.

1. **Contextual features**, such as:

   - situational factors

- status and relationships
- discourse conventions
- purposes.

2. **Interactional features**, such as:

- turn-taking
- pauses
- talk as action
- agenda-setting in conversation
- modes of address.

3. **Lexico-grammatical features**, such as:

- type of utterance
- figurative language
- rhetorical strategies.

4. **Phonological** and **graphological features**, such as:

- intonation
- word stress
- tone of voice
- accent
- pace
- volume
- typography.

Connections with other modules

You should notice how these terms and concepts fit into the systematic framework for language analysis (provided in Module 1, page 2).

The first framework deals with various factors relating to the *context* of dialogues, related to the terms *purpose*, *audience* and *genre*, which you used in analysis of texts in AS modules. Before analysing how a particular conversation works, it is important to consider who is speaking; what type of talk they are involved in; the relationship of the speakers; and their purposes.

The second framework looks at *discourse* – in other words stretches of language longer than the sentence – and examines the structure of a conversation, for example, how 'turn-taking' is managed between the participants. It includes aspects of *pragmatics*, considering what a speaker means by a particular utterance: the question form 'What are you talking about?' could be a request for clarification or a challenging or dismissive comment.

The third framework deals with *grammar* and *lexis* (vocabulary). It examines the types of utterance used by speakers (in other words interrogatives, imperatives, declaratives, exclamations and so on), and the type of vocabulary used (for example slang, jargon, taboo words, and figurative language).

The fourth framework helps us to analyse dialogue in terms of *phonology* and *graphology*. Speech is conveyed by sounds that signal much about the speaker's idiolect (their social and regional background), as well as clues to their personality and mood. However, you will be analysing written representations of speech, which can provide only some indication of sounds by graphological features such as capitals, italics, bold, information given in brackets, and so on.

It is not possible to keep these four approaches separate, as discussion of any script or transcript will refer to aspects from each of them. However, you should keep notes of the concepts and terminology under these four headings for revision.

Although these linguistic approaches were first applied to everyday conversation, the insights gained can also be applied to 'literary' representations of dialogue. As the readers or audience we interpret literary dialogue using our awareness of the conventions of talk in life. A re-construction may retain an illusion of spontaneity, but we need to be aware that in fiction and drama dialogue is written according to a range of conventions. It is important to bear in mind that the context and purposes are different, in other words that dialogue plays a role in creating plot or drama, whereas conversation has a social purpose.

Literary concepts and approaches

Some dramatists aim to create a sense of realism, to portray a convincing 'slice of life', notably in soap operas. It would be a mistake, however, to judge scripted dialogue solely on a scale of how 'realistic' it is. You may notice, first, the extent to which it replicates the style of everyday talk, but then consider the role of this dialogue – whether realistic or stylised – in the drama, prose fiction, or poetry extracts you are studying. Sections will consider the following areas:

- the role of dialogue in creating character and plot

- realistic v. stylised presentation of speech

- the use of figurative language and rhetorical strategies.

Conversation analysis

What is an everyday conversation?

The term 'conversation' refers to talk that involves more than one participant. The connotations of 'everyday conversation' may suggest an interaction that is spontaneous, private, equal, perhaps trivial, and usually polite. This would immediately create a set of simple contrasts with written dialogue. Yet conversations often have a degree of deliberation and planning; an audience beyond the participants; an unequal relationship between the participants; degrees of crucial significance; and varying degrees conflict.

ACTIVITY 1

Work in small groups to generate examples of different kinds of conversation.

Note examples on a scale from, for example:

- the most private   to   the most public

- spontaneous and unplanned   to   self-conscious and prepared

- equal status of participants   to   wide difference in power and status

- trivial topic/purpose   to   significant topic/purpose

- polite consensus   to   obvious conflict and hostility

Now read the commentary on page 126.

Research background

Although linguists turned their attention to conversation analysis comparatively recently, it has been the subject of study by sociologists (such as Harvey Sacks and Dell Hymes) and sociolinguists (John Gumperz and Erving Goffman) for much longer. In conversation analysis, one key aim is to establish the rules or conventions that determine the structure of interactive talk. There are a number of theories and frameworks – some of which will be presented in this section – but they are constantly being developed, challenged and refined, so the area is wide open for your own observations and ideas. Although you can base these on your memory of conversations, it would be better if you could tape-record some conversations and make transcripts.

Transcription conventions

Detailed transcripts of conversations attempt to show phonological features of intonation, word stress, accent, pace and volume, in order to indicate tone of voice as well as the words actually spoken. The graphological markers that are commonly used are: capitals, bold, phonemic alphabet, and so on.

But you will be looking at more basic transcripts. As in a playscript, these identify the speakers and record the words spoken. Sometimes pauses are indicated by these parentheses (.) or a row of dots . . . If the speakers overlap – speak over each other – this is shown with a forward slash / with the overlapping words shown on the line below. (See Activity 3)

Before looking at some established theories, concepts and terms, begin with your own thoughts. How do conversations work? A rule that is sometimes offered to children is 'speak when you are spoken to'. However, in Lewis Carroll's *Through the Looking-Glass*, Alice points out something illogical about this rule:

> 'Speak when you're spoken to!' the Queen sharply interrupted her.
>
> 'But if everybody obeyed that rule!' said Alice, who was always ready for a little argument, 'and if you only spoke when you were spoken to, and the other person always waited for *you* to begin, you see nobody would ever say anything, . . .'

ACTIVITY 2

- Write down your suggestions for five conventions/rules of conversation.

- Compare your five conventions with those listed by a partner. Reach a consensus for five to eight conventions of conversation.

- If there is disagreement along the lines of 'It depends . . . ', list the factors that it depends on.

- Form groups of four and repeat the activity.

- Work as a full class group to compile a list of agreed conversation conventions.

- Also make a list of the factors that these conventions depend on.

Now read the commentary on page 126.

We will look at this topic again in the section 'Principles of conversation' (page 89).

Turn-taking

Much work on conversation analysis has focused on **turn-taking**. The analogy of a game of table tennis has been used to express the fact that participants alternate turns. The analogy of a dance expresses the way that participants adapt to each other's moves and style, by echoing and slightly rephrasing each other's words. And the analogy of fencing expresses the element of conflict in some interactions.

ACTIVITY 3

- Read the following two extracts. The first is a transcript of a conversation between three men working together on a building job. The second is said to be the transcript of a radio conversation between a US Naval ship and Canadian coast guards, off the coast of Newfoundland in October 1995.

- Identify and comment on features of repetition and rephrasing in both.

- What are the significant differences in style and effect?

EXTRACT 1

GEORGE: An I went to Wickes one twenty-five one twenty-five an then you know your Carlite finish big bag

GORDON: Aye

GEORGE: I think that was (.) three pound sixty-nine for a big bag or something

FRED: Aye

GORDON: Aye

GEORGE: Three sixty-nine

GORDON: Oh well that's not bad

GEORGE: Well it's handy

GORDON: At Wickes

FRED: At Wickes is that

GEORGE: That's at Wickes

EXTRACT 2

CANADIANS: Please divert your course 15 degrees to the South, to avoid a collision.

AMERICANS: Recommend you divert your course 15 degrees to the North, to avoid a collision.

CANADIANS: Negative. You will have to divert your course 15 degrees to the South to avoid a collision.

AMERICANS: This is the Captain of a US Navy ship. I say again, divert YOUR course.

CANADIANS: Negative I say again. You will have to divert your course.

AMERICANS: This is the aircraft carrier USS *Lincoln*, the second largest ship in the United States Atlantic fleet. We are accompanied by three destroyers, three cruisers, and numerous support vessels. I demand that you change your course 15 degrees north, I say again, that's 15 degrees north, or counter-measures will be undertaken to ensure the safety of this ship.

CANADIANS: We are a lighthouse. Your call.

- In the Shakespeare play you are studying, find a dialogue that involves repetition and rephrasing.

- Comment on the effect of such repetition in that context: is it collaborative or hostile?

Now read the commentary on page 127.

Distribution and length of turns

In the previous examples, the turns were fairly evenly distributed. With a group conversation, it can be interesting to look at who has the most, and who the least, turns. What does this indicate? Is it always about status and power? Think back to a recent group conversation in the class. There can be many reasons for not participating equally in a conversation.

A conversation between two people tends to have an equal number of turns. In this case, you can look at the *length* of the turns: at who speaks most. Speaking for the longest may indicate presumption of a higher status, or it may be an agreed role in the situation. In an interview, for example, the candidate for the job would be expected to speak most.

ACTIVITY 4

Read the following extracts. One is the record of a real-life conversation, the other a literary representation of talk.

- What similarities and differences are there in the situational context of each interaction?

- Note the distribution and length of turns.

- In what ways does this reflect the situation, the roles and status of the participants?

The first is a written version of a conversation recorded on the TV programme *Big Brother*. The book produced after the show uses a mixture of techniques to record the interaction between the participants: direct and indirect speech with authorial summaries, as in a novel; a record of the words spoken as in a play script, but using speech marks.

The seven (four males and three females) participants in the TV game-show have decided to confront Nick about his apparently manipulating the votes by showing pieces of paper with two names written on them.

EXTRACT 1

Darren asks where the pieces of paper are and Nick says most of them are destroyed. 'Most of them' alerts Darren and Nicky who both want to know how many there were and where they were.

Craig speaks again: 'No one wants to make a fool of themselves. I went into the box a couple of weeks ago and said in front of five million people and my family and friends that you are a genuine guy and I would like to spend the duration with you. I feel a c . . . in all honesty. I feel you're responsible for making me feel a c . . . in front of millions of people. I would like to see the paper with my name on it.'

Darren's indignation takes over: 'You're a grown man. I can't believe you would do this in a situation where we're being watched by so many millions. There's no kind of excuse. You're a grown gentleman. That's childish. Pathetic.'

TOM adds: 'Last week you came past me and you said to me "Craig's the traitor" as if to say Craig was the one who voted for me.'

'What game are you playing?' Nicky asks.

Darren says: 'There's no traitor in here. As much as I may talk to Anna, when it comes to nominations I can nominate her. Why is Craig a traitor? Is it a boy/girl game? Is that what you think? What's the game to you? I'm not here to get the girls out. I'm seriously shocked at the fact that you're showing people's names. That's fucking sick.'

'You're making more of a fool of yourself by saying you only put two names on there,' says Craig. 'You've been caught out and you're blatantly lying about it. Will you go and get the paper?'

NICK: 'I will not do that.'

CRAIG: 'Will you give me permission to go through your things?'

Nick shakes his head. 'I'll pack my suitcase and go.'

CRAIG: 'That's your decision, but you've dug your own grave.'

NICK: 'I accept that.'

DARREN: 'Do you really want that £70,000?'

NICK: 'I've done something wrong.'

DARREN: 'Not just in front of us, in front of millions. I feel sick.'

CRAIG: 'I've lost all respect for you. I thought you were a clever guy.'

NICKY: 'A lot of people had respect for you. Caroline used to sing your praises at night-time. I'm gutted. Caroline's name could have been on one of those pieces of paper as well, and you were telling her "Caroline you're fine, you're not going this week, you'll be fine" and you were flashing her name in front of other people. She'll be so disappointed in you. It makes me feel sick.'

(From *Big Brother, The Unseen Story* by Jean Ritchie, 2000)

The second extract is from the play *Light Shining in Buckinghamshire* by Caryl Churchill. This short scene from Act 1 is set in a courtroom during the Civil War in 17th-century England. Margaret Brotherton, barely audible, is on trial for vagrancy. (JP stands for Justice of the Peace, the title of the magistrates or judges in the court.)

IST JP: Is this the last?

2ND JP: One more.

IST JP:	It's a long list.
2ND JP:	Hard times.
IST JP:	Soft hearts. Yours.
2ND JP:	Step forward please.
IST JP:	I still say he should have been hanged.
2ND JP:	He'll die in jail. Name?
BROTHERTON:	Margaret Brotherton.
IST JP:	That's no example, nobody sees it.
2ND JP:	Margaret Brotherton. Begging. Guilty or not guilty?
BROTHERTON:	I don't know what you mean . . .
IST JP:	You're not of this parish?
2ND JP:	Where do you come from?
BROTHERTON:	Last week I was at Aston Clinton, and before that from Northampton.
IST JP:	I don't want to be told every place you've ever been. Where were you born?
BROTHERTON:	Long Buckby.
IST JP:	If you belong fifty miles away what are you doing here?
2ND JP:	Have you relations here? Friends you could stay with?
IST JP:	Tell us about your third cousin's wife's brother who has work for you. No? Or have you been told you get something for nothing here?
2ND JP:	It's only our own poor who get help from this parish.
IST JP:	And we don't give money. So you can't drink it. It's your system of poor relief that brings them – they hear there's free bread and cheese, free fuel, there's no parish for miles that does that.
2ND JP:	We can't help every vagrant in the country.
IST JP:	You must go back to where you were born.
2ND JP:	If her parents didn't come from there they won't take her.
IST JP:	Her father's parish.
2ND JP:	She's never been there.
IST JP:	The parish she last lived in.
2ND JP:	They turned her out for begging.

IST JP:	Exactly, and so do we.
2ND JP:	Why aren't you married?
BROTHERTON:	. . .
IST JP:	Can we please agree on a sentence.
2ND JP:	First offence. Let's be lenient.
IST JP:	It's only fair to warn you in advance that the next council meeting may reconsider the whole question of poor relief.
2ND JP:	Margaret Brotherton, we find you guilty of vagrancy and sentence you to be stripped to the waist and beaten to the bounds of this parish and returned parish by parish to . . .
IST JP:	Where she was born.
2ND JP:	To the parish where you were born. Next please.

- In the Shakespeare play you are studying, find a passage in which the length and distribution of turns are unequal.

- Comment on the effect of this feature of turn-taking.

Now read the commentary on page 127.

Types of exchange

A sequence of turns is called an **exchange**; each turn in the exchange is termed a **move.** Some exchanges are completed in two moves. These are termed **adjacency pairs.** Examples are:

Utterance function	*Expected response*
Greeting: *Hallo there.*	Greeting: *Hi!*
Congratulation: *Well done!*	Thanks: *Oh, thank you.*
Apology: *I'm so sorry.*	Acceptance: *That's all right.*
Leave-taking: *Goodbye.*	Leave-taking: *Bye.*

Question – answer

A common exchange, or adjacency pair, is the question and answer:

What's the time?
Nearly midday.

The Birmingham School of linguists analysed classroom talk and found that there is often a third move added to this exchange, which occurs because this type of question functions to check knowledge already known by the questioner.

Question – answer – comment

What is the capital of Singapore?
It's Singapore!
That's right.

In fact exchanges often last for more than two turns, or moves. Consider the following examples:

Request – response – acknowledgement

Have you got any cash?
Yes, here you are.
Thanks.

Statement – comment – response

K: So he walked over, right big 'I am' and he had tattoos up his arms right, an anchor here and a microwave here.

P: He didn't.

K: He did. He said do you want a drink or do you want a kick up the bum with an open-toed sandal. I said get you Eamon Andrews.

P: You didn't.

K: I did. I said I'll have a pint of Babycham, some pork scratchings and a yellow cherry and if I'm not here when you get back I'll be in t'toilet putting hide and heal on my love bites.

P: You didn't.

K: I did.

(From a comedy sketch by Victoria Wood.)

ACTIVITY 5

- Read the following extract from the comic novel *Three Men on the Bummel* by Jerome K. Jerome.

- Pick out examples of this type of three-part exchange.

- Do you consider it a fair or an exaggerated representation of classroom talk?

- What attitudes and values are conveyed by this representation?

'No, no,' interrupted the Professor. 'I do not want you to repeat the poem. I want you to tell me in your own words what sort of wood it was where the girl lived.'

The Professor tapped his foot impatiently; the top boy made a dash for it.

'Please, sir, it was the usual sort of a wood.'

'Tell him what sort of a wood,' said he, pointing to the second lad.

The second boy said it was a 'green wood.' This annoyed the Professor still more; he called the second boy a blockhead, though really I cannot see why, and passed on to the third, who, for the last minute, had been sitting apparently on hot plates, with his right hand waving up and down like a distracted semaphore signal. He would have had to say it the next second, whether the Professor had asked him or not; he was red in the face, holding his knowledge in.

'A dark and gloomy wood,' shouted the third boy, with much relief to his feelings.

'A dark and gloomy wood,' repeated the Professor, with evident approval. 'And why was it dark and gloomy?'

The third boy was still equal to the occasion.

'Because the sun could not get inside it.'

The Professor felt he had discovered the poet of the class.

'Because the sun could not get into it, or, better, because the sunbeams could not penetrate. And why could not the sunbeams penetrate there?'

'Please, sir, because the leaves were too thick.'

'Very well,' said the professor. 'The girl lived in a dark and gloomy wood, through the leaf canopy of which the sunbeams were unable to pierce. Now, what grew in this wood?' He pointed to the fourth boy.

'Please, sir, trees, sir.'

'And what else?'

'Toadstools, sir.' This after a pause.

The Professor was not quite sure about the toadstools, but on referring to the text he found that the boy was right; toadstools had been mentioned.

'Quite right,' admitted the Professor, 'toadstools grew there. And what else? What do you find underneath trees in a wood?'

'Please, sir, earth, sir.'

'No; no; what grows in a wood besides trees?'

'Oh please, sir, bushes, sir.'

'Bushes; very good. Now we are getting on. In this wood there were trees and bushes. And what else?'

. . .

'Please, sir, there was a torrent there.'

'Quite right; and what did the torrent do?'

'Please, sir, it gurgled.'

'No; no. Streams gurgle, torrents . . . .?'

'Roar, sir.'

'It roared. And what made it roar?'

This was a poser.

No commentary.

However, the classroom situation is not the only one where such protracted question-and-answer exchanges take place, nor is their function the same, as the next Activity shows.

ACTIVITY 6

Read Extract 1, based on the TV quiz show *Who Wants to be a Millionaire?*, is an invented exchange between the programme presenter and a contestant.

Also read Extract 2, from the play *Educating Rita* by Willy Russell, which is an exchange between a university lecturer and a mature student.

- Suggest reasons why the question–answer exchanges are protracted in each.

- What does it suggest about the situation, the purposes of the conversation, and the status and relationship of the participants?

EXTRACT 1

(The contestant has been offered a question plus four possible answers.)

PRESENTER: Is it A . . . B . . . C . . . or D?

CONTESTANT: Can I ask the audience?

PRESENTER: Right, audience on your key pads . . . 60% say D.

CONTESTANT: That's what I thought.

PRESENTER: You don't have to take their answer. They have been wrong before!

CONTESTANT: No, I'll go with the audience. D.

PRESENTER: Not C?

CONTESTANT: No. D.

PRESENTER: Final answer?

CONTESTANT: Final answer.

PRESENTER: That's where we have to take a break. Jane is on £2,000. Come back after the break to see whether . . .

EXTRACT 2

In this extract from *Educating Rita*, Frank, a university lecturer, is holding a tutorial with Rita on E. M. Forster's novel *Howards End*, when she suddenly asks:

RITA: Are you married?

FRANK: [*Moving back to the swivel chair.*] It's – ogh . . .

RITA: Are y'? What's y' wife like?

FRANK: Is my wife at all relevant?

RITA: What? You should know, you married her.

FRANK: Well, she's not relevant. I haven't seen her for a long time. We split up. All right?

RITA: I'm sorry.

FRANK: Why are you sorry?

RITA: I'm sorry for askin'. For bein' nosey.

FRANK: [*Sitting in his swivel chair.*] The thing about *Howards End* is that . . .

RITA: Why did y' split up?

FRANK: [*Taking off his glasses and looking at her.*] Perhaps you'd like to take notes! When you have to answer a question on Forster you can treat the examiner to an essay called Frank's marriage!

RITA: Oh go way. I'm only interested.

FRANK: [*Leaning towards her; conspiratorially.*] We split up, because of poetry.

RITA: Y' what?

- Try to find examples of question–answer exchanges in the Shakespeare play you are studying. Are these protracted beyond two moves?

- What is the effect of this extended exchange?

Now read the commentary on page 128.

Initiating turns

In each sequence of turns, you can look at who *initiates* the turns. This first move may be in the form of an **interrogative**, but could also be a **declarative** or an **imperative**.

Interrogative: What did she say to you?
Declarative: I can't stand people who agree with you all the time.
Imperative: Well, say something.

Such initiating utterances signal the need for a response from the other participants. You can notice whether there is a response and how it functions in the conversation. The person who initiates exchanges clearly exerts an influence on the conversation, in the sense that the other participants need to react and respond. Does this mean that the initiator is assuming more power and status? After discussing the next activity, think about the roles adopted by your friends in a group conversation.

ACTIVITY 7

The following three exchanges are taken from a longer conversation that you will analyse in Activity 21.

*   Identify the form of the initiating utterance.

*   What is the function of the responses?

*   What does this suggest about purpose of the conversation and the roles and relationships of the participants?

EXTRACT 1

SAM: That's what pisses me off I'm sorry but Sally puts in like three pounds but what's two extra pounds?

CHRIS: I know that's exactly what pissed me off oh my god three pound!

EXTRACT 2

SAM: Exactly look what we've just done for –.

CHRIS: Yeah (.) we put in at least six quid for that jumper.

EXTRACT 3

SAM: I think it was absolutely disgusting.

NICKY: Yeah me too I think Sally and Maria could have made the effort.

Now read the commentary on page 129.

Allocating turns

It is also interesting to look at the way turns are passed from one to another. It usually happens smoothly, without much pause between turns. In fact, there seems to be a desire to avoid lapses in a conversation. Perhaps this is because periods of silence can be uncomfortable, unless the participants are close friends, or family. Activities 26 and 27 will look at the effect of pauses and silences in conversations.

The obvious way for turn-taking to happen is that one person clearly finishes and the next takes over. But how do we know they have finished? One signal is a completed grammatical structure. In the following examples, this is marked by the symbol].

In spoken conversation we can also use intonation clues: a rising intonation on the first two complete grammatical structures suggested that the speaker had not finished; a falling intonation on the third suggested the speaker had come to the end of their turn.

SAM: It's like two pound] I would never do that] three pounds is like nothing]

NICKY: That's what I said to my Mum

Sometimes the turn is allocated by *naming* another person:

NICKY: Her Mum asked me and I felt so embarrassed didn't she Steph she said who else is (1.0) I didn't know what else to say

CHRIS: I know

Sometimes the speaker seizes a turn by *interrupting* an unfinished utterance, marked in scripts and some transcripts by a row of dots. This **self-selection** can be done in a range of ways, from subtle to aggressive.

NICKY: And I think we mean a lot to Beth like to somebody else like Sally or someone like that we don't really . . .

SAM: But she was bullied, she had no friends like me when she came to college

When one speaker **overlaps** the other, it is often marked in transcriptions with a forward slash / , with the first speaker's words continuing on the next line after the interruption.

CHRIS: I know, my Mum and Dad couldn't even give me a lift /

SAM: Personally I don't think /

CHRIS:

          down and they'd been drinking but my Dad gave me a lift down.

SAM: I don't think the present should come from anyone else but us

Back-channel behaviour

On the other hand, a listener can indicate that they want the speaker to continue by uttering short encouraging sounds or words, such as 'yeah . . . mmm . . . oh . . . right'.

The term for this is **back-channel behaviour**. Gardner outlines seven different types of listener contributions that are common in casual talk in English:

- *Continuers* hand the floor back to the last speaker (such as 'mmhm', 'uh', huh')

- *Acknowledgements* express agreement with or understanding of the previous turn ('mm', 'yeah')

- *Assessments* express some form of appreciation of what has just been said ('how awful', 'wonderful')

- *Newsmarkers* mark the speaker's turn as news ('really', 'is it!')

- *Questions* either (a) indicate interest by asking for further details, or (b) seek to correct some misunderstanding

- *Collaborative completions* finished another's utterance

- *Non-verbal vocalisations* (laughter, sighs, frowns)

Topic changes

Another factor to consider when looking at turn-taking is the fact that conversations usually swing from one topic to another. This is another area of interest – seeing how transitions are managed. Phrases like 'by the way . . . that reminds me . . . talking of . . . anyway' are used as **framing moves.**

It is also interesting to note *who* establishes the topic of conversation. In the Specification, this is referred to as **agenda-setting**. 'Changing the subject' is a familiar way of avoiding talking about a topic, as the next activity shows.

ACTIVITY 8

Read the following extract from *Cloud Nine* by Caryl Churchill.

* How does Betty avoid answering questions about her decision to leave her husband?

* What do you infer from her lack of response?

The mother, Betty, is talking in the park to her daughter, Victoria; her son, Edward; their friend, Lin; and Lin's daughter, Cathy.

BETTY: . . . Well I am rattling on. I like your skirt dear but your shoes won't do at all. Well do they have lady gardeners, Edward, because I'm going to leave your father and I think I might need to get a job, not a gardener really of course. I haven't got green fingers I'm afraid, everything I touch shrivels straight up. Vicky gave me a poinsettia last Christmas and the leaves all fell off on Boxing Day. Well good heavens, look what's happened to that lovely painting.

[CATHY *has slowly and carefully been going over the whole sheet with black paint. She has almost finished.*]

LIN: What you do that for silly? It was nice.

CATHY: I like your earrings.

VICTORIA: Did you say you're leaving Daddy?

BETTY: Do you darling? Shall I put them on you? My ears aren't pierced, I never wanted that, they just clip on the lobe.

LIN: She'll get paint on you, mind.

BETTY: There's a pretty girl. It doesn't hurt, does it? Well you'll grow up to know you have to suffer a little bit for beauty.

CATHY: Look mum I'm pretty, I'm pretty, I'm pretty.

LIN: Stop showing off Cathy.

VICTORIA: It's time we went home. Tommy, time to go home. Last go then, all right.

EDWARD: Mum did I hear you right just now?

CATHY: I want my ears pierced.

BETTY: Ooh, not till you're big.

(Much later after talking about Betty's beads, which Cathy likes, Betty announces she's leaving.)

. . . Well it's been lovely seeing you dears and I'll be off again on my little walk.

VICTORIA: You're leaving him? Really?

BETTY: Yes you hear aright, Vicky, yes. I'm finding a little flat, that will be fun.

              [BETTY *goes.*]

Look at an extract from the Shakespeare play you are studying.

• Identify ways in which the turn-taking is managed.

• What is the effect of these features?

No commentary.

Situational factors

It is important to bear in mind that the conventions for managing turn-taking vary from one social context to another. Age is also a factor. If you compare the morning news programmes – BBC1, *GMTV*, *Big Breakfast* on Channel 4 – you will notice different conventions for turn-taking. There is a younger audience for *Big Breakfast*, and the conversation conventions appear loud and chaotic to older ears. Similarly, BBC1 may seem too leisurely and staid to younger ears.

If you have any data recorded from TV chat shows, radio phone-ins or live conversations, this can be used for the following activity, which practises the type of analysis you will undertake in the first examination question.

ACTIVITY 9

Read the following transcript of part of a conversation, and then organise your comments by using the framework provided in the Specification (pages 66–67 of this module.

• What can you tell about the context: the status and relationship of speakers; the purpose of the talk; and the situation (phone or face to face)?

• Justify your comments by reference to interactional features: turn-taking; pauses; back-channel behaviour; overlaps, and so on.

• Also refer to lexico-grammatical features: type of utterance; vocabulary; and repetitions.

• Is there any indication of phonological features?

A: hallo

D: oh hi A it's D here

A: oh hi D have you (.) not left yet?

D: just about to go

A: right

D: I was just going to say (.) that comic book stuff /

A: yeah /

D: it's um I've put it on the
sideboard so if you want to call round some time /

                                          oh brilliant thank you /

                                            when K's in

A: yeah (.) so are you driving down with K?

D: no no I'm going on the train

A: oh right (.) is it fairly direct then?

D: no I have to change in London unfortunately but er /

                                         right /

                                        just two trains /

                                            right

good/

D: the Littlehampton train goes from Victoria /

                                       mmm /

                                        so it's not a big er a big

haul really /

A: right (.) you taking your laptop?

D: I am yes /

              yeah /

               hope the damn thing will work /

                                yeah /

                                when I'm down there

A: and did you say there wasn't a phone there?

D: there isn't no

A: but you've got your mobile?

D: I have yes yeah (.) and I've got a hotmail number /

                                        oh good /

                                        so I can email /

                                            mmm

A: oh well if you want to send me an email I'll (.) that will include your hotmail (.) will it?

D: yes it will

A: right (.) yeah 'cos then you can have a sort of social life by email

D: yes I did send my hotmail number off to a few people (.) I forgot to send it to J so I gave it to her yesterday /

                    yeah /

                        yes yes yeah (.) so I will send it to you er yeah

A: oh well have a (.) really productive time (.) two weeks is it?

D: yes mmm (.) well I hope so

A: it will be a strange experience which could be quite good for writing a murder story

D: yes it's er I'm curious to see what it's gonna be like /

                        mmm /

                        you know er feeling

interested but quite apprehensive

Now read the commentary on page 129.

Representation of phonological features

The term **idiolect** refers to the distinctive features of an individual's language use. It is generally much easier to identify a person from their speech than from their writing. Once all traces of pronunciation have gone, we are left only with clues such as choice of vocabulary and, possibly, some typical sentence structures. In the previous transcript, for example, there was the question form: 'have you (.) not left yet?' This structure – 'have you not?' rather than 'haven't you?' – is a feature of some Northern dialects. However, the pause in this case suggests that the speaker began with one structure planned – 'have you left?' – and had to rethink and rephrase, when it was obvious that D hadn't left.

As you are analysing written versions – scripts and transcripts – of speech, there is a limited representation of phonological features. There are some graphological conventions for indicating emphasis, volume, tone of voice and accent, for example.

Emphasis is often shown by	italic print
Volume by	capital letters
Intonation by	punctuation (question or exclamation mark)
Tone of voice by	authorial comment or stage directions
Pauses or *interruptions* by	a row of dots or a forward slash
Accent by	spelling changes

Representations of dialect variations

Every speaker has an accent, but the use of standard spelling in a transcript suggests that there is nothing remarkable or significant about the speaker's accent. The reader can 'hear' the voice as they choose. However, a director or actor will decide on a particular accent for a part, thus indicating some aspect of their interpretation.

The use of non-standard spelling is generally confined to regional accents, even though any pronunciation of English is not accurately represented by its spelling. For example, the standard pronunciation [inuf] is always written as 'enough'. This means that standard pronunciation passes without emphasis as the norm, whereas regional accents are highlighted as a deviation from the norm. You might have noticed this is your study of texts in Module 2. It is rare to find a work written mainly in non-standard spelling. However, in Module 6 you will be commenting on an extract from the novel *Trainspotting* by Irving Welsh, which is written in Glaswegian **vernacular**.

In his poem 'Them & [uz]', Tony Harrison recalls the reaction of his English teacher at Leeds Grammar School to his northern accent:

> I played the Drunken porter in *Macbeth*.
>
> 'Poetry's the speech of kings. You're one of those
> Shakespeare gives the comic bits to: prose! . . . '

While there may be no graphological indication of different accents in Shakespeare plays, producers often cast an RP (**Received Pronunciation**) accent for the heroic, noble characters, and choose various regional accents for the minor, comic characters. The assumption, perhaps, is that poetry should be spoken with the standard accent, whereas prose is more 'common'.

In the Shakespeare play you are studying you should note which characters speak in prose, and which in blank verse or other verse forms, then consider what effect this creates. If you watch a performance of the play, notice which accents are used for the characters.

ACTIVITY 10

Read Extract 1 below, taken from *A Phenomenology of Working Class Experience* by Simon J. Charlesworth. Then read Extract 2, from the novel *White Teeth* by Zadie Smith.

- Note all the indications of phonological features.

- Comment on the different methods of representations in transcript and novel.

- Evaluate their use and effect. Bear in mind the fact that non-standard spelling draws attention to itself and takes more time to interpret.

- Imagine 'What if . . . the speech was written in standard spelling?' How would this change the effect?

EXTRACT 1

S is the researcher; X is a male interviewee

S: Ah you still on't buses?

X: Naow . . . I've bi'n finished eighteen months.

S: What've yer bi'n do'in?

X: Nowt. I've bi'n on't dole all't time. I'll likely nivver [never] work age'an.

S: Ahr do yer find bein' unemployed?

X: Terrible! It's fuckin' shit.

S: Ahr do yer mean?

X: I nivver feel rait. I feel rait depressed all time and ill, like. I think it's shit. It gets me dahn [down] rait bad, I'm just rahn [round] 'ouse all't time, 'cept [except] fo' if I cum dahn 'ere. [Pauses] Still, tha can't grumble can yer? Life gu's on and all that, eh? Tha just 'as to mek best yer can and 'ope fo' best.

EXTRACT 2

(Hortense came to England from Jamaica with her young daughter, Clara, who married Archie, born and bred in London. Irie is their daughter, visiting her grandmother for the first time in years.)

'Irie, look at you! Pickney nah even got a gansey on – child must be freezin'! Shiverin' like a Mexico bean. Let me feel you. Fever! You bringin' feber into my house?'

It was important, in Hortense's presence, never to admit to illness. The cure, as in most Jamaican households, was always more painful than the symptoms.

'I'm fine. There's nothing wrong with-'

'Oh, really?' Hortense put Irie's hand on her own forehead. 'That's fever as sure as fever is fever. Feel it?'

Irie felt it. She was hot as hell.

'Come 'ere.' Hortense grabbed a rug from Darcus' chair and wrapped it around Irie's shoulders. 'Now come into the kitchen an' cease and sekkle. Runnin' roun' on a night like dis, wearing flimsy nonsense! You're having a hot drink of cerace and den gone a bed quicker den you ever did in your life.'

Irie accepted the smelly wrap and followed Hortense into the tiny kitchen, where they both sat down.

'Let me look at you.'

Hortense leant against the oven with hands on hips. 'You look like Mr Death, your new lover. How you get here?'

Now read the commentary on page 129.

Principles of conversations

In Activity 2, you listed conventions for conversations that work well. Now think about the opposite: why do some conversations seem *not* to work? There are self-help manuals that give advice on making conversations work. One example of advice is offered via two questions: 'How many ears have you got? How many mouths? Well, remember that in a conversation!' In other words, try to *listen* more than you speak.

Of course, it depends on the context for the conversation – a job interview will work in different ways from a chat or an argument. Most people would expect to speak more than listen, when they are the interviewee. You might do the same in an argument, if you were determined to win. For the next activity, consider what makes sociable talk work when the purpose is to co-operate.

ACTIVITY 11

- Write down five maxims for friendly conversations, expressed as 'Do's' and 'Don'ts'.

- Compare these in a 'pyramiding' exercise: work in pairs first and try to reach agreement on three to five maxims; then form groups of four; then eight and so on, until there is a full group discussion.

Now read the commentary on page 130.

The co-operative principle

Grice claims that his maxims (see the commentary to Activity 11, page 130) can account for the way meanings are created and conveyed in conversations between two people. For him, these maxims are based on the principle of co-operation. This does not mean that speakers always abide by the maxims. Grice uses the term **flout** for the deliberate departure from a maxim. He suggests that this departure from the norm **implies** a meaning; the listener is encouraged to **infer** some meaning from the flouting of a maxim. If, for example, a person avoids answering a question and makes an apparently irrelevant comment, the listener will look for a reason for this, as you saw in the extracts from the plays *Educating Rita* and *Cloud Nine*.

Grice uses the term **violate** for an apparently unintentional departure from the maxims. For example, if someone gives too much information, or seems to be rambling on in an irrelevant way, the listener might infer that the speaker is lonely or needs to talk.

ACTIVITY 12

Use any recordings you have made of conversations, or recall conversations where one participant said:

- too much

- too little

- something irrelevant

- something untrue

- something obscure or ambiguous.

What did the speaker imply? What did the listener infer?

No commentary.

If Grice's framework helps to explain how meanings are constructed in everyday conversations, then it can also help us to interpret dramatic dialogue. For dialogue to be dramatic, we expect it to reveal conflict and tension, rather than co-operation; moreover, constructed dialogue may often imply, rather than state explicitly. The next activity asks you to apply this framework to an extract from *Hamlet* and then to evaluate its effectiveness.

ACTIVITY 13

- Read the following extract from Shakespeare's *Hamlet*.

- Which of Grice's maxims are flouted?

- Why? What is the apparent effect on Claudius/on you as audience?

- What do you infer about the character of Hamlet?

Hamlet has just killed Polonius and is now being questioned by Claudius, who is planning to send Hamlet abroad to be executed.

CLAUDIUS: Now Hamlet, where's Polonius?

HAMLET: At supper.

CLAUDIUS:	At supper! Where?
HAMLET:	Not where he eats, but where 'a is eaten; a certain convocation of politic worms are e'en at him. Your worm is your only emperor for diet: we fat all creatures else to fat us, and we fat ourselves for maggots; your fat king and your lean beggar is but variable service – two dishes, but to one table. That's the end.
CLAUDIUS:	Alas, alas.
HAMLET:	A man may fish with the worm that hath eat of a king, and eat of the fish that hath fed of that worm.
CLAUDIUS:	What dost thou mean by this?
HAMLET:	Nothing but to show you how a king may go a progress through the guts of a beggar.
CLAUDIUS:	Where is Polonius?
HAMLET:	In heaven; send thither to see; if your messenger find him not there, seek him i'th'other place yourself. But if, indeed, you find him not within this month, you shall nose him as you go up the stairs into the lobby.
CLAUDIUS:	Go seek him there.
HAMLET:	'A will stay till you come.

Now read the commentary on page 131.

The limits of the co-operative principle

There are various objections to the usefulness of Grice's framework. (This discussion is in preparation for your study in Module 6, where you need to select those linguistic and literary approaches that seem most appropriate, and then to evaluate your choice.) One objection to Grice's approach to conversation is that it presupposes an ideal world where people are equal participants in conversations, which they use simply to co-operate with each other. What about all the situations where the participants are not equal and have conflicting needs regarding the outcome of the talk? Even in a situation with politician and interviewer, although they may seem well-matched in terms of power, neither desires to co-operate with the other as they have different purposes and agendas. Many conversations can be seen, in some ways, as a struggle for the upper hand, however restrained they appear on the surface.

ACTIVITY 14

Read the following extract from the novel *White Teeth* by Zadie Smith and then answer the following questions.

- What is each character's goal or purpose in the conversation?

- How does each character try to establish control of the discussion?

- How do you respond to this portrayal of the characters?

- What aspects of conversation analysis have contributed to your analysis of the literary effect of this passage? (Refer to the framework with four headings provided in the Specification, listed on pages 66–67.)

Samad looked at his clipboard, underlined something in pen three times and turned to the parent-governors once more.

'The Harvest Festival.'

Shifting, scratching, leg-crossing, coat-repositioning.

'Yes, Mr Iqbal,' said Katie Miniver. 'What *about* the Harvest Festival?'

'That is precisely what I want to know. What *is* all this about the Harvest Festival? What *is* it? *Why* is it? And why must my children celebrate it?'

The headmistress, Mrs Owens, a genteel woman with a soft face half hidden behind a fiercely cut blonde bob, motioned to Katie Miniver that she would handle this.

'Mr Iqbal, we have been through the matter of religious festivals quite thoroughly in the autumn review. As I am sure you are aware, the school already recognises a great variety of religious and secular events: amongst them, Christmas, Ramadan, Chinese New Year, Diwali, Yom Kippur, Hanukkah, the birthday of Hailie Selassie, and the death of Martin Luther King. The Harvest Festival is part of the school's ongoing commitment to religious diversity, Mr Iqbal.'

'I see. And are there many pagans, Mrs Owens, at Manor School?'

'Pagan – I'm afraid I don't und–'

'It is very simple. The Christian calendar has thirty-seven religious events. *Thirty-seven.* The Muslim calendar has *nine.* Only nine. And they are squeezed out by this incredible rash of Christian festivals. Now my motion is simple. If we removed all the pagan festivals from the Christian calendar, there would be an average of'– Samad paused to look at his clipboard – 'of twenty days freed up in which the children could celebrate Lailat-ul-Qadr in December, Eid-ul-Fitr in January and Eid-ul-Adha in April, for example. And the first festival that must go, in my opinion, is this Harvest festival business.'

'I'm afraid,' said Mrs Owens, doing her pleasant-but-firm smile and playing her punchline to the crowd, 'removing Christian festivals from the face of the earth is a little beyond my jurisdiction. Otherwise I would remove Christmas Eve and save myself a lot of work in stocking-stuffing.'

Samad ignored the general giggle this prompted and pressed on. 'But this is my whole point. This Harvest Festival is *not* a Christian festival. Where in the bible does it say, *For thou must steal foodstuffs from thy parents' cupboards and bring them into school assembly, and thou shalt force thy mother to bake a loaf of bread in the shape of a fish?* These are pagan ideals! Tell me where does it say, *Thou shalt take a box of frozen fish fingers to an aged crone who lives in Wembley?*'

Mrs Owens frowned, unaccustomed to sarcasm unless it was of the teacher variety, i.e., *Do we live in a barn? And I suppose you treat your own houses like that!*

'Surely, Mr Iqbal, it is precisely the *charity* aspect of the Harvest Festival that makes it worth retaining? Taking food to the elderly seems to me a laudable idea, whether it has scriptural support or not. Certainly, nothing in the bible suggests we should sit down to a turkey meal on Christmas day, but few people would condemn it on those grounds. To be honest, Mr Iqbal, we like to think of these things as more about *community* than *religion* as such.'

'A man's god *is* his community!' said Samad, raising his voice.

'Yes, umm . . . well, shall we vote on the motion?'

Mrs Owens looked nervously around the room for hands. 'Will anyone second it?'

Now read the commentary on page 131.

Politeness principles

The need to be polite accounts for various strategies in conversation. Leech proposed a **tact maxim** that can be summarised as 'minimise the cost to other, maximise the benefit to other.' For example, if we request some action that would inconvenience the other, we should use a politely indirect form of the imperative. The following examples of grammatical structures move from direct towards indirect.

Turn the music down.	**Imperative**
Would you turn the music down please?	**Phrased as an interrogative**
I wonder if I could ask you to turn the music down.	**Complex declarative**

Leech's **approbation maxim** states: 'minimise dispraise of other, maximise praise of other.' Thus, if we need to say something bad about the other person, we should choose an indirect way.

A fringe doesn't suit you.	**Direct negative statement**
Why don't you try growing your fringe out?	**Suggestion**
You'd look lovely without a fringe.	**Positive comment**

You may already have thought of some objections to this principle, along the lines of 'Yes, but surely it depends'. Friends, for example, tend to be more direct with each other and the use of politely indirect forms could seem cold and distant. Again, it is essential to consider the context for the talk – particularly the relationship of the speakers – in order to specify the conventions that work. The politeness principle may seem limited to a particularly cosy world, where social pleasantries are all. Ways of indicating solidarity differ from one social context to another. What seems straightforwardly polite to one person may seem ingratiating to another. Foreign students of English often comment on the excessive use of 'please' and 'thank you' in English conversation. Thus you need to consider the pragmatics of politeness, in other words what the speaker *means* by an utterance and what the listener *infers*.

Brown and Levinson developed a framework around the concept of **face**, which refers to our public self-image. There are two aspects to this concept: **positive face** refers to our need to be liked and accepted; **negative face** refers to our right not to be imposed on. Thus politeness involves speaker showing an awareness of the other's 'face needs'.

They suggest that speakers use **positive politeness** strategies with friends to emphasise solidarity, such as:

- shared dialect
- informal lexis
- informal grammar
- more direct requests.

Negative politeness strategies, on the other hand, emphasise respect when there is a social distance between speakers, so more indirect requests and a more formal lexis and grammar are used.

Robin Lakoff suggested another framework for a politeness principle with three maxims:

- Don't impose (Principle of *Distance*)
- Give options (Principle of *Deference*)
- Be friendly: make your receiver feel good (Principle of *Camaraderie*).

The words in brackets describe the types of rapport that Deborah Tannen suggests can be established between speakers. She emphasises the variation in the ways that types of rapport can be achieved. She notes that groups of people have different styles of interacting, for example, a 'high involvement style' or a 'high considerateness style'. Variation in styles can be related to social factors of gender, race, ethnicity, and social class. A later section ('Gender variations in conversational styles', page 99) will look more closely at gender.

ACTIVITY 15

Read the following extract from *Abigail's Party* by Mike Leigh. Beverley and Laurence have invited their neighbour, Sue, and friends, Angie and Tony, round for drinks on the evening when Sue's daughter, Abigail, is having a party next door.

- Identify the politeness strategies used by the speakers. (Include reference to questions and pronouns.)

- What do these suggest about status and relationships?

- How does Sue manage to get her own way?

BEVERLEY:	Laurence, would you put a record on for us, please?
LAURENCE:	Yes, surely. What would we like to hear?
BEVERLEY:	Demis Roussos.
LAURENCE:	No Beverley, we don't want to listen to that fat Greek caterwauling all night.
	[LAURENCE *selects a record.*]
BEVERLEY:	Darling, not *classical*.
LAURENCE:	*Light* classical, just as a background. Sue, do you know James Galway?
SUE:	Yes, I've heard of him.
LAURENCE:	A very up and coming young flautist. Do you like him?
SUE:	Yes, he's very good.
LAURENCE:	Fine, I'll put it on for you, Sue.
BEVERLEY:	Laurence, I'm sorry, we don't want to listen to classical music at the present moment.
LAURENCE:	Well, what do we want to listen to, Beverley?
BEVERLEY:	Demis Roussos.
LAURENCE:	Well, if everybody else wants to listen to *Demis Roussos*, we'll put him on.
BEVERLEY:	Tone, do you like Demis Roussos?
TONY:	Yeah, he's all right.
BEVERLEY:	He's fantastic, isn't he? Sue?
SUE:	I don't know him, I'm afraid.
ANGIE:	Oh, you'll like him. He's lovely.
BEVERLEY:	Sue, he's really great. Sue, would you like to hear him?
SUE:	Yes.
BEVERLEY:	Yup. Laurence? *Angie* likes Demis Roussos. *Tony* likes Demis Roussos. *I* like Demis Roussos and *Sue* would like to hear Demis Roussos. So please, do you think we could have Demis Roussos on?
LAURENCE:	[*Pause.*] Yes.
BEVERLEY:	Thank you.

Now read the commentary on page 132.

Lexical features of conversations

The following activities look at the ways in which choice of lexical features can indicate the assumed, or actual, relationship between participants in conversations. Speakers can construct and vary the level of intimacy through, for example:

- modes of address
- technical words (jargon)
- **taboo** words (swearing)
- slang or anti-language.

We will look at the first two.

Modes of address

There are many ways of addressing another person, and the choice of address term signals the status and relationship the speaker wishes to establish with the other participant. This may, or may not, be reciprocated by the other. Add the range of terms used to address you to the following list of examples:

First name	Alison
Title and surname	Ms Ross
Full name (first name + surname)	Alison Ross
Title + full name	Ms Alison Ross
Surname only	Ross
Title only	Miss/Mrs
Position/job name	Teacher/Chairperson
Relationship	Mum/Sister (our Alison)
Honorific	Madam
Endearment	Honey/Dear
Altered first name	Ali
Altered surname	Rossi
Nickname	Alien
Insulting name	Clever clogs

Each choice of address term indicates something about both the relationship (actual or perceived) between the speakers and also the social context. In general terms, it may be assumed that the use of address terms has a fixed value – for example, that the use of first names indicates friendliness and informality. However, you can probably think of situations in which the use of a first name was patronising or presumptuous. In service occupations, where workers wear name badges, a customer can addresss a waitress or sales·asssistant by his/her first name, but cannot be responded to in a similar form. Many older people object to the habit of calling everyone by their first name and would prefer acquaintances to use their title and surname. Conversely, the use of title and surname does not always convey respect and distance, for example when there is a sudden change from the usual first name to: 'OK then, Mr Allen, let's hear your brilliant idea.' In the extract from *White Teeth* above (Activity 14), Samad's title and surname are used often, whereas he refers only once to 'Mrs Owens'. The effect of repeatedly addressing a person by their name can be authoritative, rather than neutrally polite.

ACTIVITY 16

- In one column, rank address terms in approximate order of intimacy.

- Add a brief note about the context. Who addresses you like that, and in what situation?

- In small groups, discuss the results, for example:

  Which address terms are never used for you?

  Which are used in different situations for different effects?

No commentary.

Analysis of address terms used in literary representations of dialogue can illuminate the status and relationships of the participants. Naming is significant, particularly where the choice of address term is not reciprocated.

ACTIVITY 17

Read the following short extract from Shakespeare's *Richard III* (Act 3, Scene 4).

- Note the modes of address used by each speaker.

- What does this suggest about status, relationship, and situation?

- What other interactional features of turn-taking support this?

BUCKINGHAM: What says your Highness to my just demand?

KING RICHARD: I do remember me, Henry the Sixth
                Did prophesy that Richmond should be King.
                When Richmond was a little peevish boy.
                A king . . . perhaps . . . perhaps –

BUCKINGHAM: My lord!

KING RICHARD: How chance the prophet could not, at that time,
                Have told me – I being by – that I should kill him?

BUCKINGHAM: My lord, your promise for the earldom –

KING RICHARD: Richmond! When I was last at Exeter . . .

- Now consider Shakespeare's use of iambic pentameters (10 syllables/5 beats to each line) in this dialogue.

- Identify the points where the pattern is broken.

- What is the function of this deviation from the established rhythm?

Now read the commentary on page 133.

Taboo words

Pragmatic conventions – what the speaker is understood to convey by an utterance – change over time and across social groups. One area that is in flux at the moment is the use of taboo words. The effect of swearing ranges from giving extreme offence to seeming amusing, relaxed or friendly. Age is certainly a factor here, but gender and social class are also factors.

ACTIVITY 18

Read the following transcripts, both of which are taken from Simon J. Charlesworth's *A Phenomenology of Working Class Experience*.

* What, according to each of the speakers, is the effect of using taboo language?

* What is your reaction to taboo language?

* What variables of context are significant in the use and effect of taboo language (situation, age, gender, social class, ethnicity)?

TRANSCRIPT 1

(An interview with a woman, X.)

X: It is just getting worse all time rahnd [round] 'ere. Ah can't stand it. Last night next-door neighbours were F'in' and Blindin' it at each other an' the'r kids wo' cryin'. An' mi an' Y [husband] could 'ear 'em. An' it med me feel invaded. Ah did, Ah felt violated.

S: Ye, it's like that in town, yer walk abaht an' yer can't ignore ahr bad it is.

X: I 'ate it wi' E [*daughter*] 'cos ye'll bi walkin' along an' yer can 'ear lads an' lasses talkin', swearin' abaht sex, 'cos yer know wot the'r like nahr, [S: Ye.] an' Ah [I] 'owd [hold] 'er close t' mi an' se', 'Come on love', 'cos Ah don't want it touchin' 'er. If Ah could Si, Ah'd send mi kids to a public school t' protect 'em from all this. Owt t' get 'em aht. Ah mean it's t' late fo' us in it?

TRANSCRIPT 2

(An interview with a man, J.)

J: Ye see rest on us 'd se' sumaht [would say something] if hi wo' tranna bi clever an' usin' wrong word, one'r us 'd se' 'Shur'up yer daft fuck'. Ye' see that's your trouble. Like wi'y all get on, an' wi like t'bi corrected like that, but you wun't du that would yer?

S: Naow, I wun't. It's not right fo' mi t' du that anyway, cos Ah've got benefit o'r a priviledged education an' you lot an't.

J: Yer too fuckin' nice a bloke. Ah mean tha must bi one'r most decent men Ah've ever met but if Ah se' summaht wrong Ah'd want yer t' se', 'naow yer silly cunt, tha's got that wrong, tha means this', yer see. It's better if tha just honest.

Now read the commentary on page 133.

Gender variations in conversational styles

This section looks more closely at the notion of gendered language. Is there a distinctly male versus female way of talking? There are certainly commonly held assumptions, both about how men and women *should* behave and about how they actually do, for example: 'Women shouldn't swear; men can and do.' Edelsky shows that children at an early age have already internalised ideas of what is a 'typical' word for men or women to use.

Some assertions about language and gender have been made without any research to back them up; others are based on limited data or informal observation. Research that was done in the 1970s, for example, suggested that men interrupted more than women in mixed conversations; but there have been many objections to the validity of this claim, which is based on a restricted amount of data. Moreover, the social roles of men and women have changed since then, so perhaps social changes are reflected in changing language styles.

Imaginative representations of dialogue reflect not research, but the writer's intuitive understanding of the way that men and women talk. It is of course important to bear in mind that gender is not the only factor; age, social class and situation, and even personality, are also important.

ACTIVITY 19

Read the following extract from a romantic novel by Barbara Cartland.

- How is the woman represented through her manner of speaking?

- How is the man represented through his manner of speaking?

- What is the effect of this on you and on the ideal/assumed reader?

'God, but you are beautiful!' he exclaimed, and his voice was low and hoarse with passion, 'Why should I care what has happened to you in the past? You are mine now . . . mine . . . my wife.'

He swept her off her feet, lifting her high in his arms. The firelight revealed his face, distorted, diabolical, and it seemed to her that it was the face of a man who has suffered beyond all endurance, and become a devil.

Then, as she cried out in a fear such as she had never known before, he carried her across the room towards the shadowy darkness of the great bed.

'Vane! Vane!' she cried. 'Do not frighten me. I love you. Oh, Vane, spare me!'

Her voice was hardly audible as it came before her bruised lips, and yet he must have heard her, for he paused, looking down at her as she lay in his arms, her head flung back, her torn night-robe revealing her nakedness, her pelisse trailing from her on to the floor.

'Please, Vane. Please!' Caroline whispered again, and now she was sobbing like a child who has been frightened.

The expression on his face altered and she knew that he had heard her.

With a sudden movement, so unexpected that she screamed in sheer physical terror, Lord Brecon threw Caroline from him and on to the bed. She fell helplessly against the softness of the pillows. Then with a sound too inarticulate for her to interpret he turned from her and left the room.

Now read the commentary on page 134.

Women's language?

Barbara Cartland constructed a fictional romantic world that reflected her ideal of how men and women interacted. Like much romantic fiction, it is an extreme version of the supposed passivity of women and the supposed dominance of men. The next activity asks you to compile observations of the ways that males and females talk. The commentary summarises some research from the 1980s and 1990s. (Useful textbooks for those who want to read more about this topic are *Language and Gender* by Goddard and Patterson, and *Feminist Stylistics* by Sara Mills.)

ACTIVITY 20

- Consider the following conversation situations: (a) all male, (b) all female, and (c) mixed groups.

- Do you feel there are any noticeable differences?

- Feedback your comments to the full group.

- Compare your points with those given in the commentary.

Now read the commentary on page 134.

'Powerless' language?

O'Barr and Atkins collected data from courtroom interactions. They suggest that, rather than terming the features we have been discussing 'women's language', it would be better to term them 'powerless language'. Their data showed that more women tended to be high in 'women's language features', while more men tended to be low in these features; but it also showed that women with increased social power and experience also had a lower level of these features.

However, this reference to 'powerless language' may suggest that certain features of language can be powerful, or powerless, full stop, regardless of the context.

But as Angela Goddard points out, there's no such thing as a powerless style of language. Power isn't 'in' language, nor is it 'in' people. Rather it's the courtroom situation that makes such behaviour as hesitation signify a lack of credibility. But a lawyer or judge who used so-called 'powerful' language in the local pub would also lack credibility. Power is not linguistic but social.

Gender and genres of talk

A conversation may include various genres of talk. These may involve:

- telling stories or anecdotes

- gossiping

- expressing opinions

- telling jokes

- chatting.

Studies of conversations have suggested that there are some gender differences in the type of talk we employ. As you read the following two summaries of accounts of storytelling and gossip, consider whether these theories agree with your experience of how males and females talk. You can then analyse a transcript of conversation to see whether it gives an indication of the gender of the speakers, according to these theories.

Storytelling

These theories are taken from *Analysing Casual Conversation* by Eggins and Slade.

They suggest that:

- Women don't tell 'naughty' stories.

- Stories in which speakers show themselves in fearful, embarrassing or humiliating situations are far more likely to be told by women than men.

- Male speakers seem to prefer to feature as heroes in stories which are about danger, violence, heroic deeds etc. In our culture men do not usually tell stories about their own fears and failures.

- Women present a mundane world where problems can be shared, and usually where something is being 'done' to the protagonist rather than by the protagonist.

- Women relate incidents in which they violate social mores and are scared or embarrassed as a result.

- The purpose of narratives in women's talk is to bind women together in sustaining and creating new worlds and in experimenting with possible selves.

Gossip

It is often said that females engage in more gossip than males. But the term gossip is used in many different ways. It can refer to idle chat about daily life, to women's talk in general, or, to conversations based on rumours about other people.

Eggins and Slade suggest that gossip is a way of 'asserting social unity' and that it 'provides a means of exploring similarity and shared values'. They add: 'Gossip functions as a form of social control . . . labels the actions or the behaviour of the third person as deviant and unacceptable, so makes clear what is considered acceptable behaviour.'

Having been introduced to some theories about the relationship between language and gender, consider them in the light of the following extract from a conversation.

ACTIVITY 21

Read the following transcript of part of a conversation. (The writer of the transcript has used some punctuation marks not usually present in transcriptions.)

- Do you feel confident about assigning a gender to the speakers?

- What else can you tell about the social context (age, social background, relationship, situation, purposes)?

- Identify features of the conversation that lead you to these assumptions, for example:

      genres of talk
      ways of interacting and turn-taking
      grammatical features
      lexical choice.

- In which senses might you label this conversation 'gossip'?

CHRIS: I know it's awful honestly Sam if everyone did that to me I would be crying my eyes out

SAM: If that was me I would be crying I wouldn't even talk to them, I'd be like fuck off! I don't want your bloody present!

CHRIS: I know exactly I would be crying my eyes out.

SAM: No not being funny but gifts, even if we brought Beth the world it wouldn't make up for like them not being there /

CHRIS: exactly /

CHRIS: and who turns up and I feel
ashamed 'cause Luke asked me to organise it and who to come and it's like /

SAM: yeah,
he knows it's like not you, we got there and said Luke look, Luke we are fucking
disgusted we can't believe how many have turned up and we said Sally's excuse
and he was like (.) and he said well the main ones are here, her main friends
and I said exactly, the ones that care about her have turned up.

CHRIS: Yeah exactly

SAM: It's just seeing her I could see that she was hurt I could see it in her eyes I know

CHRIS: It was visible, she wasn't happy I mean its not just 'cause it was us but she
wasn't happy because people she thought were her friends weren't there and I
thought she was mad at me or /

SAM: exactly /

CHRIS: something 'cause I wasn't well and I was
all (.) and I don't know (1.0) and even with Luke she didn't look happy she was
like (.)

SAM: Yeah, I think she was probably I think she was like well you know what about
the other (.) and even Anna is like and even Anna is not that friendly with a lot
of people but even she I told her when you were rang me that night I rang her
about an hour after I said oh look Anna everyone's going round Beth's and she
didn't even have the decency to ring me up and say are we going round Beth's?!

CHRIS: Yeah fuck you you know don't even bother! Like this morning I was like I'm
going to work but I've got to see if I'm meeting people that if anyone needs a
lift that's why I phoned you and I was about to phone you

SAM: Mmm

Now read the commentary on page 135.

If there are certain expectations about the styles of talk used by males and females
in various everyday situations, then an audience will bring these assumptions to
their interpretation of *literary* dialogue. The characters may be constructed in ways
that confirm the expectations, or may behave in unexpected ways.

ACTIVITY 22

The following extract is from the play *Oleanna* by David Mamet. John is a
lecturer at an American university, Carol is a student on his course. In this
scene, she has come to his room for help.

- Before reading it, first consider the context of the dialogue: situational
  factors; status and relationships; discourse conventions; purposes.

- Note your expectations of the relative power of the two participants and the ways they are likely to interact in this conversation.

- Does the representation of their conversation follow your expectations?

- Refer to interactional features and also lexical and grammatical features to support your points.

JOHN: What do you want me to do? We are two people, all right? Both of whom have subscribed to . . .

CAROL::   No, no . . .

JOHN: . . . certain arbitrary . . .

CAROL: No. You have to help me.

JOHN: Certain institutional . . . you tell me what you want me to do . . . you tell me what you want me to . . .

CAROL: How can I go back and tell them the *grades* that I . . .

JOHN: . . . what can I do . . . ?

CAROL: *Teach* me. *Teach* me.

JOHN: . . . I'm trying to teach you.

CAROL: I read your book. I read it. I don't under . . .

JOHN: . . . you don't understand it.

CAROL: No.

JOHN: Well, perhaps it's not well *written* . . .

CAROL: [*Simultaneously with* 'written'] No. No. No. I want to *understand* it.

JOHN: What don't you understand? [*Pause*]

CAROL: *Any* of it. What you're trying to say. When you talk about . . .

JOHN: . . . yes . . . ? [*She consults her notes.*]

CAROL: 'Virtual warehousing of the young' . . .

JOHN: 'Virtual warehousing of the young.' If we artificially prolong adolescence . . .

CAROL: . . . and about 'The Curse of Modern Education.'

JOHN: . . . well . . .

CAROL: I don't . . .

JOHN: Look. It's just *a course*, it's just a book, it's just a . . .

CAROL: No. no. There are *people* out there. People who came *here*. To know something they didn't *know*. Who *came* here. To be *helped*. To be *helped*.

So someone would help them. To *do* something. To *know* something. To get, what do they say? 'To get on in the world.' How can I do that if I don't, if I fail? But I don't *understand*. I don't *understand*. I don't understand what anything means . . . and I walk around. From morning 'til night: with this one thought in my head. I'm *stupid*.

JOHN: No one thinks you're stupid.

CAROL: No? What am I . . . ?

JOHN: I . . .

CAROL: . . . what am I, then?

JOHN: I think you're angry. Many people are. I have a *telephone* call that I have to make. And an *appointment*, which is rather *pressing*; though I sympathise with your concerns, and though I wish I had the time, this was not a previously scheduled meeting and I . . .

CAROL: . . . you think I'm nothing . . .

Now read the commentary on page 136.

Pragmatics

This section recaps on some of the terms and concepts introduced over the course and adds a few more. (For those who want a good introduction to the subject, *Pragmatics* by Jean Stilwell Peccei is recommended.)

You will remember that the emphasis in pragmatics is not so much on what *sentences* mean, as on what *speakers* mean when they utter them. This distinction is also expressed in the terms: **form** and **function,** sentence and utterance. Although the term 'utterance' is usually understood to refer specifically to spoken language, it is used here to refer to the sentence in context, whether spoken or written.

In order to interpret pragmatic meanings, the context must be taken into account. So, for example, taboo words might imply aggression, offence or friendly bonding. Eggins and Slade suggest that if you know the other person well, the conversational style tends to be more confrontational and **elliptical** (shortened or abbreviated in some way). Forms of friendly banter and insults are often a feature of intimate conversations, but would be interpreted as inappropriate or hostile in talk with acquaintances.

The style of talk between friends may flout Grice's maxims of manner and relevance (see the commentary on Activity 11, page 130), in that the speakers need not make all their contributions clear and unambiguous and can introduce apparently irrelevant comments.

Talk between friends may also flout Leech's tact maxim (see page 93), as the use of formal conventions of politeness in a conversation with a close friend can signal coldness and distance. Conversely, Eggins and Slade suggest that if you don't know the other person very well, then the talk is more supportive, aiming for consensus. There is likely to be more careful adherence to principles of politeness and co-operation.

Because of the varying styles and conventions of talk in different social contexts, there is always the possibility of misunderstanding utterances. The listener needs a wide social awareness in order to interpret meanings, yet there can still be disagreement in interpretation.

Inference, presupposition and implicature

To infer something is to deduce it on the basis of what has gone before. In *Pragmatics*, Peccei writes: 'interpreting utterances involves a considerable amount of intelligent guesswork where the hearer draws inferences from the speaker's words to arrive at the speaker's meaning.'

Presupposition is a kind of **inference**. Peccei comments that some definitions of presupposition are narrow and sentence oriented: 'a necessary precondition for the sentence to be true.' However, in the study of dialogue it is more useful to use a broader definition of presupposition that is speaker oriented: 'anything the speaker assumes to be true before making the utterance.'

For the meaning to be conveyed to the listener, those assumptions need to be *understood* by the listener (though not necessarily accepted). This definition allows us to discuss questions and imperatives, which, unlike statements, are not strictly either true or false. For example, 'Don't lend him any more money' presupposes that you have lent him money before.

It is important to spot presuppositions in debates and arguments so that we can, for example, counter questions like 'When did you stop beating your wife?' This type of question is sometimes described metaphorically as a 'hook and pull through'. The presupposition that beating has already occurred is the disguised hook; if you reply to the question, you have swallowed the hook. Politicians are always cautious about answering any questions with a hook. Values and attitudes may be implicitly conveyed through presuppositions in texts. There is an advert in national newspapers, for example, that has the heading: 'Are you shamed by your mistakes in English?' This plays on many people's insecurity in their language use, as it assumes (a) the validity of the notion of 'mistakes' and (b) that this is a cause for shame.

The concept of **implicature,** another type of inference, is related to presupposition. Questions are not always followed by clearly relevant and complete responses. In these cases, the speaker is implying a meaning:

A: Have you done those two assignments?
B: I've done the one on turn-taking. [Implies the other one hasn't been done.]

A: Do you like my Helmut Lang jacket? It's the new dirty denim look.
B: It looks as if it needs a wash. [Implies the response 'No'.]

It is far more important to be aware of the pragmatic meanings in texts than it is to be able to identify each example as presupposition or implicature. Don't let unfamiliar terminology confuse or cloud the relevance of your comments. The underlying concept is more important.

ACTIVITY 23

Read the following exchange. It will be clearer if spoken aloud.

• What do the listeners need in order to interpret S's final comment?

Three women are sitting round a table drinking tea. S picks up a plate of biscuits and offers them to the other two women.

S: Do you want a biscuit?

A: yes please

C: no thanks

S: (addressing A) C's getting married next month.

Now read the commentary on page 136.

Talk as action

Much of our language, whether spoken or written, has the form of declaratives, such as 'It's a nice day for the time of year'. The form of these sentences might suggest that the main purpose of language is to impart information, to make propositions that are either true or false. But there are a few verbs, called **performatives**, that *do* something when spoken in the right context, for example: 'I promise', and 'I hereby pronounce you man and wife'. The **Speech Act Theory** developed by the philosophers Austin and Searle suggests that we are nearly always using language to perform some function, even if the surface structure is a declarative. The statement about the weather conditions, given above, often performs a social – **phatic** – function, that is, to establish an initial friendly rapport, usually with a stranger or acquaintance. Think back to conversations with friends: what type of initial comments have a phatic function?

Austin and Searle use the terms **sense** and **force** to distinguish between the form of the utterance and its function. We can only understand the particular force of an utterance in its context.

'It's raining.'   *Sense:* statement about weather
'I'm in the bath.'   *Sense:* statement about current location

Contexts:

'Can I go out to play?'
'It's raining.'   *Force:* refusal of request

'The phone's ringing.'

'I'm in the bath.'   *Force:* suggestion that the other person will have to answer it

Austin and Searle use three key terms in their analysis: **locution** (the sense of the utterance), **illocution** (the intended meaning) and **perlocution** (the perceived meaning). In other words, there may often be a difference between what a person intended to convey by saying something, and the effect that utterance had on a listener.

(Remember: you should use these concepts if they help you analyse the meanings and effects of a text, but beware of using terminology simply to impress. It is perfectly acceptable, for example, refer to the 'intended meaning', rather than 'illocution'.)

Misunderstandings which arise between intended and perceived meaning are often a factor in dramatic dialogue. There is also complex interplay of meanings, as in Alan Bennett's monologues, where characters are often unaware of the way their words are interpreted by the audience. The literary term 'subtext' is often used to refer to this aspect of a text. Thus, although these concepts have been introduced under the umbrella heading of *linguistic* concepts and approaches, it is hard to separate them from literary approaches and concepts. When you explain the approaches you use in your work for Module 6, it is unlikely that you will be able to distinguish purely linguistic from purely literary approaches. Each discipline has gained insights from the other. However, the following section examines some approaches and concepts that are associated with literary studies.

Literary approaches and concepts

Imaginative reconstructions of everyday talk

Representations of conversations in literature occur in prose fiction, drama, and in some poetry. The examination question on Shakespeare asks you to discuss how the characteristics of everyday talk are turned to dramatic effect. The examination question on unseen texts asks you to identify some essential differences and similarities between conversations in life and dialogue in literature.

Dialogue in literature may be written as more or less 'realistic', but it is essential to consider it in the light of dramatic purposes, i.e. its role in:

- the presentation of themes, attitudes and ideas

- character construction

- the unfolding of plot.

Although an illusion of reality can serve some purposes, drama and fiction are not intended to stand as a 'slice of real life'. Readers and audience are aware, not only of the conventions of everyday talk, but also of the conventions of the theatre, fiction, and poetry.

One important difference is that everyday conversations often involve the participants in a private, spontaneous, transitory encounter for their own shared purposes. By contrast, the dialogue of characters in literary texts, apparently talking to each other, is intended for the audience of readers or listeners who know that this dialogue plays a role in the unfolding narrative. The audience expects everything to be significant and thus attempts to interpret apparent irrelevancies that might be overlooked in everyday conversations.

It is not surprising if some features of spontaneous talk – such as pauses, repetitions, false starts, and overlaps – are 'tidied up' in imaginative constructions of dialogue, so you should not spend too long detailing the differences. If such features are included, as in the extract from David Mamet's *Oleanna* (Activity 22), you should consider the function of a naturalistic style.

However, the audience does not expect a faithful imitation of life in drama and fiction. Although it would be more 'realistic' for characters to die without being able to utter some telling last words, the needs of Shakespearean drama are served by their ability to produce articulate speeches as they die. The dramatic convention of the soliloquy – an internal monologue spoken aloud for the ears of the audience only – might well be taken as a sign of madness in everyday life.

Talk intended for a wider audience

The comparison between casual conversations and scripted dialogue also reveals wide differences in situational factors. Some real-life talk, however, is intended for a wider audience. Recorded interviews or conversations, on TV or radio for example, may not be scripted, but may nevertheless have a degree of planning in the knowledge that there is an important audience beyond the immediate participants. When people are talking 'on the record', they are much more conscious of the effect of their words than when speaking 'off the record'. When microphones are left switched on accidentally, speakers can make remarks embarrasingly at odds with their official pronouncements.

In classical times the study of rhetoric – the art of public speaking – identified strategies that help to persuade an audience to identify with the speaker. Many of these strategies are still used in political speeches and other types of persuasive speaking.

The following examples are all taken (respectively) from Shakespeare's *Julius Caesar* and John Major's speech to the Conservative Party conference in 1991.

- *Rhetorical questions* have the form of questions addressed to the audience, though an answer is not required, as it is assumed to be obvious. This helps establish a shared point of view between speaker and listeners.

  'Did this in Caesar seem ambitious?'

  'Is this the sort of world we want for our children?'

- *Balanced phrases* suggest a neat and memorable equivalence or contrast between two notions.

'The poor have cried, Caesar hath wept.'

'I thrice presented him a kingly crown, which he did thrice refuse.'

' . . . in which taxes could fall and savings grow.'

' . . . the power to choose and the right to own.'

- *Triples* provide a list of three related items, often suggesting a build up to a climax. They are so common in advertising and other forms of persuasion that they must have an emotional effect. Politicians often add on a fourth item, perhaps believing that more is better.

'Friends, Romans, countrymen, lend me your ears.'

'Not today, not tomorrow, not after the next election. Not ever while I'm Prime Minister.'

- *Vocabulary* is also very important. Words with positive connotations tend to be repeated. When referring to the opposition, words with negative connotations are used. However, a word may have different connotations in different contexts. 'Ambition', 'ambitious' can have positive connotations, but are used with negative connotations in Mark Antony's speech. 'Back to basics' and 'ordinary people' can have negative connotations, but have positive connotations in John Major's speech.

ACTIVITY 24

Read the following transcript from Prime Minister's Question Time in the House of Commons. It is part of an exchange between the Prime Minister, Tony Blair, and the leader of the opposition, William Hague, on 25 January 2001, regarding the resignation of a Labour minister, Peter Mandelson.

- What rhetorical strategies does each speaker use? You may identify strategies apart from those listed above.

TB: [Mr Mandelson's] personal courage and sense of duty in coming to the house this afternoon to answer questions on Northern Ireland before departing the government.

WH: Now you've notched up the historic achievement of being forced to sack the same minister for the same offence twice in 25 months, do you recognise that your career-long dependency on Mr Mandelson has been a monumental error of judgement?

TB: I don't suppose I ever expected you to behave graciously at all over his resignation. But I believe that the job Mr Mandelson has done in Northern Ireland well merited his position as secretary of state . . . I therefore believe it was right that he occupied that position and I also believe that he is a bigger man than many of his critics.

WH: The fact is that to reappoint . . . a disgraced minister 10 months after he was forced to resign, in breach of every convention and precedent, was a demonstration of the arrogance with which you wield your power. To spare yourself and the country going through this a third time, will you now guarantee that Mr Mandelson will not be running the election campaign of the Labour Party and will not return to office in any government led by you?

TB: Mr Mandelson has already made that clear in the statement he made earlier. I think that he has done the right thing. I think he has done the honourable thing. It is a long tradition in this house that when someone does do that, we pay tribute to it. I am only sorry that once again you have lived down to my expectations.

WH: Mr Mandelson has done the right thing, but it's a pity your judgement led him to have to do it twice within the space of one parliament. Doesn't this go wider . . . because Mr Mandelson has been central to everything you have done. It was Mr Mandelson who picked you out, who briefed the press for you, who stabbed the chancellor in the back for you, who spun all of your campaigns for you . . . In a government where standards of truth, honesty and integrity have taken second place to spin and smear, aren't you truly the first among equals?

TB: I really think that by that performance, you diminish yourself far more than you diminish anyone else. I made it clear that if people did something wrong they would pay the penalty, and he has paid the penalty.

But I also believe that he can be very proud of the record and contribution he made while in government. As for the rest of the nonsense you have spoken, I've no intention of getting into it.

- Choose a speech from the Shakespeare play you are studying and identify rhetorical strategies used.

Now read the commentary on page 136.

Realism

Much modern drama aims to give an impression of real life; this is particularly true of TV soap operas. However, one difference you are likely to notice between transcripts of everyday conversations and literary representations of dialogue is that some features of spontaneous talk –- pauses, repetitions, false starts, overlaps – are 'tidied up' in plays and novels. Even apparently natural representations of conversations in soap-opera scripts proceed with orderly conventions of turn-taking that are more typical of interviews than informal talk. It is worth considering what other features of everyday talk are retained to maintain an illusion of spontaneity.

It is not the ultimate goal of drama, however, to be 'true to life'. The Russian stage director Stanislavski suggested that the writer must be true to the aesthetic integrity of the play. The contemporary American playwright David Mamet has also challenged the importance of realism, in his *Essay on Realism*: 'In general, each facet of every production must be weighed and understood solely on the basis of its interrelationship to the other elements; on its service or lack of service to the meaning, the action of the play.' So it is not enough to demonstrate that dialogue is realistic; it is also necessary to discuss the purpose and effect of such realism. If you agree that the extract from his play *Oleanna* (Activity 22) retained many features of spontaneous conversation, what do you think is the purpose and effect of this realism?

Naturalistic dialogue

The English playwright Harold Pinter is known for his ability to capturing the flavour of everyday talk in a realistic manner. Before you comment on this aspect of his dialogue, consider the following comments from the critic, Martin Esslin, who suggests that the apparent realism in Pinter' plays functions in dramatic and poetic ways:

> . . . what sounds like tape-recorded speech is highly stylised, even artificial . . . combine the appearance of total reality with complete control of rhythm and nuance of meaning . . . every syllable, every inflection, the succession of long and short sounds, words and sentences are calculated to a nicety. And it is precisely the repetitiousness, the discontinuity, the circularity of ordinary vernacular speech which are here used as formal elements with which the ingredients from which he takes the recurring patterns and artfully broken rhythms *are* fragments of a brilliantly observed, and then hitherto overlooked, *reality*, he succeeds in creating the illusion of complete naturalness, of naturalism.

Esslin also writes:

> The dialogue and the characters are real, but the over-all effect is one of mystery, of uncertainty, of poetic ambiguity . . . The first deviation from the usual realistically constructed play lies in the element of uncertainty about the motivation of the characters, their backgrounds, their very identity.

Pinter himself comments on this lack of explicitness:

> My characters tell me so much and no more, with reference to their experience, their aspirations, their motives, their history. Between my lack of biographical data about them and the ambiguity of what they say there lies a territory which is not only worthy of exploration but which it is compulsory to explore. You and I, the characters which grow on a page, most of the time we're inexpressive, giving little away, unreliable, elusive, evasive, obstructive, unwilling. But it's out of these attributes that a language arises. A language . . . where, under what is said, another thing is being said.

Grice's maxim of quantity (see the commentary on Activity 11, page 130) states that speakers should say neither too much nor too little. A line from a song by REM captures the concern that most of us have: 'I've said too much; I haven't said enough.' Pinter has interesting comments to make about the pragmatics of silence, the fact that we infer meaning from a person's lack of comment: 'It is in the silence that they [characters] are most evident to me.' Similarly, we infer meaning from the fact that a speaker is 'rattling on'. Pinter observes:

There are two silences. One when no word is spoken. The other when perhaps a torrent of language is employed. This speech is speaking of a language locked beneath it. That is its continual reference. The speech we hear is an indication of that we don't hear. It is a necessary avoidance, a violent, sly, anguished or mocking smokescreen which keeps the other in its place. When true silence falls we are still left with echo but are nearer nakedness. One way of looking at speech is to say that it is a constant stratagem to cover nakedness.

ACTIVITY 25

Read the following extract from near the beginning of Pinter's play *The Caretaker*. The younger man, Aston, has invited the homeless Davies to his attic room and allows him to stay there.

- Note the features that suggest 'tape-recorded' speech:

  (a) lexical and grammatical features such as short utterances, colloquial vocabulary

  (b) interactional features such as turn-taking, pauses, agenda-setting, modes of address.

- Note the 'two types of silence': a character saying either too much or too little.

- How do these features help to construct the two characters and suggest the potential for conflict between them?

DAVIES: I was lucky you come into that caff. I might have been done by that Scotch git. I been left for dead more than once.

            [*Pause*]

            I noticed that there was someone was living in the house next door.

ASTON: What?

DAVIES: [*Gesturing*] I noticed . . .

ASTON: Yes. There's people living all along the road.

DAVIES: Yes, I noticed the curtains pulled down there next door as we came along.

ASTON: They're neighbours.

[*Pause*]

DAVIES: This your house then, is it?

[*Pause*]

ASTON: I'm in charge.

DAVIES: You the landlord are you?

[*He puts a pipe in his mouth and puffs without lighting it.*]

Yes. I noticed them heavy curtains pulled across next door as we came along. I noticed them heavy big curtains right across the window down there. I thought there must be someone living there.

ASTON: Family of Indians live there.

DAVIES: Blacks?

ASTON: I don't see much of them.

DAVIES: Blacks, eh? [DAVIES *stands and moves about.*]

DAVIES: Well you've got some knick-knacks here all right, I'll say that. I don't like a bare room. [ASTON *joins* DAVIES *upstage centre.*]

DAVIES: I'll tell you what, mate, you haven't got a spare pair of shoes?

ASTON: Shoes?

[ASTON *moves downstage right.*]

DAVIES: Them bastards at the monastery let me down again.

ASTON: [*Going to his bed.*] Where?

DAVIES: Down in Luton. Monastery down in Luton . . . I got a mate a Shepherd's Bush, you see . . .

ASTON: [*Looking under his bed.*] I might have a pair.

DAVIES: I got this mate at Shepherd's Bush. In the convenience. Well, he was in the convenience. Run about the best convenience they had. [*He watches* ASTON.]

DAVIES: Run about the best one. Always slipped me a bit of soap, any time I went in there. Very good soap. They have to have the best soap. I was never without a piece of soap, whenever I happened to be knocking about the Shepherd's Bush area.

ASTON: [*Emerging from under the bed with shoes.*] Pair of brown.

DAVIES	He's gone now. Went. He was the one who put me on to this monastery. Just the other side of Luton. He'd heard they give away shoes.
ASTON:	You've got to have a good pair of shoes.
DAVIES:	Shoes? It's life and death to me. I had to go all the way to Luton in these.
ASTON:	What happened when you got there, then?
	[*Pause*]
DAVIES:	I used to know a bootmaker in Acton. He was a good mate to me.
	[*Pause*]
	How many more Blacks have you got around here then?
ASTON:	What?
DAVIES:	You got any more Blacks around here?
ASTON:	[*Holding out the shoes.*] See if these are any good.
DAVIES:	You know what that bastard monk said to me? [*He looks over to the shoes.*] I think those'd be a bit small.
ASTON:	Would they?
DAVIES:	No, don't look the right size.

Now read the commentary on page 137.

Stylised dialogue

Other writers use more stylised forms of dialogue. This may be because the situation or characters are to be seen not as real and individualised, but as **archetypes** (the original or model, an exemplar of a type of person). Such stylisation can create more distance between audience and the drama, so that there is less chance of the audience being drawn into a suspension of disbelief. The German playwright Bertold Brecht wanted the audience to remain aware that they were watching a drama: he wanted his plays to appeal to the intellect rather than to the emotions.

ACTIVITY 26

Read the following extract from *Waiting for Godot* by Samuel Beckett.

Vladimir and Estragon are two tramps waiting for days on a country road for a man they have only heard of but never met, called Godot. He never turns up.

- Note features of their conversation that resemble (a) everyday talk and (b) a stylised representation.

- What is the effect of constructing dialogue in this way?

ESTRAGON: In the meantime let us try and converse calmly, since we are incapable of keeping silent.

VLADIMIR: You're right. We're inexhaustible.

ESTRAGON: It's so we won't think.

VLADIMIR: We have that excuse.

ESTRAGON: It's so we won't hear.

VLADIMIR: We have our reasons.

ESTRAGON: All the dead voices.

VLADIMIR: They make a noise like wings.

ESTRAGON: Like leaves.

VLADIMIR: Like sand.

ESTRAGON: Like leaves.

SILENCE

VLADIMIR: They all speak together.

ESTRAGON: Each one to itself.

SILENCE

VLADIMIR: Rather they whisper.

ESTRAGON: They rustle.

VLADIMIR: They murmur.

ESTRAGON: They rustle.

SILENCE

What do they say?
They talk about their lives.
To have lived is not enough for them.
It is not sufficient.

SILENCE

VLADIMIR: They make a noise like feathers.

ESTRAGON: Like leaves.

VLADIMIR: Like ashes.

ESTRAGON: Like leaves.

LONG SILENCE

Say something!
I'm trying.

Now read the commentary on page 137.

The role of dialogue in prose and drama

Apart from stage directions, dialogue is the essence of drama. It can fulfil various functions; it can:

- make the audience believe the representations are real people

- reveal aspects of character

- give the audience more knowledge than the characters possess

- create a relationship between audience and character

- relay information and imply a past which has relevance to the present

- predict the rest of the action

- move the action along

- comment on the action.

Dialogue in prose fiction can be used to fulfil some of these functions, but the writer has other resources within the narrative – thoughts can be presented; feelings can be described; flashbacks can reveal aspects of the past; point of view can be suggested; authorial comments can be made on motives; descriptions of surroundings can suggest mood; and so on.

The following extract is from the short story *Everyday Use* by Alice Walker. The narrator's elder daughter has returned home for a visit. She has changed her name from Dee to Wangero Leewanika Kemanjo, because she doesn't want a white person's name. The other daughter, Maggie, has stayed at home with her mother, whereas Dee went away to college.

ACTIVITY 27

Read the following passage of dialogue from *Everyday Use*. The visiting daughter (Wagero/Dee) and mother are looking at the quilts made out of old clothes by the grandmother. In this setting of the text, everything except the words spoken and the 'inquits' ('said x'), has been printed in italics.

- Consider whether these comments could be included in a play script as stage directions.

- List the phrases that can only be used to construct situation and character in prose fiction.

'Mama,' Wangero said *sweet as a bird*. 'Can I have these old quilts?'

I heard something fall in the kitchen, and a minute later the kitchen door slammed.

'Why don't you take one or two of the others?' I asked. 'These old things was just done by me and Big Dee from some tops your grandma pieced before she died.'

'No,' said Wangero. 'I don't want those. They are stitched around the borders by machine.'

'That'll make them last better,' I said.

'That's not the point,' said Wangero. 'These are all pieces of dresses Grandma used to wear. She did all this stitching by hand. Imagine!' *She held the quilts securely in her arms, stroking them.*

'Some of the pieces, like those lavender ones, come from old clothes her mother handed down to her,' I said, moving up to touch the quilts. Dee (Wangero) moved back just enough so that I couldn't reach the quilts. They already belonged to her.

'Imagine!' *she breathed again, clutching them closely to her bosom.*

'The truth is,' I said, 'I promised to give them quilts to Maggie, for when she marries John Thomas.'

She gasped like a bee had stung her.

'Maggie can't appreciate these quilts!' she said. 'She'd probably be backward enough to put them to everyday use.'

'I reckon she would,' I said. 'God knows I been saving 'em for long enough with nobody using 'em. I hope she will!' *I didn't want to bring up how I had offered Dee (Wangero) a quilt when she went away to college. Then she had told me they were old-fashioned, out of style.*

'But they're priceless!' she was saying now, *furiously; for she has a temper.* 'Maggie would put them on a bed and in five years they'd be in rags. Less than that!'

'She can always make some more,' I said. 'Maggie knows how to quilt.'

Dee (Wangero) looked at me with hatred. 'You just will not understand. The point is these quilts, these quilts!'

'Well,' I said, *stumped.* 'What would you do with them?'

'Hang them,' she said. As if that was the only thing you could do with quilts.

Maggie by now was standing in the door. I could almost hear the sound her feet made as they scraped over each other.

'She can have them, Mama,' she said, *like somebody used to never winning anything, or having anything reserved for her.* 'I can 'member Grandma Dee without the quilts.'

I looked at her hard. She had filled her bottom lip with checkerberry snuff and it gave her face a kind of dopey, hangdog look. It was Grandma Dee and Big Dee who taught her how to quilt herself. She stood there with her scarred hands hidden in the folds of her skirt. She looked at her sister with something like fear but she wasn't mad at her. This was Maggie's portion. This was the way she knew God to work.

When I looked at her like that something hit me in the top of my head and ran down to the soles of my feet. Just like when I'm in church and the spirit of God touches me and I get happy and shout. I did something I had never done before: hugged Maggie to me, then dragged her on into the room, snatched the quilts out of Miss Wangero's hands and dumped them into Maggie's lap. Maggie just sat there on my bed with her mouth open.

'Take one or two of the others,' I said to Dee.

But she turned without a word and went out to Hakim-a-barber.

Now read the commentary on page 138.

Shakespeare dialogues

The speech of characters in Shakespeare's plays is more stylised when in verse, more naturalistic when in prose. Because his plays were written in a very different historical period, it is difficult for modern readers to assess how natural the speech is. However, we can assume that many discourse conventions are unchanged, for example turn-taking, interruptions, not answering the question, pauses and hesitations, differences in address terms, and so on.

The following activity looks at the use and effect of questions and repetition in an extract from a Shakespeare tragedy.

ACTIVITY 28

Read the following extract from Shakespeare's *Othello*. Othello has murdered his wife, Desdemona, believing the suspicions, planted in his mind by Iago, that she had been unfaithful to him with Cassio. Emilia, Desdemona's maid, does not know that her husband, Iago, has done this.

- Comment on the use of question forms.

- How do they function in the dialogue?

- Note the way one character echoes the words spoken by the other, either by exact repetition or rephrasing.

- What is the effect of this in the scene?

OTHELLO:	Thy husband knew it all.
EMILIA:	My husband?
OTHELLO:	Thy husband.
EMILIA:	That she was false to wedlock?
OTHELLO:	Ay, with Cassio. Nay, had she been true, If heaven would make me such another world, Of one entire and perfect chrysolite, I'd not have sold her for it.
EMILIA:	My husband?

OTHELLO: Ay, twas he that told me on her first.
             An honest man he is, and hates the slime
             That sticks on filthy deeds.

EMILIA: My husband?

OTHELLO: What needs this iterance, woman? I say, thy husband.

EMILIA: Oh mistress, villainy hath made mocks with love.
             My husband say she was false?

OTHELLO: He, woman;
             I say thy husband: dost understand the word?
             My friend, thy husband, honest, honest Iago.

EMILIA: If he say so, may his pernicious soul
             Rot half a grain a day. He lies to th'heart.
             She was too fond of her most filthy bargain.

OTHELLO: Ha!

EMILIA: Do thy worst.
             This deed of thine is no more worthy heaven,
             Than thou wast worthy of her.

OTHELLO: Peace, you were best.

EMILIA: Thou hast not half that power to do me harm
             As I have to be hurt. O gull! O dolt!
             As ignorant as dirt. Thou hast done a deed –
             I care not for thy sword – I'll make thee known,
             Though I lost twenty lives. Help, help, ho, help!
             The Moor hath killed my mistress. Murder, murder!

Now read the commentary on page 138.

Using appropriate approaches, concepts and terms

In the previous activities, the tasks steered you towards the use of specific approaches, concepts and terms. When you respond to an extract of dialogue in the examination, you will need to decide for yourself which are the significant aspects of the dialogue and then use appropriate approaches in your analysis. You should begin by commenting on the wider aspects of discourse: the situational factors such as the status and relationships of the participants, their purposes, and the discourse type or genre. Then you can begin to analyse the ways in which the writer constructed these effects.

ACTIVITY 29

Read the following extract from Act 1 of Shakespeare's *King Lear*. Lear is deciding how to divide up his kingdom between his three daughters. He invites each of them to speak of their love for him.

- What characteristics of everyday talk does Shakespeare turn to dramatic effect in this dialogue?

LEAR: The Princes, France and Burgundy,
Great rivals in our youngest daughter's love,
Long in our court have made their amorous sojourn,
And here are to be answer'd. Tell me, my daughters,
(Since now we will divest us both of rule,
Interest of territory, cares of state)
Which of you shall we say doth love us most?
That we our largest bounty may extend
Where nature doth with merit challenge. Goneril,
Our eldest-born, speak first.

GONERIL: Sir, I love you more than word can wield the matter;
Dearer than eye-sight, space and liberty;
Beyond what can be valued rich or rare;
No less than life, with grace, health, beauty, honour;
As much as child e'er lov'd, or father found;
A love that makes breath poor and speech unable;
Beyond all manner of so much I love you.

CORDELIA: [*Aside.*] What shall Cordelia speak? Love, and be silent.

LEAR: Of all these bounds, even from this line to this,
With shadowy forests and with champains rich'd,
With plenteous rivers and wide-skirted meads,
We make thee lady: to thine and Albany's issues
Be this perpetual. What says our second daughter
Our dearest Regan, wife of Cornwall?

REGAN: I am made of that self metal as my sister,
And prize me at her worth. In my true heart
I find she names my very deed of love;
Only she comes too short: that I profess
Myself an enemy to all other joys
Which the most precious square of sense possesses,
And find I am alone felicitate
In your dear highness' love.

CORDELIA: [*Aside.*]   The'n poor Cordelia!
And yet not so; since I am sure my love's

	More ponderous than my tongue.
LEAR:	To thee and thine, hereditary ever,
	Remain this ample third of our fair kingdom,
	No less in space, validity and pleasure,
	Than that conferr'd on Goneril. Now our joy,
	Although our last, and least; to whose young love
	The vines of France and milk of Burgundy
	Strive to be interess'd; what can you say to draw
	A third more opulent than your sisters? Speak.
CORDELIA:	Nothing, my lord.
LEAR:	Nothing?
CORDELIA:	Nothing.
LEAR:	Nothing will come of nothing: speak again.
CORDELIA:	Unhappy that I am, I cannot heave
	My heart into my mouth; I love your Majesty
	According to my bond; no more nor less.
LEAR:	How, how, Cordelia! Mend your speech a little,
	Lest you may mar your fortunes.
CORDELIA:	Good my Lord,
	You have begot me, bred me, lov'd me: I
	Return those duties back as are right fit,
	Obey you, love you, and most honour you.
	Why have my sisters husbands, if they say
	They love you all? Happily, when I shall wed,
	That lord whose hand must take my plight shall carry
	Half my love with him, half my care and duty:
	Sure I shall never marry like my sisters,

Now read the commentary on page 139.

Examination techniques

Your preparation for this module should have provided you with an understanding of how conversations in 'life and literature' work and also with skills in analysis. In your revision time, ensure that you know the set Shakespeare play well. Remind yourself of the four frameworks for analysis provided on pages 66–67. It is better not to attempt to learn a list of impressive terms off by heart – if the concepts are not already familiar, you may use them without insight or real understanding.

In the examination room, make sure that you divide your time equally between the two questions: approximately one hour for each. Spending longer on one may improve the quantity, but not necessarily the quality, of your answer. However, a brief, rushed answer will be awarded few marks. You will need (a) time to read the extracts, (b) time to study the unseen texts, and (c) time to make a brief plan of your answer so that you cover all the points mentioned in the question. This should leave 40 to 45 minutes to write your answer.

Unseen texts

In the examination, this question asks you to compare a transcript of real conversation with a literary representation of a conversation. You should be able to comment on the following:

- differences between transcription and play script

- conventions and contexts of talk in both transcript and play script

- achievement of effects in play script

- ways in which power, conflict, and control are evident in both

- significant choices of lexis and grammar

- phonological aspects evidenced in both

- ways pragmatic meanings are conveyed in both.

When reading the unseen texts, note briefly the differences aand then concentrate on the similarities.

The differences. There will probably be features of spontaneous talk that are not present in the literary text. Consider the reasons for this: most obviously the different channel for communication – one existed as sounds, the other exists as marks on the page. Also bear in mind the different contexts, for example purposes and audience: the conversation was communication for some purpose between two people, and probably not intended for a wider audience. By contrast, the literary representation is part of a novel or play and so is intended for a wider audience and needs to play a role in the work as a whole – to develop character, plot, themes, and so on.

The similarities. In order to interpret the conversation, you need to draw on a knowledge and understanding of the ways that conversations work in ordinary life. A dramatic dialogue is likely to portray tension and conflict, using such means as different agendas, persuasive devices (rhetoric), and unequal power relations.

ACTIVITY 30

Do the sample question provided in the Specimen Units and Mark Scheme booklet in one hour.

The indicative content provides a commentary.

Then refer to the mark scheme to assess your answer.

No commentary.

Shakespeare extracts

In your response to the two extracts from the Shakespeare play you are studying, you should be able to comment on the following:

- Context, including:

  the dramatic situation

  character relationships

  status of characters

  stages in play.

The ways in which Shakespeare draws upon social and psychological aspects of talk.

The ways in which Shakespeare transforms everyday styles and conventions into theatrical art.

- The roles given to characters in dialogue, such as:

  provocative

  reactive

  collaborative.

- The differences in language use between speakers:

  Who asks questions?

  Who gives commands?

  Who insinuates?

- The ways in which features of speech convey character, including:

  prolixity (saying too much)

  taciturnity (saying too little)

  hesitancy

  modes of address.

- Literary features, such as:

  staging

  character construction

  figurative language

  rhetorical devices.

ACTIVITY 31

Do the sample question provided in the Specimen Units and Mark Scheme bookletin one hour.

The indicative content provides a commentary.

Then refer to the mark scheme to assess your answer.

No commentary.

Commentaries

Activity 1

Here are some examples. You may have thought of many more.

- Private/public. Although many conversations are heard by the participants alone, many can be overheard, and this may affect the conversational behaviour. One side of mobile phone conversations, on the train for example, can be heard by the other passengers.

- Spontaneous/planned. Often private conversations are rehearsed mentally before being spoken. If the conversation is going to be heard by a wide audience, on a chat show for example, both the questions and the responses are prepared to some extent. In the professional context of an interview, for example, both interviewer and interviewee will monitor their contributions carefully.

- Equal/unequal status. Conversations between friends may take place on an equal footing, but in many situations the roles of the participants are unequal in power and status: teacher–student; parent–child; boss–employee; host–guest; nightclub bouncer–person in queue.

- Trivial/significant. Small-talk or an exchange of pleasantries, with a stranger at the bus stop for example, usually touches on nothing of importance to either party. Other apparently trivial pieces of chat may be important in the ways they function to maintain a friendship. Many of the important issues in life are dealt with through talk, even if they are backed up with written documents.

- Polite/hostile. As children, we are taught how to be polite in conversations, but there are many situations in which one or both participants deviate from politeness conventions. This might be because of the conflict in the situation, but is also a means of friendly banter.

Activity 2

You may have mentioned some of these points (though there are others):

- take turns

- don't interrupt

- don't hog the conversation

- be polite

- be truthful.

Disagreement probably relates to 'situational factors', such as:

- who the speaker is (age, gender, and so on)

- the relationship between the speakers (friend, boss, stranger)

- the setting of the conversation (phone or face to face)
- the purpose of the conversation.

Activity 3

In the first conversation, the three men often echo each other's words either by exact repetition: 'Aye . . . at Wickes', or by slight rephrasing: 'three pound sixty-nine/three sixty-nine . . . Oh well that's not bad/Well it's handy.' This type of repetition is supportive behaviour, endorsing each other's words, as they also co-operate in the physical sharing of work.

The second text has been passed around by email. It may be authentic, but might be a type of urban myth, as it seems so perfect in the way it builds up gradually to a punchline. The stylised form of repetition and rephrasing could be a factor of the situation, where set phrases must be used in such radio communication. However, instead of stating the crucial information immediately, the Canadians simply echo the formal instruction: 'divert your course', with the only change being 'North' to 'South'. The withholding of key information allows the American ship to include a long, threatening account of their naval might, which is then capped by the effectively brief: 'We are a lighthouse.' The effect of the repetition is a form of sparring and blocking, rather than co-operation.

Activity 4

Both interactions are a form of interrogation and trial, though the first is an actual, informal conflict and the second a fictional representation of an official court scene. However, the participants of the first situation are well aware that they are being filmed and that millions will be watching, so it is not a private conversation. In the second extract, the character, Margaret Brotherton, is in the relatively powerless position of a defendant in front of two judges, who have the authority to jail, beat, expel or even hang people.

The person 'on trial' in the *Big Brother* scene has always enjoyed an equal status with the others and has broken only the rules of a game show, so the stakes for him may not seem to be as high.

The *Big Brother* extract begins with a significant question about where the pieces of paper are. Nick's evasive answer that 'most of them' have been destroyed is followed by each of the others expressing their shocked reaction to his behaviour. Each takes a relatively long turn, with Darren and Craig dominating, whereas Nick remains silent until Craig makes the crucial request to 'go and get the paper'. The exchange then moves in turn between Craig and Nick, with Darren adding more expressions of his shock at such manipulation (thereby suggesting his own straightforward honesty and fair play). Nick's brief contributions are contrite. There is little he can do in this situation, outnumbered by previous 'friends' who are now opponents, and exposed in front of an avid TV audience. By taking on the role of spokesman for a sort of collective outrage, Craig's status on the show improved and he was the eventual winner. Darren was also quite successful, but many viewers found him rather smug.

In the play, the two JPs' alternate turns, so they seem to be working in tandem, like a comedy duo or a bad-cop, good-cop pair: 'Hard times/Soft hearts.' They continue their conversation while addressing the defendant almost as an afterthought. Their questions to her are curt and they want only short answers. After her first four responses, she does not get a chance to speak again. The two JP's first fire questions without waiting for answers, then begin talking between themselves about the cheek of the poor from other areas expecting help; they start referring to her in the third person (she) rather than addressing her directly until the question: 'Why aren't you married?' Her lack of response is indicated by a row of dots. This is an unanswerable question and not within the usual factual matters. Margaret Brotherton's lack of turns indicates both her powerlessness and the JPs' dismissive attitude. In a real courtroom scene, the authority figures might be expected to speak for longer and to ask all the questions, but this representation uses the farcical, yet menacing, element of the pair enjoying their own repartee, while considering the defendant as a distraction. They move quickly to sentencing her without having considered her case.

Activity 6

This type of protracted and ritualised exchange is common in public conversations like televised quiz shows. It may also be a feature of conversations crafted for dramatic or humorous effect. As you saw in the conversation between on American ship and a Canadian lighthouse (Activity 3), tension and humour are heightened by the delay in getting to the point. Whereas it may be desirable in real-life situations to achieve the purpose as quickly as possible, there needs to be some dramatic tension in dialogue constructed with a purpose and audience in mind.

Although Rita is the student and she is having a tutorial in the room of her university tutor, the play often shows her taking the initiative and pushing Frank to acknowledge other ways of seeing the world than from his academic viewpoint. So she interrupts the usual question-and-answer exchange from tutor to student by inserting her own personal question. 'Are you married?' is the form of question usually termed a Yes/No question as opposed to a 'Wh- question' such as 'Who did you marry?' or 'When did you get married?' Her form of question suggests that the option for Frank's answer is either yes or no. As often happens with awkward questions, Frank sidesteps it first by not giving an answer, then by responding with questions of his own. This is the pragmatic area of language use – not so much what the sentence means, as what the speaker means when s/he utters it. Once he has Rita answering his questions again, he reverts to the academic topic, but she returns to the personal interest, asking 'Why did you split up?' Again he avoids answering the question and, when pushed for an answer, gives an obscure and unexpected response that refers to poetry – his academic domain. This exchange functions to portray the unusual shift in the tutor-student relationship that is an important feature of this play. Frank seems unable to engage on a personal level, but expresses this only obliquely. Rita is generally more direct, admitting her lack of knowledge and confidence in academic matters.

Activity 7

Exchange 1 is initiated with an interrogative. The response is supportive of the speaker's implied meaning: 'I know that's exactly . . . '

Exchange 2 is initiated with an imperative. Again the response is supportive with the confirmation: 'Yeah.'

Exchange 3 is initiated with a declarative, to which the response is again: 'Yeah me too.'

Judging from this evidence, the participants are friends talking with the purpose of sharing annoying experiences, with the comfort of knowing that the others agree about their reactions.

Activity 9

The two participants appear to be talking on the phone, as the opening 'hallo' is followed by the other speaker giving her/his name, which would not be necessary if they were face to face. The relationship seems quite informal and friendly, as the more polite greeting 'hallo' changes to 'hi'. The topic of the talk is D's trip, so A asks most of the questions and D's turns are longer to provide the information, with A inserting back-channel comments: 'yeah, right, good, mmm.' These often function in a phone conversation to show that the listener is still there and A is encouraging the speaker to continue.

It would be interesting to know how you assessed the relationship of the speakers on the evidence of this transcript. They are primarily work colleagues, who also meet socially, so you may have noted a polite friendliness in the interaction. It would also be interesting to know how you assessed the age, gender and social class of the participants. There are few indications of phonology, apart from 'yeah', which these days is a pronunciation that is widespread, rather than limited to very informal situations. There are abbreviated grammatical structures, typical of spoken language, such as 'you taking your laptop? . . . two weeks is it?' There are also some quite extended, complex sentence structures that suggest this speaker is in articulate mode: 'it will be a strange experience which could be quite good for writing a murder story.' The lexis ranges from informality to more formal terms: 'that comic book stuff . . . really productive time'; includes reference to modern technology: 'laptop . . . hotmail number', but also terms like 'sideboard' that are less modern. Perhaps a person's choice of expletive: 'the damn thing' is a good clue to social group? The topics suggest something about the world of these two people. Their conversation deals with quite mundane details of train journey, mobile phone and email in detail, with comic books and writing a murder story mentioned briefly, presumably commonplace topics for the speakers.

Activity 10

The transcript uses different spelling for many of the words to indicate the Northern accent of the speaker. This is not done in a strictly consistent way, but is intended to help the reader hear the voice. Some of the words spelt differently are glossed in brackets, in case the reader cannot understand. It does present some problems as writing is taken in by the eyes, but should be easy to follow if heard. However, the presence of a 'translation' suggests, as the use of subtitles for a regional accent on film or TV would, that this is a marginal or minority pronunciation.

The novel makes fewer changes to standard spelling to indicate Hortense's Jamaican accent. Most readers are used to reading apostrophes signalling an abbreviation to the first or final sound: 'freezin' . . . 'ere.' The other changes indicate some of the changes in pronunciation of consonants: 'dis . . . sekkle.' However, this is not done in a consistent way, probably with the ease of reading in mind: 'feber' once mentioned, becomes the standard spelling of 'fever'.

Imagine dubbing the voices of Mafia mobsters in films into a standard English accent, or even an accent from the American Deep South. Changing the distinct voice and variety of English can be as significant as changing the style of sentences or choice of words. It is another version of the text and the effect will be different (comical in the above examples).

The writers of these two extracts have to balance the need to convey the individual voice with the needs of a reader interpreting visual marks on the page. The researcher, Simon Charlesworth, is investigating working-class experience and wants to base his research on people's own accounts. He wants their own words, spoken in their own way. In the novel, the character of Hortense is conveyed largely through the way she speaks (rather than authorial description and comment). It is important for the reader to have a sense of her individual voice. This is done not only by pronunciation features, but also by characteristic phrasing, grammatical structures, and choice of lexis: 'Runnin' roun' on a night like dis, wearing flimsy nonsense!'

Activity 11

The 'maxims of conversation' devised by by philosopher Paul Grice are based on what he calls the principle of co-operation.

Quantity: Give the right amount of information:

- Make your contribution as informative as is appropriate.

- Do not make your contribution *more* informative than is appropriate.

Quality: Try to make your contribution one that is true:

- Do not say what you believe to be false.

- Do not say that for which you lack adequate evidence.

Relevance: Be relevant.

Manner: Be clear:

- Avoid obscurity of expression.

- Avoid ambiguity.

- Be brief (avoid unnecessary wordiness).
- Be orderly.

Activity 13

Hamlet's responses flout Grice's maxims of quality, quantity, relevance, and manner. Presumably his underlying purpose is to avoid giving the true answer (maxim of quality), which would lead to his own death. He may also know that it is just a matter of time, but enjoys taunting his uncle in this fashion: the king is placed in the less powerful position of struggling to follow (maxim of relevance) and of having to repeat his question. Hamlet first gives a misleadingly short answer to the question 'Where is Polonius?' As he elaborates, giving more comment than needed (maxim of quantity), he flouts the maxim of manner, by speaking in an obscure way. The audience can share the 'joke', knowing what Claudius does not, and enjoy his discomfiture. Hamlet has little power in the situation, except his power with words.

Activity 14

Samad Iqbal wants to get the time taken for Harvest Festival celebrations used for some more Muslim celebrations. In doing so, he wants to make the point that there is an imbalance in the school's policy, despite their claims to represent a range of religious groups. The headteacher, Mrs Owens, is on the defensive; she wants to maintain her decision (and is backed up by other members of staff and parents) without appearing to offend Samad's beliefs.

Samad is more obviously confrontational in his argument, whereas the teachers maintain a surface deference. He opens with a curt reference to the topic of concern: 'The Harvest Festival.' Katie Miniver's response is polite on the surface, addressing him by full name, but the question form 'What *about* the Harvest Festival?' with the indicated emphasis is a familiar way of expressing hostility or contempt. Samad echoes it, thus regaining control, and adds on a list of related questions. The headteacher gives a relatively long statement (thus holding the floor) with a list emphasising the range of cultures represented. Her choice of lexis is formal, indicating some authority. She uses his name at the beginning and end of her statement, as a politeness feature, which can be interpreted as patronising, as is her use of the phrase: 'as I am sure you are aware'. (Later she uses the word 'surely' also with the implication: you would have to be unreasonable to disagree with me on this.) Samad's response is contrastingly brief and his use of a question about pagans baffles her. Once he is in the position of offering explanations, he quotes lists and figures to add authority to his opinion. Mrs Owens uses exaggeration again suggesting the absurdity of the other side: 'removing Christian festivals from the face of the earth.' She adds a more deprecating piece of personal reference to 'stocking-stuffing' to take the sting out of it. Samad caps this with his own humorous caricature of Harvest Festival. Mrs Owens' style reverts to a formal register using words such as 'laudable . . . scriptural' using emphatic terms (adverbs) like 'surely . . . precisely . . . certainly.' Her final utterance opens with 'To be honest', where a possible implication might be 'in contrast to you', and she uses the pronoun reference 'we' to exclude Samad from a group of people who care about 'charity' and 'community', both of which are indicated by italics as stressed. Her neat contrast between 'community' and 'religion' is immediately capped, by Samad's rephrasing: 'A man's god *is* his community!' Mrs Owens does not wish to continue the argument, but moves to her winning proposal: 'shall we vote on the motion?'

This dialogue has been constructed by Zadie Smith as one scene in her novel about various cultural groups living in London. The context of the reader plays a role in any interpretation of texts. (See the section on reader response theorists in Module 6, page 167) Your response and interpretation may be different. This particular reader remembers confrontations with her children's headteacher and various struggles for power in meetings between parents and governors, all of which were won by the headteacher. Thus I read the extract with delight, seeing Samad, although not the winner of the confrontation in practical terms, to have all the best arguments and strategies. The portrayal of the headteacher is read as patronising and manipulative. Apart from constructing her part in the dialogue, the author adds comments to steer a negative response, such as 'genteel . . . fiercely cut blonde bob.'

This analysis concentrated on length of turn, repetition and rephrasing, use of question forms, modes of address, use of formal lexis, and the pragmatic effects of some sentence forms. You may have found other features that contributed to an analysis of the ways in which control of the conversation is achieved. In Module 6, you will be required to make your approach explicit.

Activity 15

Each character is superficially polite during this exchange, though it is obviously a battle of wills between husband and wife. Laurence feels that classical music is more 'classy' than his wife's taste and tries to enlist the support of Sue, rather than Beverley's friend, Angie. Because of their status as guests, the others say nothing to directly disagree with them. Only Angie expresses any strong opinion about the choice of music; Sue and Tony are half-hearted in their agreement, but this is rephrased by Laurence or Beverley as ammunition for their point of view:

BEVERLEY:	Tone, do you like Demis Roussos?
TONY:	Yeah, he's all right.
BEVERLEY:	He's fantastic, isn't he?

Use of question forms. Both Laurence and Beverley ask questions of their guests that encourage them to express agreement: 'Do you like . . . ?' Beverley uses question forms to Laurence that function as strong requests: 'do you think we could have Demis Roussos on?' Laurence uses questions in a sarcastic way: 'Well, what do we want to listen to, Beverley?'

Use of pronouns. Both Laurence and Beverley use the first-person plural 'we' to suggest reference to the whole group, though it clearly indicates their personal preference, in opposition to their spouse's preference: 'we don't want to listen to classical music.' Each seeks to gain support by addressing the guests directly as 'you'. Laurence turns his choice of classical into a favour for Sue: 'I'll put it on for you, Sue.' Beverly sums up her case by referring to each person in turn in the third person, before returning to referring to the whole group as 'we'.

Laurence uses a definite 'No' in response to Beverley's suggestion of Demis Roussos, whereas Beverley modifies her reaction with a term of endearment: 'Darling, not *classical.*' Laurence is the only one who uses derogatory terms: 'we don't want to listen to that fat Greek caterwauling.' Beverley leaves her opinions implied and is superficially polite; when Laurence reluctantly concedes to her request/order, expressed with a 'please', she responds with 'Thank you.' She gets her own way in this scene, as in every other scene of the play. Laurence is fighting a losing battle.

Activity 17

Each time he speaks, Buckingham addresses King Richard by a title – 'Your Highness . . . my lord'. The king does not use any term of address, but refers to other parties by name instead. Buckingham is being deferential to his king and the king is ignoring both his request and his name. This suggests that Buckingham is in a weak position; he is forced to reiterate his request, begging for a straight answer, even though he probably suspects it will be negative. The pragmatic meaning of a lack of response is usually negative. The length of turns also suggests the relatively low status of Buckingham in this exchange, though he does interrupt the king as he begins to hesitate and repeat himself. This lack of politeness is a sign of his desperation to get an answer.

There is deviation from the norm of iambic pentameters at the points where one speaker interrupts the other. The two missing beats in the line 'perhaps . . . perhaps' suggest pauses as the king stops speaking, but holds the floor. There is also a missing beat in the line 'your promise for the earldom', perhaps because of the extra syllables in the previous line, where the king's words run on beyond ten syllables. Shakespeare's use of iambic pentameter heightens the aspects of holding and seizing turns.

Activity 18

The woman in Transcript 1 is upset by the use of swearing by her neighbours. She refers to swearing in general, but does not mention any of the words used. Such language affects her to the point of feeling 'invaded'. She worries most about the effect on children and tries to shield her own daughter from it. Language is referred to in concrete terms as 'touching' her daughter, so she would not agree with the saying 'Sticks and stones may break my bones, but words can never hurt me'. She feels the use of taboo language is connected with social class, because she believes that a public school would protect her children. (Do you think this is likely?)

The man in Transcript 2 uses both of the strongest taboo words himself and sees it as a sign of honest communication between friends. He comments that the interviewer is 'too nice' because he does not use swear words and could be 'just honest' if he did so. The interviewer expresses the opinion that it would not be 'right' because of he has the benefit of privileged education. It's not clear whether he means it's not right for educated people to use taboo language, or more generally, not right to correct people so abruptly.

The interviewer, Simon Charlesworth, makes the following comments on this issue:

This forthrightness, which is seen as a mark of respect to the other person, is a form that is demonstrated in postures and gestures that contravene the petit-bourgeois order perceived as 'poshness', and any form of 'aloofness' which working class men and women tellingly equate with teachers, librarians, council workers, Social Security officials and politicians. As another man warned, 'Never trust men in suits, men wi' silly smiles, like fucking Tony Blair and . . . '

As another man counselled, 'Tha too nice, Sime, tha wants to try insertin' the words 'fuck off' int' thi' vocabulary.' It is as though this world solicits hardness as a way of avoiding having to deal with threat and actual violence; as though a certain comportment and expressivity is called for in order to avoid ingress into one's personal existence.

Activity 19

The woman speaks in a frightened or quiet voice. She hesitates and repeats herself. Of course this may also be a factor of the situation. The man also speaks quietly, but it seems to be a deliberate choice, rather than one he cannot avoid. He speaks without hesitation or repetition, seeming more confident and articulate. She is overwhelmed by the situation and he is responding as the dominant figure, or an owner, as his words 'You are now mine . . . mine . . . my wife' show. This representation of male–female relationship is popular with the many readers of Cartland, who, we may assume, are women rather than men, and older rather than younger women. Perhaps the ideal reader is one who enjoys imagining a powerful man and a helpless woman, as a comfortable world far removed from their experience? The absence of taboo language or details may also be a comfort. You are unlikely to be part of this ideal readership and reactions may range from amusement to hostility.

Activity 20

Here is a brief summary of some theories about language and gender:

'Lakoff and Dale Spender characterise women's speech as more hesitant, less fluent, less logical, less assertive than men's speech. Women, in their view, are more silent, interrupt less frequently than men, use tag questions and modal verbs more than men, use co-operative strategies in conversations rather than competitive ones.' (Sarah Mills)

These are their proposals, but they do not have research proof. You could apply these hypotheses to your own informal observations.

Hiatt claims that women use 'really' more often than men (but this is research into writing).

Pamela Fishman uses the term 'conversational shitwork' for conversational strategies such as prompting questions, supporting information and suggests that these generally supportive and minimal contributions are more typical of women than men. (*Analysing Casual Conversation*, Eggins and Slade)

Interrogatives are ways of offering the turn. It has been suggested that women in mixed-sex conversations ask more questions and these tend to be 'wh- forms' with open-ended answers, rather than polar – closed Yes/No questions – which men prefer.

These are some phonological, lexical and grammatical features that some researchers suggest are typical of women's language. This may not accord with your observations of the ways that males and females talk. Some people feel that other factors are more significant than gender, such as power or lack of it.

Activity 21

Did you assess the speakers as young, female, student friends spending some free time together, talking about an event which upset all of them?

If you used the term 'gossip', was this because you thought this was 'idle talk' or 'women's talk'? Perhaps you felt that one of the functions of such a conversation is to 'explore similarity and shared values' and to 'label the actions of the third person as deviant and unacceptable'. In your experience, do males engage in such talk?

Here are some features identified by the author. You may have concentrated on others.

- There is evidence of supportive responses and back-channel behaviour indicating the friendly purpose and relationship: 'I know . . . I know exactly . . . yeah exactly'.

- There are words relating to a teenage way of life: friends, presents, parties, ringing up, lifts.

- Some phrases are sayings that might be used by older people: 'not being funny but . . . even if we brought B the world . . . I could see it in her eyes . . . She didn't even have the decency.'

- There is much reference to emotions: 'crying my eyes out . . . I feel ashamed . . . I feel ashamed . . . we are disgusted . . . I thought she was mad at me.' Was this a feature that helped you identify the speakers as belonging to a particular age, social or gender group?

- There is use of taboo language – assumed by the woman in a previous extract to be something to protect young girls from by sending them to public school – in a casual way to express emphasis. There are other words (adverbs) used to add emphasis: 'it's awful *honestly* . . . *exactly* . . . don't *even* bother.'

- The use of phrases such as 'she was like . . . she was all . . . ' to introduce reported speech is suggested as a feature of young people's language (Sal Tagliamonte). Also the expression 'mad at me' seems a marker of a young age group, whereas the non-standard expression 'A is not that friendly' could be used by a wider range.

Activity 22

In this context, John has the power and authority of his position as Carol's lecturer. If Carol needs help, she is likely to feel particularly insecure. You might expect John to control the conversation – even if Carol is the one who needs to initiate some questions – perhaps by having longer turns, speaking fluently, challenging or correcting Carol's comments or interrupting. Carol might be expected to 'speak when she is spoken to', listen politely to John, be more hesitant in expressing herself.

The conversation does not follow these expectations. The following comments refer to the following features: interruptions, length of turns, contradictions, imperatives, interrogatives, rhetorical strategies, level of lexis (vocabulary).

John seems in control in the first utterance, as he asks a question which can be interpreted as hostile: 'What do you want me to do?' Carol interrupts in mid-structure, rather than at a more convenient point, with a flat negation, which she repeats when John attempts to finish his utterance: 'No.' She is firm in her demand: 'You have to help me', then echoes his last phrase and turns his question around: 'you tell me.' He sounds knocked off balance by her imperatives: 'Teach me.' John also breaks in and interrupts her speech on a couple of occasions, notably when she tries to tell him she doesn't understand his book, 'any of it'. He makes self-deprecating comments: 'perhaps it's not well written', and: 'it's just a course. It's just a book.' But this provokes a relatively long and uninterrupted speech from Carol, emotion conveyed in the use of clipped utterances, repetition and rhetorical strategies, such as building up similar structures: 'So someone would help them. To do something. To know something.' She ends on the statement 'I'm stupid', which is immediately contradicted by John, but challenged twice by Carol: 'What am I then?' John's response to this is his longest uninterrupted speech, where he uses formal lexis and stock diplomatic phrases, such as 'I sympathise with your concerns'. Carol breaks him off in mid-sentence with the blunt: 'you think I'm nothing.'

Activity 23

S's meaning presupposes a world where it is necessary for a woman to lose some weight in order to look her best in her wedding outfit. If the listener does not understand this, the final utterance may seem like a change of topic, rather than an explanation for C's refusal of biscuits.

Activity 24

William Hague asks a number of *loaded questions*, which remain unanswered by Tony Blair. He uses *triples* on several occasions: 'It was Mr Mandelson who picked you out, who briefed the press for you, who stabbed the chancellor in the back for you, who spun all of your campaigns for you'; 'standards of truth, honesty and integrity'.

Tony Blair uses *balanced phrases* in his replies: 'you diminish yourself far more than you diminish anyone else'; 'if people did something wrong they would pay the penalty, and he has paid the penalty.'

Emotive words with positive connotations are used by Blair to refer to Mandelson: 'courage, duty, a bigger man, honourable.' Emotive words with negative connotations are used by Hague to refer to Blair (rather than Mandelson, who is no longer a threat): 'dependency, error of judgement, arrogance, spin and smear.'

Flat *insult* is used by Blair in response: 'nonsense.'

Activity 25

The grammatical structures and vocabulary are typical of colloquial speech, for example the inverted question structure 'You the landlord are you?', and such elliptical structures as 'Family of Indians live there'. Vocabulary such as 'caff' and 'Scotch git' suggest the idiolect of Davies. Their use of pleasant cliché indicates a desire to be friendly: 'You've got to have a good pair of shoes. Shoes? It's life and death to me.'

Davies initiates nearly all the exchanges either with questions or comments, to which Aston makes little response. Davies' greater amount of talk might indicate his confidence, or nervousness – he is, after all, a visitor in someone else's home. Aston's reluctance to take up any of the conversational gambits might indicate a coldness, a lack of interest or his natural reticence. His actions are kind, in contrast to his brief responses. In fact, he begins to take more part by asking questions, once the topic changes from details of *his* life to details of Davies' life: 'What happened when you got there, then?' At this point, Davies avoids answering, so perhaps both are cautious about revealing too much detail about themselves. Davies' topics of conversation jump around from topic to topic, when there is no response from Aston. Although getting a pair of shoes is important to him, he seems equally concerned about the neighbours and returns to 'How many more Blacks you got around here then?' Strangely, when Aston offers him a pair of shoes, Davies returns to his earlier anecdote and then dismisses the shoes without trying them on.

The two characters seem an awkward combination. Though not openly confrontational, Davies appears so demanding and suspicious that this might prove a problem for the passive host, if he is pushed further. Davies lacks the awareness to realise when he has gone too far. The play ends with Aston asking him to leave.

Activity 26

The two men pick up on each other's short utterances, repeating, adding and rephrasing, as happens in everyday talk. However the topic, control and patterning shares more with poetry than conversation:

All the dead voices.
They make a noise like wings.
Like leaves.
Like sand.
Like leaves.

This exchange, and others with similar patterns, ends when Estragon repeats exactly the same phrase, rather than adding a new variant.

They seem to be playing with words, perhaps simply to pass the time, which hangs heavily when waiting for something. Estragon suggests it is a way of avoiding thinking. Perhaps this is the other type of 'silence' that Pinter refers to: 'a constant stratagem to cover nakedness.'

Activity 27

Actions can be shown as stage directions in drama, such as: 'she breathed again, clutching them closely to her bosom.' The actor would have to suggest aspects of characterisation, such as: 'like somebody used to never winning anything, or having anything reserved for her.'

But some of the narrative could not be included in a play script, such as flashback narrative: 'I didn't want to bring up how I had offered Dee (Wangero) a quilt when she went away to college. Then she had told me they were old-fashioned, out of style.'

Unless the device of soliloquy is used, internal thoughts cannot be expressed in plays: 'something hit me in the top of my head and ran down to the soles of my feet. Just like when I'm in church and the spirit of God touches me and I get happy and shout.'

The narrative is from the *perspective* of the mother, but a play could not show that this is how her mother sees her: 'it gave her face a kind of dopey, hangdog look.'

Activity 28

Here it is interesting to note how Shakespeare makes use of questioning. It comes at a very dramatic point in the play. Othello believes he has done an honourable thing in killing Desdemona: 'Yet she must die, else she'll betray more men.' For the first time he tells Emilia that it was Iago, her husband, who suggested Desdemona was unfaithful. Emilia smells a rat.

Shakespeare creates here a sense of information being processed by the recipient and repeated in disbelief to gain time because it cannot be believed. Emilia then fails to listen and respond appropriately to Othello's next statement. The audience stays with her words. The exchange is rapid and this adds to the dramatic tension since you know they are not building a conversation – they are heading for a row. Emilia seeks confirmation and persists in disbelief and growing alarm. The information-giver, unable to realise it is a lie, becomes frustrated and states back to her in two different ways to try and break the deadlock. He is focusing on the wrong part of Emilia's statement. She does not mean: Did you say my husband? She is saying: I cannot believe you said my husband; why would he say a thing such as that when it is not true, and why would you be such an idiot as to believe him?

Activity 29

In this scene, Lear wishes to be in complete authority, both as king and father. Thus, he intends the conversation to follow a certain pattern: each daughter in turn will swear her love to him and he will reward each with a gift of lands. Two daughters are happy to play this conversational game according to his rules and get the better of him by flattery. One daughter maintains her independence and integrity.

In Lear's first speech, he establishes control of the dialogue by posing his egocentric question via imperative structures: 'Tell me, my daughters . . . Goneril . . . speak first.' Goneril's speech is full of extreme comparisons ('Dearer than eye-sight') so that the audience/reader might wonder how arrogant a father must be not to recognise this as hyperbolic flattery. Lear rewards her with lands and then asks the next daughter to speak. The style of extreme claims is echoed in Regan's speech.

In drama, as well as fables, folk tales and jokes, the conventions of posing the same question/task to three daughters/sons is that the first two will follow a similar pattern, but the third and youngest will break away from this. This expectation is reinforced by Cordelia's use of asides (comments unheard by the other participants, but intended for the ears of the audience). Her short utterances contrast with the longer speeches of her sisters and refer to love and silence, suggesting that the two go together. In discourse conventions, short and simple can signal sincerity. Her father phrases his question in a way that make's it absolutely clear that she is speaking of love in order to win a prize. His perfunctory imperative 'Speak' is matched by a brief response with a strange combination of the negative 'Nothing' and the respectful 'my lord'. His one-word echo conveys his sudden, stunned lack of words. Cordelia's response uses no politeness strategies to disguise the negative 'Nothing' repeated back to Lear. There is a sort of battle and stalemate by the four turns each repeating the word 'Nothing'. Lear asserts his authority with the demand 'Speak again'. This is a very blunt way of allocating a turn. Her ambiguous reply 'no more nor less' does not provide enough clear detail for her father's needs. Cordelia is flouting Grice's principle of co-operation and Lear infers, mistakenly, that she loves him less than her sisters do. Certainly, he cannot tolerate her brief, plain replies and tries to force her to say what he wants to hear with another imperative and a threat: 'mend your speech a little, lest you may mar your fortunes.' Cordelia's response is now clear and truthful and says that her father can share 'half my love' with her husband. She is not playing the conversational game that Lear tried to set up – all she has to do is speak lying words of love like her sisters in exchange for a share of Lear's kingdom. She has thwarted his need for this type of power by refusing to respond as instructed.

This, the synoptic module, is worth 20% of the final A Level mark.

ASSESSMENT OBJECTIVES

AO1   communicate clearly the knowledge, understanding and insights gained from the combination of literary and linguistic study, using appropriate terminology and accurate written expression (2.5%)

AO2ii   respond with knowledge and understanding of texts of different types and from different periods, exploring and commenting on relationships and comparisons between them (7.5%)

AO3ii   use and evaluate different literary and linguistic approaches to the study of written and spoken language, showing how these approaches inform their readings (5%)

AO4   show understanding of the ways contextual variation and choices of form, style and vocabulary shape the meaning of texts (2.5%)

AO5   identify and consider the ways attitudes and values are created and conveyed in speech and writing (2.5%)

The weighting given to this module (20%) should alert you to the fact that more is being demanded of you than at AS. In order to demonstrate 'understanding' of texts you must be able to apply different approaches to explain and interpret them. You must also be able to justify the framework you choose to use when examining the texts.

The examination of your pre-release texts

Three days before the examination you will be provided with the pre-release pack, which will contain 10–12 texts from both literary and non-literary genres. Some will be from earlier historical periods, and there will be representations of spoken language, both scripted and unscripted; these materials take the place of a set text. You will have *two* questions to answer in the examination, based on a collection of texts on a particular topic in the pre-release pack. The two tasks are related:

1.   the first requires discussion of the texts themselves,

2.   the second asks you to comment on the methods you used in this discussion.

The first question is more heavily weighted with 50 marks; the second question has 20 marks. So in the two hours allocated for writing, you should spend more time on the first question. However, the second question is the opportunity to meet AO3ii.

As this module is based on pre-release materials, your work begins in the days preceding the examination with a thoughtful reading and annotation of the texts. You also have the first half hour of the examination for reading the two unseen texts, and during this time you can begin to prepare for some of the Assessment Objectives.

You should remember that AO2ii is the most heavily weighted. This assesses your ability to explore the relationships and comparisons between the texts in the Anthology. In the reading and preparation stage, you should consider the types of relationships and comparisons that may be made between texts. During the course of your study you have been introduced to a number of conceptual frameworks for the study of language and literature, and these will be reviewed in this final section. You are not expected to apply *all* the frameworks, but to choose those you find most useful. The second question asks you to explain and evaluate your choices. The activities in this section will provide you with the opportunity to apply a variety of approaches.

Reading and classifying the pre-release texts

As you read the pre-release texts, you may decide to classify them in order to reveal types of relationships between them. Earlier modules introduced a number of frameworks for classification. But before reviewing some of these frameworks, we need to look at some of the problems inherent in any system that attempts to classify. Descriptions of the natural world, for example, attempt to find categories into which everything will fit neatly, with no overlaps and nothing left out. Such systems are often based on **binary** opposites, for example animate/inanimate. Broad classifications of this kind are often very useful, but there is always the danger that they may obscure the rich complexity of the material they try to organise, and also that they will be accepted as 'natural' and inescapable.

In your study of the Anthology for Module 1, you were encouraged to classify texts according to such paired concepts as formal/informal, speech/writing, standard/non-standard, and so on. Although you may find it useful to use these simple distinctions as a preliminary classification of the pre-release material, you should be aware of their shortcomings, for there is always a danger that any *simple* classification may hide other significant factors – factors which it is important to explore.

In Module 2, for example, you were introduced to the concept of variations across two axes: the synchronic (variations at a single point in time), and the diachronic (variations over time). Placing a text at a point on a 'vertical' axis is not always a sufficient classification as it suggests that all texts produced at a particular historical moment share the same essential qualities. The 'horizontal' axis in this particular framework indicates other significant factors, such as social dialect, geographical dialect, register, and idiolect.

We can now review some of the frameworks you have used before, looking this time at their limitations.

Literary/non-literary

Module 6 assumes a non-problematic classification of 'literary' texts, deliberately ignoring any difficulties over the distinction between literary and non-literary. However, you will have noticed that this is a tricky distinction to maintain. What category would letters, journals or autobiography come into? Is an on-line chat-room exchange a conversation? What is the columnist doing every week in a newspaper – is it non-literary when the aim is to persuade, and literary when the aim is to 'entertain'?

So while you may find it useful to begin by classifying texts as either literary or non-literary, it may well be more rewarding to explore the areas of overlap and thus challenge the distinction as over-simplified or misleading.

Poetry/prose/drama

The familiar classification of literature into poetry, prose and drama is a seemingly neat and useful distinction between three main genres (it is a system widely used in bookshops and libraries), but it is one that overlooks revealing areas of overlap such as the poetry in Shakespearean drama, dramatic monologues classed as poetry, and autobiographical texts written as novels.

Genre/purpose/audience

In your study so far you may well have found these concepts very useful. But even here there are complications. There are, for instance, many examples of overlapping genre. And while in your work on the production of texts in Module 3 you used a simple framework of four primary purposes, you probably found that it was tricky to state a *single* purpose for your texts. In order to persuade, for example, you need to inform; and to inform, you need to engage and entertain your audience. Similarly, if you produced poetry, fiction or drama, it is conventional to classify the purpose as being to 'entertain', but this is clearly an over-simplification. If a writer's intention is to shock and disturb, the term 'persuade' might be closer to the mark, though it might not exactly account for the purpose or effect of the text.

It is also hard to specify a single audience for a text. A play attracts a range of people, an Internet site can be visited by anyone with access to it, and some children's stories are avidly read by adults: the Harry Potter books, for example, and *Alice in Wonderland*.

Conversation/dialogue

Module 5 explored the distinction between real-life conversations and literary representations of dialogue. Further exclusive categories in this area include spontaneous/planned, and private/public.

Yet areas of overlap are apparent here, too. In a discussion group, the speaker rehearses or crafts what it is s/he wishes to say to make sure that the point is put across effectively. The speech is not written down *word for word* – but nor will what is said be unplanned. Is it 'spontaneous' speech?

Politicians will often receive briefing papers written by aides to keep them up-to-date with important issues. When interviewed, the politician will interweave the information presented in writing into a spoken response. Occasionally the politician does not answer the interviewer's question but gives a party point of view – what was an informative interview is transformed into a medium for persuasive propaganda.

Literary/linguistic approaches

The distinction between linguistic and literary approaches suggested in AO3 is also difficult to maintain. For as the frameworks mentioned in the previous paragraphs attempt classification in terms of language features, so they may also be termed 'linguistic' approaches. Close analysis of style is sometimes referred to as **Stylistics** and thought of as a more linguistic approach than its literary counterpart, **Practical Criticism**. You will be offered further guidance on these two important approaches in Activity 10 (page 152).

We have now looked briefly at the issues you need to consider when classifying the pre-release texts. The approach to Module 6 in the rest of this section will provide the following:

- an account of what is meant by context (AO4), and an opportunity to consider the range of contexts there may be for texts you have already studied

- a revision task which allows you to practise your skills of analysis

- suggestions on the frameworks you can use when reading the materials

- advice on how to approach the writing of your evaluative commentary

- guidance on AO5, which relates to the ways attitudes and values are created and conveyed in speech and writing

- advice on how to approach the reading preparation and annotation of the pre-release materials

- further advice on preparing for the examination

- an anthology of texts on the theme of Dreams.

Some of the materials are accompanied by activities and worked examples of the possible ways of approaching the examination questions. The rest are provided for you to use as mock materials.

ACTIVITY

This activity – a research project – should be set at an early stage in the teaching of Module 6, and a date agreed for the presentation of the materials.

- As a group, agree a topic or theme and then collect a range of materials relating to it. Here are a few suggestions to set you thinking:

    Winning and losing
    Fame
    Money
    Appearances
    Food
    Friends
    Entertainment.

You may think of many others. Ensure that you choose materials from a variety of sources and that they are of an appropriate length to be included in a pre-released source materials pack.

- Use some of the terms and concepts discussed above to carry out a preliminary classification.

- Note interesting areas of overlap, relationships and comparisons between texts.

- How useful did you find the various frameworks?

No commentary.

The contexts explored

It's helpful to begin by considering a few related questions about the concept of 'literature'; these will allow you to focus on the issues of audience, purpose and context.

ACTIVITY 1

- What *is* literature?

- *Who* decides what is to be considered literature?

- Why study literature?

- Read through the following statements and decide what they have in common:

1. Poetry is not a turning loose of emotion, but an escape from emotion; it is not an expression of personality, but an escape from personality.
   T. S. Eliot, 1919

2. It [literature] helps to shape the personality, refine the sensibility, sharpen the critical intelligence.
   Bullock Report into Education, 1974

3. Literature . . . is any kind of writing which for some reason or other somebody values highly.
   Terry Eagleton, 1983

Now read the commentary on page 186.

In order to bridge the divide between language studies and literary studies, it has become necessary to find a common term that allows an interdisciplinary approach to literature. The term now widely used is *text*, which removes the distinction between the literary and non-literary, and has been used as an inclusive category by, for example, linguists and those engaged in cultural studies. Indeed, learning more about cultural studies can help to develop a new understanding of literature. Cultural studies values all expressions of a culture, just as linguists value all texts (and not just 'literary' ones). A bus ticket, a script for a film, a talk show, a soap opera, a piece of text in an advertisement, a play – all have the potential to tell us something about language and its conventions, and also something about the lives, values and attitudes of particular groups at particular times.

This brings us to the continuing debate about the nature of literature and the content of courses offered to students. In recent years attempts have been made when drawing up programmes of study to acknowledge the literature of English-speaking peoples around the world; examples include Caribbean and Indian literature. The number of writers who are still alive when their works are studied has also grown. (The choices students would make, however, rarely form part of the discussion.)

Until recently it has been assumed that all GCSE students should study a Shakespeare play as part of their English Language course, and so proposals to change the contents of the GCSE course met with a range of strong reactions. Here is one side of the argument.

Are Britains to become the dunces of the Western world?

Daniel Johnson

What teachers call the canon – not just Shakespeare, but everything from Chaucer to Joyce – is to be dropped from English GCSE. If the Government accepts these proposals, as it almost invariably does, nobody will be obliged to study any major work of literature. Gone will be the two compulsory Shakespeare plays, to be replaced by an amorphous 'drama', mainly based on Hollywood, pop videos and soap operas.

The Daily Telegraph
8 February 2001

ACTIVITY 2

- Draw up a list of texts you would recommend for the literature part of a course in Language and Literature at A Level.

- What criteria would you use to make the selection?

- Would you include Shakespeare? Why?

No commentary.

One of the ways in which the study of text is changing is in the emphasis now placed on *context*. As many people have been puzzled by the term, it is worth spending some time considering what it covers.

Context: commerce

Visit any bookshop or on-line book service and you become aware of just how many books are available. You can find anything. Or can you? It is worth considering how much control and free choice the reader really has.

Who decides what to print? On what basis is this decided? Perhaps you can name some of the big publishers. Publishing is an extremely expensive activity, and like other businesses, publishing companies want to minimise their risks and maximise their profits in order to survive. However, this necessity can mean that only books that have the potential to sell *well* are published. Many publishers now want writers with a 'saleable image'.

For those who have access to the Internet, there are many new texts to be found there. But even texts on the Internet need to be seen in the context of the commercial world. Recently the American best-selling author Stephen King withdrew his latest novel, *The Plant*, from publication on the Internet because too few people were prepared to pay the small fee he was asking.

Therefore an important consideration of those publishing a text is: Will it make money? Publishing houses decide what to offer the public on the basis of careful financial calculations. A text can be made more popular by competitions and literary prizes (such as the Booker Prize and the Orange Prize), or even by being chosen as a set text by an examining board – but its first appearance in the world of the reader comes about because someone believes it is going to make money. Of course there are exceptions, such as writers who can get their works funded by grants, or who can self-publish on a small scale. Nevertheless, there may be thousands of other texts you *might* have found fascinating – but you will never even know of their existence.

Still, it's relatively easy to obtain novels and books of poetry; but how do we gain access to plays, which are performed works? Of course you can just read a play; but that isn't how the writer considered it would be experienced. Nor can you decide to go to a particular play just when you feel like it – it is advertised for specific dates in a specific place at a specific time. Finally, you cannot decide, halfway through the particular performance, to stop watching the play and come back to it at another time.

ACTIVITY 3

Think about the practical and commercial aspect of putting on a play.

• What arrangements need to be made for the production?

• What jobs do the members of a theatre company have to perform? (You don't need to know their technical names.)

Now read the commentary on page 186.

Context: audience/reader

Although the term 'audience' is used to describe all the people seeing a production, it would be wrong to assume that they will all form the same view of what they have seen. Different perspectives can arise simultaneously amongst those who are present at a production. Their motives for being there in the first place could differ greatly.

ACTIVITY 4

In Module 5 you worked with a Shakespeare's play. Remind yourself of the first scene of the play. (You may have seen video productions or a live stage version.)

- Write the following headings on a sheet of paper: Actor – Member of the audience – A student of English.

- Consider first *why* they are there, and then list the different viewpoints that they could have.

No commentary.

How do we as modern readers identify the potential for alternative readings of a text? This next activity will help you to develop an approach that can be called 'reading against the grain'. First used by the German critic Walter Benjamin to describe a way of reading history (see his collection of essays *Illuminations*), this technique allows us to question texts as we read them, exposing in particular the many assumptions they embody. The German dramatist and poet Bertold Brecht held a similar view; you have already touched upon this approach in Module 4, when you were directed to be aware of the 'gaps and silences' in texts (page 4).

This next activity will need to be planned as part of a library visit or self-directed study. Your results should be discussed in class.

ACTIVITY 5

Go to a library and find the fiction section. You need a watch that shows seconds.

- Open any book of fiction and time how long it takes you to identify which characters are male and which are female.

- How did you recognise this? Was it clearly identified by such markers as names or pronouns?

Now read the commentary on page 186.

ACTIVITY 6

Read the following poem, 'Meeting at Night' by Robert Browning.

- What picture do you get of the people in the poem? What is their gender?

- From whose point of view is the action in the poem described?

- What do you think is the reason for the meeting?

> The grey sea and the long black land;
> And the yellow half-moon large and low;
> And the startled little waves that leap
> In fiery ringlets from their sleep,
> As I gain the cove with pushing prow,
> And quench its speed in the slushy sand.
>
> Then a mile of warm sea-scented beach;
> Three fields to cross till a farm appears;
> A tap at the pane, the quick sharp scratch
> And a blue spurt of a lighted match,
> And a voice less loud, through its joys and fears,
> Than two hearts beating each to each!

Now read the commentary on page 187.

Context: the writer and the reader

You may have learnt that critics in the past believed it was possible and preferable to be 'objective' about a text. The categories *objective* and *subjective* work alongside other assumptions such as fact and fiction. These absolute categories do not help when considering many aspects of existence. If you are studying history, you will have already encountered this problem. Many events occur – but who decides at a given time what is important and what should be written as 'history'? You cannot possibly list every *fact* which occurred even in one second of existence on this planet. You do not have the information on record and, even if you did, the task would take for ever. Students of history rely on the written or spoken versions others have supplied – in other words other people's *texts*: contemporaneous sources or the writing of those classified as 'historians'. There are such things as historical facts: for example, on 1 July 1916 the Battle of the Somme began. That is a fact and is as objective as one can be. However, what can one do with that fact? As soon as we want to learn more we are in the hands of others. What were the causes of the First World War? Different people have different versions. What was it like to be in the war? That depends on such factors as who you were, where you were, your rank and so on.

ACTIVITY 7

Write your life story in one paragraph, and then consider the following questions and tasks:

- Did you begin 'I was born . . . '?

- Did you include details relating to schools, parents, home, and so on?

- What was the last event or fact you recorded?

- Consider the number of words spent on one topic. Does this seem an accurate reflection of the importance of that topic?

- Are there important points missed out?

- Try to assess why you included certain bits of material and left others out.

(The authors gratefully acknowledge Keith Green and Jill LeBihan as the originators of this activity and thank them for giving permission to reproduce it here.)

Now read the commentary on page 187.

What sense we as readers make of any text relies heavily upon the contexts we bring to it. We may not share the social class, education, race, customs or values of the writer. The development of our character and the influence of psychological factors during our development will also affect how we respond. If we have studied other people's ways of reading texts or have a particular moral, religious or political outlook, then these factors too will affect what we notice and engage with in a text.

ACTIVITY 8

Read out your autobiographical paragraph to a partner and ask her/him to identify what additional information you would need to supply for it to make sense to someone from another culture – either someone in another part of the world, or someone who will find your text one hundred years from now.

Now read the commentary on page 187.

Context: culture

The term 'culture' is sometimes used as an evaluative term to describe the arts favoured by the few. But here it is used to identify the distinctive activities, values and beliefs of groups of people. In order to see how cultural contexts work, it is useful to examine a text written about a different culture. A good example is *Wild Swans* by the Chinese writer Jung Chang, a personal history of three generations of the author's family.

ACTIVITY 9

Read the following extract from *Wild Swans* (1992).

- What is the effect on you of the first five sentences?

- How does Chang describe the appearance and manner of her grandmother? (Of course Jung Chang would not have known her grandmother as a young woman.)

- Which aspects can be explained by the cultural context and values of the period and place?

My grandmother was a beauty. She had an oval face, with rosy cheeks and lustrous skin. Her long, shiny black hair was woven into a thick plait reaching down to her waist. She could be demure when the occasion demanded, which was most of the time, but underneath her composed exterior she was bursting with suppressed energy. She was petite, about five feet three inches, with a slender figure and sloping shoulders, which were considered the ideal.

But her greatest assets were her bound feet, called in Chinese 'three-inch golden lilies' (*san-tsun-gin-lian*). This meant she walked 'like a tender young willow shoot in a spring breeze,' as Chinese connoisseurs of women traditionally put it. The sight of a woman teetering on bound feet was supposed to have an erotic effect on men, partly because her vulnerability induced a feeling of protectiveness in the onlooker.

My grandmother's feet had been bound when she was two years old. Her mother, who herself had bound feet, first wound a piece of white cloth about twenty feet long round her feet, bending all the toes except the big toe inward and under the sole. Then she placed a large stone on top to crush the arch. My grandmother screamed in agony and begged her to stop. Her mother had to stick a cloth in her mouth to gag her. My grandmother passed out repeatedly from the pain.

Now read the commentary on page 187.

Context: history

You will have been made aware during this course of the historical contexts that apply when you study any text. For example, the research you undertook when you looked at a Shakespeare play may well have involved considering such factors as Elizabethan staging conventions; politics and the monarchy; the period in which Shakespeare *set* his play, and the historical figures he represented in it. Contemporary literary theorists who focus on the over-riding importance of the historical context are known as **New Historicists,** and they are particularly interested in Renaissance literature. Stephen Greenblatt, for example, has studied the historical evidence of the mid-sixteenth century, when the English Protestant authorities abolished the Catholic concept of Purgatory. For Catholics, Purgatory is the place where the souls of the dead go to be purified. The living pray to God for the dead person and in time that person's soul is admitted to heaven.

During the Middle Ages, money was also used to ease a soul's passage through Purgatory, and this brought enormous wealth and power to the Catholic Church. These facts are particularly relevant for the study of *Hamlet*.

The website hosting Greenblatt's book (http://pup.princeton.edu.titles/7024.html) offers the following comments on the approach:

> Greenblatt argues that the human desires to commune with, assist, and be rid of the dead were transformed by Shakespeare – consummate conjurer that he was – into the substance of several of his plays, above all the weirdly powerful ' Hamlet'. Thus, the space of Purgatory became the stage haunted by literature's most famous ghost.

And the critic Frank Kermode writes:

> My understanding of the traditions concerning *Purgatory*, both learned and popular, has been gratifyingly deepened by the rich detail of Greenblatt's study . . . The nature of the ghost of Hamlet's father is an old scholarly puzzle, but Greenblatt's book raises the discussion to a new level, and does so . . . with the subtle acceptance of the ambiguities inherent not only in the Ghost but in the great play as a whole.

Greenblatt is arguing that whilst Shakespeare does not refer to the issue overtly, his works have within them elements which would *at the time* have been recognised as directly relevant to this particular contemporary concern. For the first audiences of *Hamlet*, the appearance of ghosts and the concerns of the living for the recently dead were important issues. There was much debate about the rights and wrongs of forbidding the practice of remembering the dead, for many people believed that the souls of the dead would suffer close by until released by prayer.

The point is that authors often respond to contemporary concerns, but not always directly; later readers have to rely on historical research to make these concerns explicit. Finding out about the issues and concerns of a period can be as important as investigating the author's life and personal beliefs.

Context: genre

One of the first ways to look at a literary text is to identify the genre it uses and then see how it conforms or deviates from the typical features of that genre. This approach, which was favoured by many early twentieth-century English and American academics, is known as Practical Criticism. Developed by I. A. Richards, William Empson and F. R. Leavis, it came to dominate much of the practice of twentieth-century literary studies and still exerts a major influence today. For those who practise Practical Criticism, the literary text is seen as a self-sufficient work of art. The reader's task is to examine form and style very carefully, for a detailed analysis of techniques is able to reveal the fine moral perceptions embedded in a work. Readers need to know nothing of the author or of the period in which a work was written: a great work is 'timeless'.

It is worth exploring some of the limitations of this approach precisely because it is so widely practised. Some critics of Practical Criticism would say if the words on the page are the only elements to be considered, then a great deal is left unsaid about the text — and yet social, political, psychological and cultural factors may be very important in forming a response to a work. Practical Criticism discourages the search for different interpretations, and also resists the view that interpretations may change over time.

If Practical Criticism was the mainstay of English Literature studies, then Stylistics became the mainstay of linguists when they analysed the language of literature. According to the American academic Stanley Fish:

> Stylistics was born of a reaction to the subjectivity and impressionism of literary studies. For the appreciative raptures of the impressionistic critic, stylisticians purport to substitute precise and rigorous linguistic descriptions and to proceed from these descriptions to interpretations for which they claim a measure of objectivity.

In the analyses that follow you will be given two different responses to Browning's poem 'Meeting at Night' (see Activity 6): the first based on Practical Criticism, the second on Stylistics.

ACTIVITY 10

Read the following analyses of 'Meeting at Night'.

* Where do they overlap?

* How do they differ?

Practical Criticism

The poem is written in two stanzas with a **rhyming scheme** of a b c c b a. The rhyming scheme throws emphasis on two centres of action: the response of the waves in the first stanza, and the bringing of light in the second. The poem proceeds through a series of descriptions and, though there is no main verb, human movement is implied by the effects on the water of action ('fiery ringlets'). The effect of the **enjambment** ('little waves that leap/In fiery ringlets') is to enhance the sense of movement. This is also conveyed by the changing lengths of the lines, which rise from eight syllables to nine and then ten, underlining the movement of the poem's subject and building a sense of expectation.

Nature is described to evoke a sensuous pleasure. Symbolically the dominating presence is the moon, the main connotations of which are love, fertility, femininity, and madness. The poet links the dual action of the oar stirring the water into ringlets and the reflection of the moon on the waves. There is a sense that nature is reinforcing human passion. The **imagery** of this sensual pleasure is also present in the 'warm sea-scented beach'. **Alliteration** creates the sound unities of 'large and low', 'pushing prow', and 'slushy sand'. There is a precision of action too created by the poet's use of single-syllable words.

The references to touch, prompting effects that began with the waves, continue in the second stanza. A sequence of events leads again to an effect or response, this time on the person receiving the secret visitor.

Stylistics analysis

The sentence structures of this poem are immediately **foregrounded** by their deviation from the norm: there is no **main clause** in either stanza. The first begins with a list of **noun phrases** that increase in length:

> The grey <u>sea</u> and
> the long black <u>land</u>; And
> the yellow <u>half-moon</u> large and low; And
> the startled little <u>waves</u> that leap/In fiery ringlets from their sleep

There is description of the scene, but no explicit action. The noun phrases build up to a **subordinate clause**: 'as I gain the cove . . . and quench its speed . . . ' This creates a sense of increasing anticipation and of something unstated. The images of sea and moon and the muted colours have vaguely romantic connotations, which take on more specific human reference with the words used to describe the waves: 'startled little', 'leap', 'fiery ringlets', 'sleep'. The associations of these terms suggest awakened passion – female, rather than male. The 'I' persona in the poem is linked with words formed from verbs – 'gain', 'pushing', 'quench', 'speed' – that suggest a sense of urgency and a striving for some goal. These are more active than the reactive word 'startled' and the word used to describe the sand, 'slushy'.

The second stanza also lacks a **main verb**, but one sequence of noun phrases has a **verbal noun** (formed from a verb) as the headword:

> A <u>tap</u> at the pane,
> the quick sharp <u>scratch</u>
> And a blue <u>spurt</u>

These verbal nouns convey stealthy physical actions, though without an explicit verb. The final couplet remains as a subordinate clause, but introduces human, abstract terms from the semantic field of romantic love:

> voice
> joys and fears
> two hearts beating each to each.

Compared with the precision of description of physical surroundings that leads up to the meeting, this moment is rather vague and clichéd. Has a polite veil been drawn over the meeting of what seems to be two illicit lovers, in line with Victorian conventions? The female persona, who was waiting, is diminutive like the 'little' waves; her voice is 'less loud' than the sound of hearts beating. (You may remember the female character in the Barbara Cartland extract in Module 5 (Activity 19) also struggles to speak audibly.)

No commentary.

Consolidation: Context

You have now begun to establish ways of considering context. Think about what you needed to know to help you with your study of texts. The historical period; the politics of the time; the social groups and power struggles; the values of the period; the conventions of staging in Shakespeare's day; language use at a particular time; changing cultural values – all these aspects may help you. There will not be time when you are studying the pre-release materials for a study of the historical conditions in which a text was first produced; but you need to demonstrate an awareness of the possible influences this aspect can have. As a systematic way of looking at context can help you to organise your responses, the main aspects are summarised below.

Context can refer to:

- *Audience:* the original audience and the modern; the age, ethnic identity and gender of the reader/audience; the social status and values and attitudes that might be held.

- *Purpose*: the function(s) of the text, for example to inform, persuade, instruct or entertain.

- *Mode* of text: for example, written or spoken language, or representations of the spoken.

- *Social, economic and political structures*: for example, how society was organised, who had power, what the issues of the day were, what movements there were which opposed those in power.

- *Historical background*: society's view of the arts, the events which were considered significant, the real people upon whom the texts are based (Shakespeare's 'real people', for example).

- *Genre*: a play, a poem, a short story or novel – each has its conventions within or against which the writer has produced the text.

- *Cultural practices and values*: for example, the accepted ways of behaving; the rituals, values and beliefs which bind groups together and make them recognisably different from other groups.

ACTIVITY 11

With a partner, choose severals text and then:

- Consider a context which is important to your understanding of each text.

- Give an example of a particular aspect.

The first one is completed for you:

Text	Context	Aspect of context
1. *Much Ado about Nothing*	Genre	Dramatic conventions of comedy

No commentary.

Applying the notion of contextual variation

In the examination, the first question requires you to discuss relationships and comparisons between texts on a similar topic. The sample question in the Specification refers specifically to the ways the topic is presented for various *audiences* and asks for discussion of the ways variation in *genre* and *context* shape meaning. You should also discuss how *attitudes* and *values* are conveyed and refer to the writers'/speakers' choices of *form*, *style* and *vocabulary*.

In your preparation of the pre-release material, you should consider *all* the aspects italicised above. You may make annotations on the texts to take into the examination room: this can be in the form of highlighting or underlining, or marginal notes in the form of brief phrases. But you may *not* include notes for the planning of essays, nor add any extra material such as 'post-its'.

As practice for this task, the following activity provides three extracts on the film *Chocolat*, which is based on a novel by Joanne Harris.

ACTIVITY 12

Read the three extracts below and then work through the following:

- What are the attitudes and values conveyed in each extract? Make notes of any interesting similarities and differences.

- Make brief notes on the contexts of each extract, considering aspects you think significant to the ways attitudes and values are conveyed, for example:

    genre
    audience
    purposes
    historical, social, cultural, psychological situation/contexts.

- What are the relevant features of form, style and vocabulary?

Extract 1 is a transcript of a conversation. James is a second-year A Level English Language student who has applied to do Film Studies at university. Jen is his tutor. James is responding to her question, 'Who has seen *Chocolat*?'

JAMES: I thought it was heavy on the schmaltz (.) it were like trying to be nice (.) too emotional (.) pulling at the heart strings (.) sort of forcing you to be sympathetic if you know what I mean (.) it's a bit farfetched (.) like just one woman opening a chocolate shop could change the entire outlook of the village sort of thing but er you could see that er some people might like that you know because it has a fairy tale quality to it you know sort of because it's in a picturesque French village like one of those picture postcards (.) it's got obvious villain flat character sort of thing.

JEN: Yeah but

JAMES But overall it's like erm a sweet film like er ha which is ironic.

JEN: So not for you?

JAMES It were enjoyable (.) there were some funny moments in it and Johnny Depp's good he's not in it much.

JEN: What are the funny bits then?

JAMES Er one which is running through it is the couple and they've no (.) life at all and wife going in to the shop an er woman who owns shop gives them chocolates and says er liven up her life ye know implied sex yeah.

JEN: Yeah

JAMES And her husband eats all these chocolates and it's all nice and she keeps popping in for these chocolates (.) there are these sub-plots.

JEN: This is one of those?

JAMES Yeah.

EXTRACT 2

This is an extract from an article by Jonathan Romney, first published in *The Independent on Sunday*, 4 March 2001.

Lasse Hallstrom's *Chocolat* is the screen equivalent of one of those dainty, decorative sweetmeats seen in French patisserie windows – a melt-in-the-mouth gobbet of caramelised nothing.

The townspeople are at first outraged that this seemingly godless single mother should open a chocolaterie just when they're all sternly denying themselves for Lent . . . Nevertheless, they are soon addicted to Vianne's ever-so-slightly risqué *friandises* ('Try a nipple of Venus'), which have a strange way of stirring the passions. A middle-aged woman finds her husband suddenly leering hotly over her haunches while she's on all fours scrubbing the grubby porcelain . . .

Chocolate and passion: you could think of this as a glorified Flake ad. However the film's sexuality is terribly tame, little more than coy flirtation plus a dusting of Gallic sauciness. Vianne eventually gets together with Johnny Depp's suave and altogether ludicrous blues-playing Irish Gyps – but it's apparently no more than a starlit reverie from which they both quickly spring fully clothed . . .

What makes *Chocolat* annoying is that the hedonism is so smug. Fine, enjoy chocolate – it'll rot your teeth but for heaven's sake, it won't make you a nobler person. Yet the terms of reference are grindingly banal. Crabby, intolerant people bad; joyous, sensual choccie-gobblers good. When the film touches on anything serious, such as domestic violence, it tidies it away with flip comedy.

For the dissenting critic, it's a no-win situation. Snort at such a harmless fairy tale and you look like the film's Scrooge-ish mayor: what's wrong with a little sweet-toothed gratification?

EXTRACT 3

Extract 3 is from an article by the writer Michèle Roberts, first published in *The Independent*, 24 February 2001.

As a child I worshipped in two churches, one dominated by men and the other by women. As a very religious little girl I enjoyed all the mystical, swooning raptures of the Mass, the curious experience of taking in the Host and believing in the Real Presence. I also enjoyed returning home from church and watching my mother, aunt and grandmother prepare the feasts of Sunday breakfast and Sunday lunch, working their alchemy. To me they were as powerful as any priest. Their food was an equally real presence and, of course, much more delicious than the insubstantial Host.

 . . . The simplistic Catholic split lives on, of course, in the form of oppositions between men and women, good and evil, body and spirit. Joanne Harris's novel *Chocolat* depicted a French village community re-enacting them. Harris reverses the opppositions, so that to the sympathetic reader, the female chocolate-maker is Good and the repressive male priest is Bad. The struggle is between the pagan forces of darkness, or dark chocolate, and heavenly light. Harris's heroine – played by Juliette Binoche in the film version . . . – opens a sweetshop called La Céleste Praline and serves up handmade confections that she shapes and decorates herself. . .

The witchy *chocolatière*, gifted with telepathy, could have become a professional magician, but she prefers her 'domestic magic'. . .

The writing in *Chocolat* is unremarkable, often loose and unfocused, but rises to poetry when different kinds of sweeties are named and precision is called for. Then invocations tumble out like ingredients in spells: 'Chocolate curls, white buttons with coloured vermicelli, *pains d'epices* with gilded edging, marzipan fruits in their nests of ruffled paper, peanut brittle, clusters, cracknels, assorted misshapes in half-kilo boxes'.

Read the commentary on page 188 before working on the second task required in the examination.

- In small groups, compare the points you each made with the points made in the commentary. Note the similarities and differences.

- Why do you think your interpretation and analysis was slightly different from others?

Now try the second task in the examination:

- Explain the methods you chose to examine these texts and evaluate how useful they were in contributing to your own understanding of and response to them.

No commentary.

This section of the module has explored the notion of context and consolidated some of the approaches and methods that you have already encountered over the Language and Literature course. We can now look at the question of attitude and values.

Attitudes and values

This section will look at AO5, which asks you to *identify and consider the ways attitudes and values are created and conveyed in speech and writing.*

The work you have done in Module 4 on text transformation and the more recent activity on *Wild Swans* in Activity 9 above should have given you some insights into the ways in which values and attitudes are conveyed. When looking at a text an important question to ask is: Am I being encouraged to share the writer's particular outlook or assumptions? This is certainly the aim of a great deal of journalism (which is what this section will analyse). The follow-up question is: *How* am I being encouraged to share the writer's outlook, or agree with the writer's view?

ACTIVITY 13

Read the following travel article by Will Storr, which appeared in **loaded** magazine in January 2001.

- Who are the intended readers of this piece?

- What attitudes and values are conveyed?

- How are these created?

Barcelona
The capital of the Catalan region of Spain, famous for its football, Gothic area and, er, egg and chips

Founded by the Romans in 15BC and initially named 'Barcino', the Spanish city of Barcelona has for 1,985 years been a nice place to go for your holidays. The weather's hot, the sea is Mediterranean (if slightly pooey) and everything looks stunning. The architecture, the women, even the pigeons are better-looking in Barcelona. It's the capital city of the Catalonian region and has a lovely aquarium. If you want to spend a weekend in the city let **loaded** be your guide as we whisk you away on a magical Spanical tour.

Currency   There's about 270 pesetas to the quid and you should generally find the eating and drinking is fairly cheap. Unless you come from Doncaster, where you can buy 10 barrels of beer and a packet of Wotsits for under 10p.

Where to stay   For the action, you could do worse than getting one of the many hotels around La Rambla, which is a long tree-lined street resplendent with bars (normal and strip), burger joints and witches selling their sordid wares in spider-spooky corners. Staying here will wang you within walking distance of three big nightlife centres: Port Vell, Port Olimpia and the tall ancient streets of the Gothic area. Book well in advance, though, or you could end up paying far too much for a rubbish hotel that's miles away from anywhere, like we did.

Getting around   The underground is clean, efficient and pretty cheap. A three-day pass will cost you 1,600 pesetas (£6) and you can zip all over the shop. Alternatively, you can buy a ticket on the Bus Turistic. They run two circuits (red and blue); one circles the north of the city, the other the south. You buy a day pass for 2,000 pesetas and can hop on and off as you please, as several buses drive each circuit simultaneously. They do get busy, though. Cabs are also fairly cheap, and there are plenty of them to go round.

Where to eat   Although eating out is cheap, you should be wary of the real budget end of the market. We seemed to eat nothing but cack for the whole weekend. A big plate of steak, egg and chips can seem a bargain at 800 pesetas (£3), but ours arrived marinaded in grease and slime, with the steak tougher than an old lady's J-cloth. And don't eat at El Rebujito De Moncho's in Port-Olimpia. We had paella there which was just foul. Don't bother with Blau Marie on the beach, either. If you want a truly awesome eating experience for a good price, try the restaurant at the Abba Saints Hotel (Sants Estacio metro). Bloody lovely. Nice plates, too.

What to do   During the day, there isn't a great deal to get up to. The cable car looks a good idea, but you spend ages walking to it, it takes about five minutes and it's a bit like staring at a postcard for ages. The aquarium (Drassanes tube), however, is excellent. You can go in an 80ft tunnel and look at sharks and these ridiculous things called ocean sunfish which have clearly been built all wrong. I was a little disappointed that I didn't get to feel a crab, and I also smacked my chin on a badly constructed display case. You should watch out for that.

One of Barcelona's main attractions is Gaudi's Sagrada Familia cathedral. It looks like a candle that Salvador Dali has melted with his mucky subconscious, and you can apparently go up the enormous steeples. Don't make the mistake of thinking it's closed down because it's full of cranes, like we did.

Football fans should take the metro to the legendary Camp Nou stadium (Les Corts tube), home of Barcelona FC. It's the biggest ground in Europe – capacity 109,000 –and has a museum attached that will shortly be displaying the goalposts from Wembley, where Barca won their first European Cup in 1992. Parc Güell (Lessups tube) is a big garden full of typically Spanish madness (think Miro, think Dali, think loads of acid and watching blobby shapes), and is great for running around and climbing things. I pretended it was my own garden and planned a massive barbecue in my head.

Where to go out   The old part of the city is the Gothic area (Liceu tube), just east of La Rambla. Its close medieval streets contain countless bars and boozeries. Jamboree is the local hip-hop/R'n'B club, and is packed with hoods nodding their heads and saying things like 'Mmmmmm, phat'. It's on the Place Reial, which is a square in the centre of the Gothic area. Although this is a bit of a 'hub' on a Friday and Saturday night, don't go down late on a Sunday. You'll find the place packed with tramps, pissed gringos and smoking coppers. Of all the bars in the area that we visited, Fonfone on Carrer Dels Escudellers was the nicest. They pull off the cool-club-chic-with-resident-DJ-and-comfy-seating thing excellently. On the same street, the Zoo Bar has an agreeably eclectic clientele.

But if bright lights rather than smoky bars are your thing, head down to the Baja beach club in Port Olympia (Villa Olimpica tube). They've got bikini girls dancing on the bars and a DJ in a speedboat, and it doesn't close until 6am. Alternatively, you could head north-west to Carrer de Provenca (Hospital Clinic tube), which is also lined with interesting places to get off your noggin. Try the Aloha! Polynesian bar for voodoo tomfoolery and sparklers in your cocktail. But bear in mind that although on a Friday and a Saturday the city will kill you with its staying power, on Sundays everything closes at about 12.

Interesting Barcelona fact   Dr Mick is currently living in Barcelona. We saw him three times in one night, all in different places.

Now read the commentary on page 189.

In Module 4 you were made aware of how in *Antony and Cleopatra* Shakespeare used a character (Enobarbus) to offer a particular viewpoint to the audience. Writers in magazines and journals often cultivate an opinionated style that overtly criticises others – readers enjoy the wit and cruelty involved. Below are two such examples.

ACTIVITY 14

- Create your own rules for writing 'character assassination' articles.

- Read the two magazine articles below and then compare them for subject matter. Look in particular for what they have in common.

- Which writer is more unflattering to his/her subject?

- List the devices each uses to persuade the reader that s/he is justified in taking the view s/he does.

- Compare your rules with the methods used by the writers.

EXTRACT 1

This piece, by Julie Burchill, appeared in *The Guardian Weekend*, 7 April 2001.

Some irritants, like an eyelash in the eye or a fly buzzing against a window pane on a hot afternoon are, in themselves, no big deal. You wouldn't think of letting them spoil your day, and when they've been dealt with, you think no more of them. But that itching and that droning do have a way of insinuating themselves in one's gorgeous life, and then they need seeing to.

I've been only vaguely aware of a character called 'Hunter Davies' over the past few decades. I remember a radio run-in with the lovely 80s pop star Marilyn, during which he tried to humiliate the tempestuous pouting beauty; 'What sort of name is Marilyn for a man?' he squeaked. There was a pause.

'I don't know', admitted Marilyn in his surprisingly deep' n' hunky voice. 'What sort of name is Hunter?'

Oooo! Then there was a book of essays I reviewed for the *Spectator*, which left me with the burden of knowledge that Mr Davies has a writing style that makes Charles Pooter look like Nabokov. Photographs shudderingly glimpsed over the years have informed us that Mr Davies has been, for some time, in receipt of the very same moustache that Peter Mandelson shaved off because it made him look 'too camp'. (Too right.) And then, for as long as I can remember, butch old Hunter had been taking joyless pops at me – obviously one of the legions of sad-sack, pay-your-dues-laddie penny-a-liners who never really forgave *moi* for the fact that, by the age of 25, I was on £125k a year and eating out with (I said *with*) the cutest commissioning editor gals in Fleet Street, while they had to make it t'hard way by spending a decade on provincial papers only to fetch up to a swift half in The Stab in the Back.

So it did my hard little heart good to see that the great man's latest effort, a book called The Quarrymen, is a thoroughly and pleasingly rancid example of My Dead Beatle Syndrome, wherein invariably male, always middle-aged hacks, who usually make a great show of loathing the modern, trashy, meretricious world, and who would spit from a great height on kiss-and-tell girls, suddenly come over all red misty, and when they wake up there's a sizeable book, or at least a 2,000-word article on what great mates they were with Johnny-Boy and what he said to them that wet weekend in Bootle in 1964. And by succumbing to this automatic spirit-writing business on a regular basis, they end up making almost as comfy a living off Lennon's corpse as his widow does.

EXTRACT 2

This second article, by Will Storr, appeared in **loaded** magazine in January 2001. It was printed beneath a cut-out target board of the TV presenter Anthea Turner.

Anthea turner

Due to the extraordinary depths of hatred felt by Britain towards this month's subject, we have temporarily cancelled Celebrity Dartboard. For one month only, in honour of Anthea Turner, the black-hearted harpy of television, we present Celebrity Missile Range. Darts aren't good enough for Turner – only intercontinental thermonuclear devices will do.

But why do we hate her so? It's not the televisual slurry that she's schlocked out for 10 years now. It's not her *Daily Mail*-fantasy vacant eyes or her mashed-potato-bland delivery that particularly offend. What made us take this drastic step of encouraging you to cut out her fat-jawed face and fire an eight-megatonne warhead at it is the way she's shat rump-gravy all over the literary world by releasing a book. Her autobiography, *Fools Rush In*, is an insult to us all.

In the book, we enter Anthea's worthless world of light entertainment and ludicrously self-reverential preening. We hear how 'News at Ten made Grant's return the top item . . . above a major breakthrough in the Northern Ireland peace negotiations.' And we're meant to be impressed. We're meant to thrill over her soiree at Philip Schofield's house and the *Lord of the Dance* party held in honour of Michael Flatley. As if this is the life we all aspire to. It's a suffocatingly tasteless experience, like drowning in heavily diluted milk.

Of course, not everyone hates her. In her book, she thanks ponce-faced hairdresser Nicky Clarke, 'who went on to craft and style my hair into what it is today'. You can just picture them, sitting in her mansion – Nicky pleasuring her with his curling tongs – while watching looped videos of her daytime TV appearances. Go on, cut her out, take aim and fire. It'll make you feel better. It worked for Bruno Brookes.

Now read the commentary on page 190.

So far in this section written materials have been presented. The following offers the opportunity to work on attitudes and values as conveyed by spoken language.

ACTIVITY 15

Read the following texts and then:

- Compare the two texts for the features of spoken language you have observed.

- Comment on the attitudes conveyed.

EXTRACT 1

In the first extract, the American film director Quentin Tarentino (T) is being interviewed by Adrian Wootton (AW) about his film *Jackie Brown*. At this point he is answering questions from the audience.

QUESTIONER 1: You didn't seem to have the amount of high quality in-your-face carnage In this film as we normally expect. What is going on? (Laughter)

T: In America different journalists would ask me, "Whoa, did you consciously tone down the violence in this film?" I didn't more consciously tone down the violence in this piece than I did crank up the violence in *Reservoir Dogs* or *Pulp Fiction*. They were just the services of the story. If Elmore Leonard had more people getting killed, I would have killed them!

QUESTIONER 2: There was a lot of the use of the word "nigger" when it should have been a "mother fucker" or a "bitch" instead.

T: Well, that is your opinion.

AW: Do you want to just say that again to the mike?

T: Say that again, yes.

QUESTIONER 2: What I said was there was a lot of the use of the word "nigger" when may be you could have thrown in a "mother fucker" or a "bitch".

T: You are saying "may be" now. You said "should have been". (Laughter)

QUESTIONER 2: There was a part of Pulp Fiction which I know we don't want to talk about, but you used the word "nigger" yourself, and I know here if any white guy says "nigger" to a black man, you had better put up or die.

T: You'd do that to a good friend of yours?

QUESTIONER 1: None of my good white friends call me nigger.

T: They don't have that kind of relationship with you.

QUESTIONER 2:	No, we've got a great relationship.
T:	You might have a very great relationship, but you don't have that kind of relationship.
QUESTIONER 2:	I think we have that respect for each other where we aren't going to go there.
T:	Then you are not that kind of guy. Sam Jackson is, and I was in that movie.
QUESTIONER 2:	I still don't agree with it, because I know a lot of people – almost every black guy I spoke to who saw the movie was, like, fantastic film, brilliant dialogue, but, hey, he isn't going to get away with that.
T:	I do. (Applause)
QUESTIONER 3:	I notice a little bit of Oprah Winfrey in Pam Grier, not in any physical sense but in the way she has the two voices; the white voice she used when she is in mainstream society, and the black voice that comes up sometimes. Is that something that was really difficult for you to write, as someone who is marginal to black culture but who grew up within it?
T:	No, that is not difficult for me to write at all; that is the easiest stuff for me to write in the whole script. We all have different voices. Blacks in America in particular have two voices. It is called "getting a job". The way they are with their friends or their family is not the way they present themselves in the work place. I am not talking about everybody. I am not making sweeping generalisations here, but by and large people can move in and out of dialects. If we are going to talk specifically about blacks, that is a specific thing about blacks. We all do that. We all have different voices. We all have completely different voices. I definitely have a different voice when I am angry. If I am going to fuck you up, I am going to have a completely different voice than I am having standing here right now. We all have that, and that is highlighted by a different dialect going on inside of a white community.

EXTRACT 2

This extract is from the novel *Riding the Rap* by Elmore Leonard.

Louis was letting it become 'we' to get next to Bobby and know what he was thinking, and because they were both in the life and had done state time. Bobby for shooting a man Bobby said pulled a gun on him instead of paying what he owed and went up on a manslaughter plea deal. Louis convicted no felony firearms charges when he took part in the drive-by of a dwelling with MAC10's converted to full auto. Louis went up without copping – naming any names to have his time cut – and was respected among the population, all the homeboys up at Starke, where he met Bobby Deo. After they'd got to know one another some Bobby said to him, 'How come you homes call each other *nigga*?'

Louis said, 'Mostly when you trippin' on some motherfucker, giving him a bad time, you say it. Understand? Or you say it, you not trippin' but vampin' on him some and you say it like you calling him "my brother." Either way is fine.'

So what happened, Bobby Deo tried him that time in the yard at Starke. Looked Louis in the face with kind of a smile and said, 'Yeah, nigga. Like that?' To see how Louis would take it, the man standing there waiting.

Louis said to him, 'Yeah, like that. Only it ain't fine for somebody to say it ain't a brother. Understand? Unless you being P.R. has nigga in you?' Louis looking Bobby Deo in the face the same way Bobby was looking at him, eye to eye.

Bobby said, 'You asking me, uh? You not accusing me of having mixed blood or what some call tainted? No, I'm not one of you.'

Louis saying then, 'So I know you and you know me, who we are. You know you fuck with me you got the whole population of homes on your untainted ass.' It was a question of respect was all.

Now read the commentary on page 190.

The Specification encourages you to explore the different ways texts can be read: *A Level courses in English Language and Literature should broaden and deepen students' knowledge and understanding, encouraging them to evaluate different analytical approaches to the interpretation of texts.* The activities that follow are designed to focus your attention on the variety of ways it is possible to respond to text.

ACTIVITY 16

Read the following statements about the novel *The Wasp Factory* by Iain Banks.

- What are the key differences in opinion between the two reviewers?

The first extract is the publisher's blurb:

Enter – if you can bear it – the extraordinary private world of Frank, just sixteen, and unconventional, to say the least.

'Two years after I killed Blyth I murdered my young brother Paul, for quite different and more fundamental reasons than I'd disposed of Blyth, and then a year after that I did for my young cousin Esmerelda, more or less on a whim. That's my score to date. Three. I haven't killed anybody for years, and don't intend to ever again.'

'It was just a stage I was going through.'

The following are reviews printed on the back cover:

Why you should (or shouldn't) read this book . . .

The Wasp Factory is a first novel not only of tremendous promise, but also of achievement, a minor masterpiece perhaps. There is no label. It is an obsessive novel, a bad dream of a book. Death and blood and gore fill the pages, lightened only by the dark humour, the surreal touches, and the poetry of the thing. There is something foreign and nasty here, an amazing new talent. *Punch*

It is a sick, sick world when the confidence and investment of an astute firm of publishers is justified by a work of unparalleled depravity.
There is no denying the bizarre fertility of the author's imagination: his brilliant dialogue, his cruel humour, his repellent inventiveness. The majority of the literate public, however, will be relieved that only reviewers are obliged to look at any of it.
Irish Times

Now read the commentary on page 191.

In the other subjects you are studying for A2, you may have come across the view that in your essays and presentations you should not use 'I'. You will have been told that you are learning about others' theories – social, psychological, economic, historical or scientific – which rest upon bodies of evidence far more extensive and therefore more valid than your own experiences and observations.

But in English Language and Literature your responses, and those of your peers, are important. The responses of others will show you that there is not just one way to regard a text, and the views of critical theorists will help you organise your approaches to text. Above all the emphasis is on (a) being aware of your responses, and (b) being able to support them with convincing references to the text.

ACTIVITY 17

As a group, discuss your views on a recent or well-known film or pop song video you have seen.

- Note your own immediate thoughts about the production.

- Discuss in small groups and then feed back to the whole group.

- Note in particular where you agree.

Now read the commentary on page 191.

In the second half of the twentieth century, under the influence of theories about language, the emphasis in literary studies shifted to the reader and the reader's response. Hans Robert Jauss observed: 'A literary work is not an object which stands by itself and which offers the same face to each reader in each period. It is not a monument which reveals its timeless essence in a monologue.' In other words, the reader is of crucial significance.

The French critic Roland Barthes played a leading role in this development. In 'The Death of the Author', an essay published in 1968, Barthes challenged the assumption that it is the author who is of essential importance in the study of text, and that only the author knows what the text 'really' means. As the title of the essay suggests, he wanted to give the authority traditionally accorded the author to the reader.

At first this may seem a ridiculous view. After all, the author did *write* the text – you may have seen her or him on TV collecting a prize for writing it. Bookshops and libraries will provide the book if requested by its title and the author's name. These are displayed on the front cover, referred to by critics, and identified by examination boards. You might well ask: If the author doesn't know what his/her text means, then how can anyone else? And if the author says it should be interpreted in a certain way, then who are we to argue?

But the importance of the reader's role is often overlooked. Readers will have encountered many texts, learned many values and ways of thinking specific to their time and culture, and it is this 'baggage' that they bring to their readings. It is in the process of reading that a text acquires meaning: the reader in fact *constructs* meanings through the act of interpretation. As an 'active reader' you made connections and predicted action in Modules 1 and 2; when, in Module 4, you intervened to change a text, you reconstructed it based on your own responses as a reader.

In *Is There a Text in This Class?*, The American scholar Stanley Fish asserted that the reader *creates* the text as s/he reads it. He believes that informed readers form 'interpretive communities' – that is, groups who share ways of understanding and interpreting texts.

Another way of looking at this approach is offered by Wolfgang Iser: 'One text is potentially capable of several different realisations, and no reading can ever exhaust the full potential for each individual reader will fill in the gaps in his [sic] own way.'

These theorists have been labelled **reader-response theorists**.

ACTIVITY 18

Read the following extract from the novel *Complicity* by Iain Banks.

- As you read the text, monitor your responses.

- What reactions to the events are you being encouraged to feel?

You enter through the back door using a crowbar; the door and the lock are both heavy, but the frame has rotted beneath its layers of paint over the years. As soon as you're in you take the Elvis Presley mask from your day-pack and slip it on, then pull the surgeon's gloves from your pocket and snap those on too. The house feels warm from the afternoon; it faces south and has an uninterrupted view out over the links of the golf course towards the estuary, so it catches a lot of sun.

You don't think there's anybody in yet but you aren't sure; there wasn't time to watch the place all day. It feels and somehow sounds empty. You slip from room to room, feeling sweaty beneath the slick latex of the mask. The late evening sun has turned the faint, high clouds over the sea pink and the light falls into every room, filling them with rose and shadows.

Now read the commentary on page 191.

ACTIVITY 19

Think up a brief plot that involves people meeting. Use the prompts of *who*, *when*, *where*, *why* to help you.

- How far can you write using *you* and *I* to disguise the gender of the participants? How easy was this to achieve?

- Read it out to your partner and note down the genre they believe you are working in, for example: mystery, romance, detective, thriller, horror, science fiction.

- Ask your reader to explain a little more what they have found to suggest a certain genre.

- Then choose someone else and repeat the process, noting down the response.

- Repeat this activity one last time and note the response.

Now read the commentary on page 191.

In the introductory comments to this module, your attention was drawn to the problematic nature of classification. We saw that categories such as literary/non-literary, spoken/written, and private/public are frequently subverted *in real life*.

As a final Activity before we turn to the task of examination preparation, look at the following text. It was the winning entry in the *Guardian* Text Message Poetry Competition, 2001. Entrants were instructed to use no more than 160 characters in all. The poet U. A. Fanthorpe was one of the judges and her comments follow.

ACTIVITY 20

Which categories does the text best fit:

- literary/non-literary?

- spoken/written?

- formal/informal?

> txtin iz messin,
> mi headn'me englis,
> try2rite essays,
> they all come out txtis.
> gran not plsed w/letters shes getn,
> swears i wrote better
> b4 comin2uni.
> &she's african
>
> Hetty Hughes

Now read U. A. Fanthorpe's comments below, and then:

- Identify the features in the poem that, according to Fanthorpe, make it the winner.

- Have a go at writing your own poem using Fanthorpe's guidance.

There is a quality of jokiness about English poetry, and the Guardian's terse verse contest encouraged that. So did its text message format, which has affinities with the resourceful stratagems of the old telegram. I like a poem that starts 'Pls, stop sendg msgs2ths'. The reader is being tested, as with a crossword puzzle or a Shakespeare play.

Poetry has always enjoyed fiddling around with the shapes of words and numbers of words or number of syllables: haiku, cinquain, englyn, and so on, and I have to admit to writing a poem about a road sign, in road sign language, which consists partly of words with their vowels extracted and partly of shorthand versions of place names. So in a way, the newest thing about the Guardian's competition was not the text message style, but the precise number of characters available.

It was interesting to see how inventive the competitors were. Some wrote fairly normal poems (as far as style is concerned); some wrote with as much technical resourcefulness as possible. The results were disappointing in some ways, in that the subjects tended to be rather predictable – the usual subjects, in fact: love/sex predominated, along with 'special moments'.

I've recently been judging another (more familiar) poetry competition, where the range of subjects was infinitely more surprising. But it is, of course, difficult to get far with such a small word count; you have, on the whole, to be sure that the reader understands what you're writing about from the start. And limitation of form means that it's difficult to achieve very much complexity of feeling.

I was looking for wit and technical inventiveness in the more technologically adventurous poems, and for imagination, density and the magical quality of take-off in the others. On the whole, the less technical did better – partly because the more technical had struggles with layout, and characteristically became unstuck with the last line, which is always where a poem either works or doesn't.

There were some poems which I shall remember with delight, but which didn't achieve the Final Seven because there wasn't enough substance to them: I treasure particularly two.

'They phone you up, your mum and dad.'

'Basildon: imagine a carpark.'

It was surprising how many competitors used rhyme, I suspect as a substitute for imagery. The form allowed only exceptionally gifted writers to develop an image to any extent, whereas the inevitable brevity made it quite easy to make something of a rhyme, if not exactly a rhyme-scheme. I was moved and amazed at how much feeling could be introduced in so small a space: there was great tenderness, spirit, imagination in the best entries.

On the other hand, it was sad to see how some, faced with such a small canvas, squandered words when they could have used the possibilities more fruitfully.

Now read the commentary on page 191.

Countdown to the examination

The pre-release materials are made available approximately three days before the examination. *Make sure you know when this will be and plan to use the time effectively.* Be realistic about the amount of time you have for this preparation. If you have a part-time job you will need to ensure that you will have enough time for your preparation. It is easier to do this if you have a clear idea of the days and dates preceding the examination date.

In this next section you will find a collection of materials typical of the type presented in the pre-release materials for the final examination. There is a theme – dreams – and the materials are drawn from a variety of sources. The first two are analysed; the rest provide unaided practice.

Before the examination you must read and annotate in ways which will be helpful to you. Writing at length on the materials is *not* permitted, but brief notes, highlighting, underlining and cross-referencing are encouraged. Decide on the referencing system you are going to use. *Remember: you have approximately three days to prepare for the examination.*

Analysing your texts

Your analysis of the texts can be divided into three phases.

Phase 1

When you first obtain the materials, it is a good idea to skim-read them and find the answers to these two questions:

- **What is it?**

    An extract from a novel? A newspaper article? A transcript of a conversation? Look at the title, if there is one, and then at the statement of the texts' source. Look at the layout of the text on the page. Read until you can establish what the text is.

- **When was it written/undertaken?**

    If a date is given, put a ring around it. Use the front of the booklet to keep a tally of the materials by page number.

Phase 2

Then return to each piece and begin the task of considering how each is *relevant to the chosen theme*. For example, the word 'dream' means many different things in the passages that follow. After reading each text in the Anthology, write a short definition of how the word is used in each extract:

Dream =

Phase 3

You will then ready to proceed to the more detailed level of preparation.

In the sample question, you are guided with three bullet points:

- the writers'/speakers' choices of form, style and vocabulary

- variations in genre and context

- how attitudes and values are conveyed.

This indicates the areas your answer should cover – but *not* in the order in which they should be discussed in the examination. In other words don't *begin* by commenting on form, style and vocabulary; that comes later.

AO4 assesses your understanding of the ways *contextual variation* and choices of form, style and vocabulary shape the meanings of texts. In order to discuss this in a productive way, you would need, first, to have considered the 'meanings of texts'. This should include consideration of the 'attitudes and values' referred to in AO5.

In your planning for the first question, it would be better to reverse the order of the bullet points above. In this way, you would use reference to aspects of form, style and vocabulary to support your discussion of attitudes and values conveyed and variation in genre and context.

Your answer to the first question should show understanding of:

- different genres (including mixed genres and areas of overlap)

- the ways audiences are addressed

- different (or similar) contextual factors

- the ways attitudes and values affect reader response.

This should be supported by the analysis of the distinctive linguistic features of the texts in terms of:

- grammar

- lexis

- phonology

- morphology

- graphology.

In your answer, you will have to refer to one of the pre-release texts and one of the unseen texts. You then need to select other texts that allow you to draw out some interesting relationships and comparisons. You should remember that one important Assessment Objective (AO3ii) refers to both *spoken* and *written* language, so it is likely that one or more of the spoken language texts will be compulsory.

Worked example

Below is an example of the approach to the task of preparation outlined above. Read the passage – which is taken from the novel *Written on the Body* (1992) by Jeanette Winterson – and then read the comments that follow.

It was a hot August Sunday. I paddled through the shallows of the river where the little fishes dare their belly at the sun. On either side of the river the proper green of the grass had given way to a psychedelic splash-painting of virulent Lycra cycling shorts and Hawaiian shirts made in Taiwan. They were grouped the way families like to group; dad with paper propped on his overhang, mum sagging over the thermos. Kids thin as sea-side rock sticks and sea-side rock pink. Mum saw you go in and heaved herself off the stripey fold-out camping stool. 'You should be ashamed of yourself. There's families out here.'

You laughed and waved, your body bright beneath the clear green water, its shape fitting your shape, holding you, faithful to you. You turned on your back and your nipples grazed the surface of the river and the river decorated your hair with beads. You are creamy but for your red hair that flanks you on either side.

'I'll get my husband to see to you. George come here. George come here.'

'Can't you see I'm watching television?' said George without turning round.

You stood up and the water fell from you in silver streams. I didn't think, I waded in and kissed you. You put your arms around my burning back. You said, 'There's nobody here but us.'

I looked up and the banks were empty.

Phase 1
- **What is it?**

  An extract from a novel written by a female.

- **When was it written?**

  Late twentieth century.

Phase 2
The reader is puzzled by the surreal elements. At the end of the extract the reader is not able to be sure whether the narrator 'imagined' the people or whether what is implied is that in disgust they got up and left.

Phase 3
- **Attitudes and values:**

  Note down the descriptions and the actions of the 'I' and 'you'.

  Now do the same for the other people who are described.

  Who is the author presenting in a positive way?

  What attitudes are readers encouraged to take to the people in the text?

  What could be shocking about the behaviour of the *I* and *you*?

Remind yourself of the Deconstruction approach used in Module 4 (page 31) when reading the story *Dr. Chevalier's Lie*. It will be useful when looking at this text if you think about the way opposites are being used.

- **Contextual factors:**
  The text was published in 1992. It is an extract from a novel and this would suggest that the primary purpose of the piece is to 'entertain'. However, depending on the reader's attitude to the nudity and the sexuality portrayed, the effect could also be 'persuasive'. The reader is led to consider the issue of tolerance and intolerance and the forms they take – not just in this text, but also in everyday life.

- **The ways the audience is addressed:**
  The reader, whilst not being directly addressed, works hard to make sense of the text because of the strangeness of some of the descriptions and references.

- **Genre:**
  It is fictional prose that uses the conventions of plot, narration, description and dialogue.

- **The distinctive linguistic features:**
  These have been set out below. (Note: the two-column layout below is given for ease of reading. The pre-release materials will *not* provide a column as such, but you can make use of the margins for your brief notes.)

It was a hot August Sunday. I [1] paddled through the shallows of the river where the little fishes dare their belly at the sun. On either side of the river the proper green [2] of the grass had given way to a psychedelic splash-painting [2] of virulent Lycra cycling shorts [3] and Hawaiian shirts [3] made in Taiwan. [4] They [5] were grouped the way families like to group; dad [5] with paper propped on his overhang, [4] mum sagging [4] over the thermos. Kids [5] thin as sea-side rock sticks and sea-side rock pink [4]. Mum [5] saw you go in and heaved herself [4] off the stripey fold-out camping stool. 'You [5] should be ashamed of yourself. There's families [5] out here.' [6]	1. 1st-person narrative. 2. Opposites: nature and colours. 3. Clothes, not people 4. <u>Negative connotations</u> 5. Opposites: people 6. Use of speech 7. <u>Positive connotations</u>
You laughed and waved, [7] your body bright [7] beneath the clear green water, its shape fitting your shape, holding you, faithful to you. You turned on your back and your nipples grazed the surface of the river and the river decorated your hair with beads. [7] You are creamy [7] but for your red hair [7] that flanks you on either side.	
'I'll get my husband to see to you. George come here. George come here.' [6]	
'Can't you see I'm watching television?' [8] said George without turning round.	8. Deliberately making strange
You stood up and the *water fell from you in silver streams.* [7] I didn't think, I waded in and kissed you. You put your arms around my burning back. You said, 'There's nobody here but us.' [6]	
I looked up and the banks were empty. [8]	

Summary of responses

The text poses many opposites (2 and 5):

'I' and 'you' / 'kids', 'mum', 'dad'
'I' and 'you' / 'families'
'proper green of grass' / 'psychedelic splash-painting'

The text gives no clue as to the gender of 'you' and 'I'. The first-person narrative (1) builds up the point of view of *us* from whom to pose an oppositional *they*.

People are referred to by their clothing (3). The word 'virulent' links with disease and contagion, adding to the sense of something undesirable. The green of the grass is 'proper' because it is natural.

The use of informal naming – 'kids', 'dad', 'mum' – creates a familiarity but also a sense of contempt. This is developed by the writer's use of negative descriptions (4): 'overhang' and 'sagging'. The narrator is uncomplimentary to the mother, father and children.

There are surreal challenges offered to the reader (8): the father is watching TV in the open air; people vanish.

There is a deliberate destabilising of accepted ways of describing people and therefore a deliberate making strange of what the reader expects to find familiar. Their clothes and their positions on the banks make them seem like an alien species to be recognised by their posture, clothes and behaviour.

The writer has used speech (6) to create a determined display of disapproval in the mother. Speech also adds to the surreal sense that this is not happening. Dad breaks Grice's 'maxim of quality' (see Module 2, page 102 of the AS book) by claiming that he is watching TV. The narrative viewpoint identifies as *other* what the reader may well assume is *centre* – 'respectable' heterosexual human behaviour – and thus may challenge values and attitudes.

The author encourages the reader to wonder whether the narrator has imagined the disapproving people.

Dreams: An anthology of pre-release materials

The points for discussion here arise from how 'dream' is being used in the context of the passages. You will see that each extract is slightly different in its application of the word 'dream', and your task is to identify and comment upon the different uses to which it is put. Then compare the passages for points of similarity and difference. The first two extracts have been analysed already to demonstrate the three-phase approach introduced above.

Analysis of Item 1

The text appears on page 178.

Phase 1
- **What is it?**
  A gentleman's journal? Non-literary prose is a reasonable guess. But it does not fit neatly into that category.

- **When was it written?**
  1750. The date leads the modern reader to speculate as to the target audience. Who would have had access to such a publication at that time, and what were its circulation figures? Further thought can also be given as

to the motive for having a twice-weekly journal in which such pieces appeared: Why would anyone be interested, and would anyone else have published so many of Johnson's essays?

Phase 2

'Dream' as used in this passage allows the author to give the impression of a recurring dream whilst asleep and also an obsessive desire for inherited wealth. In this case, the dream was not attained.

Phase 3

- **Attitudes and values:**
  The effect seems to be self-ironic and betraying a motive ('which sickness requires'). The reader considers whether Dr Johnson was punctual because he was a dutiful nephew, or because he wanted merely to be seen as concerned by his aunt.

- **Contextual factors:**
  Cultural and historical contexts can be commented on. The modern reader is made aware of English eighteenth-century views about inheritance. The male heir assumes he should inherit the property of the maiden aunts.

- **The ways the audience is addressed:**
  As this text was for publication we would have to ask whether Johnson wished the reader to think of him as selfish and money grabbing . He writes candidly of his thoughts, hopes and actions.

- **Genre:**
  Factual and personal viewpoint. Personal family events are seen as worthy topics to read. There may also be a moral message to the piece and in this sense there is a similarity with a religious parable. He uses simple past tense to imply a straightforward re-telling of events.

- **The distinctive linguistic features:**
  These have been set out below.

I [1] differed only from my father by the freshness of my cheeks, [2] [3] and the vigour of my step; [2] [3] and, like him, gave way to no thoughts but of [4] enjoying the wealth which my aunts were hoarding. At length [5] the eldest fell ill. I [1] paid the civilities and compliments [2] which sickness requires with the utmost punctuality. I [1] dreamed every night of escutcheons* and white gloves,*[2] and inquired [6] every morning at an early hour, whether there was any news of my dear aunt. At last a messenger was sent to inform me that I [1] must come to her without delay of a moment. [5] I [1] went and heard her last advice, but opening her will, found that she had left her fortune to her second sister.	1. 1st-person narration 2. Balance in the noun groups 3. Language change: descriptions of youth 4. Language change: negative form 5. Language change: time 6. Language change: spelling *escutcheons: the family shield and coat of arms *white gloves: symbol of gentility and wealth

Analysis of Item 2

The text appears on page 178.

Phase 1
- **What is it?**
  A transcript of spoken language.

- **When was it written/undertaken?**
  1995

Phase 2
'Dream' as used in this passage means a real dream experienced whilst asleep. In this sense it is similar to the way it was used in the Dr Johnson passage, though here there is not the added dimension of dream as conscious desire.

Phase 3
- **Attitudes and values:**
  The listener is encouraged to consider the strangeness of a dream experienced as a reality. It was memorable enough for the speaker to recall in detail when asked to talk about 'strange experiences'. The listener is asked to believe it because the speaker describes it as true.

- **Contextual factors:**
  (a) We recognise the use of the conventions for transcribing speech.
  (b) The speaker expects to have the floor until the account is completed.

- **The ways the audience is addressed:**
  A listener is implied.

- **Genre:**
  According to the linguist William Labov, oral narrative demonstrates a specific structure (see Module 1, page 11). There is the same chronological treatment of a personal experience as in Dr Johnson's passage, but here expressed in speech.

- **The distinctive linguistic features:**

I had this dream and I was in a car in the back of the car and there were two other people that I knew in the front (.) we were driving up a hill and there were traffic lights on either side of the hill (.) and on the left hand corner there was a pub (.) and at the top of the hill there was a big roundabout with a carpark in the middle (.) okay right (.) and on about halfway round the roundabout there was a co-op a big big co-op (.) erm and then about a year ago just after I had the dream (.) we were going up this hill and I was in the back of the car and my mum and dad were driving (.) ye we were on us way to Chesterfield (.) and (.) I'd never been before but I thought I recognised it (.) and then my dream came back to me (.) and I said to my mum this is strange I had a dream where there were two traffic lights on either side and a pub (.) and there was a roundabout but in my dream there was a co-op halfway round (.) and my mum said oh well that must just be a coincidence (.) and we got round the roundabout and there was a sign saying co-op but it had been sort of disguised from view before (.) and there you go	1. Abstract 2. Orientation 3. Complicating action 4. Evaluation 5. Result or resolution 6. Coda

Now choose any of the remaining passages and prepare your own responses using the guidance given above. Try to find pieces which have some obvious similarities and compare these.

Item 1

This item is from *The Rambler*, a twice-weekly periodical issued from 20 March 1750 to 14 March 1752. All but five editions were written by Dr Samuel Johnson, who also issued the periodical.

> I differed only from my father by the freshness of my cheeks, and the vigour of my step; and, like him, gave way to no thoughts but of enjoying the wealth which my aunts were hoarding.
>
> At length the eldest fell ill. I paid the civilities and compliments which sickness requires with the utmost punctuality. I dreamed every night of escutcheons and white gloves, and inquired every morning at an early hour, whether there was any news of my dear aunt. At last a messenger was sent to inform me that I must come to her without delay of a moment. I went and heard her last advice, but opening her will, found that she had left her fortune to her second sister.

Item 2

This second extract is from *Some Things to do with English Language* (1995), Sheffield Hallam University. It is a transcript of a student's response to a request to describe a dream to a listener.

> I had this dream and I was in a car in the back of the car and there were two other people that I knew in the front (.) we were driving up a hill and there were traffic lights on either side of the hill (.) and on the left hand corner there was a pub (.) and it at the top of the hill there was a big roundabout with a carpark in the middle (.) okay right (.) and on about halfway round the roundabout there was a co-op a big big co-op (.) erm and then about a year ago just after I had the dream (.) we were going up this hill and I was in the back of the car and my mum and dad were driving (.) ye we were on us way to Chesterfield (.) and (.) I'd never been before but I thought I recognised it (.) and then my dream came back to me (.) and I said to my mum this is strange I had a dream where there were two traffic lights on either side and a pub (.) and there was a roundabout but in my dream there was a co-op halfway round (.) and my mum said oh well that must just be a coincidence (.) and we got round the roundabout and there was a sign saying co-op but it had been sort of disguised from view before (.) and there you go.

Item 3

'On Receiving a Jamaican Postcard' by Grace Nichols.

Colourful native entertainers
dancing at de edge of de sea
a man-an-woman combination
choreographing
de dream of de tourist industry

de two a dem in smiling conspiracy
to capture dis dream of de tourist industry

an de sea blue
an de sky blue
an de sand gold fuh true

an de sea blue
an de sky blue
an de sand gold fuh true

He staging a dance-prance
head in a red band
beating he waist drum
as if he want to drown she wid sound
an yes, he muscle looking strong

She a vision of frilly red
back-backing to he riddum
exposing she brown leg
arcing like lil mo
she will limbo into de sea

Anything fuh de sake of de tourist industry
Anything fuh de sake of de tourist industry

Item 4

From *Trainspotting* by Irvine Welsh.

More terrors. Am ah asleep or awake? Who fuckin knows or cares? No me. The pain's still here. Ah know one thing. If ah move, ah'll swallow ma tongue. Nice bit ay tongue. That's what ah cannae wait for ma Ma giein us, just like of in the old days. Tongue salad. Poison your children.

Ye'll eat that tongue. That's a nice, tasty bit ay tongue thair son.

YE'LL EAT THAT TONGUE.

If ah don't move, ma tongue will slide down ma gullet anyway. Ah can feel it moving. Ah sit up, consumed by blind panic, and retch, but thir's nowt comin up. Ma heart's thrashing in my chest, and sweat's lashing from my emaciated frame.

Is this sllllleeeeeeeeeepppppppp.

Oh fuck. Thir's something in this room wi me it is comin oot the fuckin ceilin above the bed.

It's a baby. Wee Dawn, crawling along the ceilin. Greetin. But it's lookin doon it us now.

– You let me fuckin diieeeee, it sais. It's no Dawn. No the wee bairn.

Naw, ah mean, this is fuckin crazy.

The bairn has sharp, vampire teeth wi blood drippin fae them. It's covered in a sick yellow-green slime. Its eyes are the eyes ay every psychopath ah've ever met.

– Yefuckinkilledme litmefuckinindie junkedupootyirfuckininheids watchinthefuckinwaws ya fuckindopejunkycunt ah'llfuckinripyefuckinopen n feedoanyirfuckinmiserable sickgreyjunkyflesh . . .

Item 5

From *Some More Things to do with English Language*, Sheffield Hallam University.

This is a story that one of my students told me last year about her grandmother (.) her grandmother had lost a very precious ring (.) it was precious because grandfather had given it to her (.) and grandmother searched high and low in the house for this ring and she'd lost it literally for about twenty years and grandfather had died in that time (.) and then one night this grandmother had a dream and she dreamt this ring was down the back of a wood partitioning (.) and she woke up and she mentioned it to her son and she described the partitioning and he said that's in the bathroom let's go up there and take the panel off (.) and do y'know when they took the panel off there was the ring so she'd actually dreamt about the actual real place where the ring was.

Item 6

From *A Level Psychology* (1996) by Mike Cardwell, Liz Clark and Claire Meldrum.

Freud . . .viewed the imagery of dreams as symbolic of hidden needs, wishes and fears stored in the unconscious. He referred to the remembered imagery of dreams as the 'manifest content', while the hidden meanings were the 'latent content'. Dream analysis was an important component of Freud's psychotherapeutic technique, in which he would interpret the symbolism of the dream imagery, usually in terms of repressed sexual desires. By bringing these to the surface they could be resolved and the patient's conflicts and neuroses removed.

Unfortunately the whole technique depended on subjective report by the client and the personal interpretation of Freud. There is no independent confirmation of the link between dream imagery and repressed sexual content and indeed it is hard to imagine any scientific way of assessing the meaning of dream imagery.

Item 7

'Sweet Dreams (Are Made Of This)' by the Eurythmics.

Sweet dreams are made of this
Who am I to disagree?
I travel the world
And the seven seas –
Everybody's looking for something.

Some of them want to use you
Some of them want to get used by you
Some of them want to abuse you
Some of them want to be abused.

Sweet dreams are made of this
Who am I to disagree?
I travel the world
And the seven seas –
Everybody's looking for something.

Hold your head up – Keep your head up – Movin' on
Hold your head up – movin' on
Keep your head up – movin' on
Etc.
Sweet dreams are made of this
Who am I to disagree?
I travel the world
And the seven seas –
Everybody's looking for something.

Item 8

From the short story *Goat or Scoundrel* by Anton Chekhov.

A sultry afternoon. A young lady of about 18 is reclining on a couch in the drawing room. Flies are wandering over her face, an open book is lying at her feet, her mouth is slightly ajar, and her breath is light and even. She is asleep.

A small, elderly man of the Gogolian old-lecher genre enters the drawing room. Seeing the young lady asleep on the couch, he grins and tiptoes over to her.

'Oh . . . how lovely she is!' he whispers, smacking his lips. 'Ho, ho . . . a sleeping beauty. What a pity I am not an artist! Just look at that head, that little arm!'

The old man bends over the girl's hand, caresses it with his gnarled fingers, and plants a kiss on it. The girl sighs deeply, opens her eyes, and looks at the old man in bewilderment.

'Oh . . . is that you *mon prince?*' she mutters, struggling to wake up. 'Forgive me, but I seem to have fallen asleep.'

'Yes indeed, you were asleep,' the prince croons. 'And you are still fast asleep, yes, and dreaming of me, yes, seeing me in your dreams . . . sleep, sleep.. I am but a dream.'

The girl believes him and closes her eyes.

'How sad', she whispers, as she drifts back to sleep. 'All I ever see in my dreams are goats or scoundrels.'

The prince, somewhat rattled, tiptoes off.

Item 9

From a speech delivered on the steps at the Lincoln Memorial in Washington D.C. on 28 August 1963 by Martin Luther King, Jr.

I say to you today, my friends, that in spite of the difficulties and frustrations of the moment, I still have a dream. It is a dream deeply rooted in the American dream.

I have a dream that one day this nation will rise up and live out the true meaning of its creed: 'We hold these truths to be self-evident: that all men are created equal.'

I have a dream that one day on the red hills of Georgia the sons of former slaves and the sons of former slaveowners will be able to sit down together at a table of brotherhood.

I have a dream that one day even the state of Mississippi, a desert state, sweltering with the heat of injustice and oppression, will be transformed into an oasis of freedom and justice.

I have a dream that my four children will one day live in a nation where they will not be judged by the color of their skin but by the content of their character.

I have a dream today.

I have a dream that one day the state of Alabama, whose governor's lips are presently dripping with the words of interposition and nullification, will be transformed into a situation where little black boys and black girls will be able to join hands with little white boys and white girls and walk together as sisters and brothers.

I have a dream today.

I have a dream that one day every valley shall be exalted, every hill and mountain shall be made low, the rough places will be made plain, and the crooked places will be made straight, and the glory of the Lord shall be revealed, and all flesh shall see it together.

This is our hope. This is the faith with which I return to the South. With this faith we will be able to hew out of the mountain of despair a stone of hope. With this faith we will be able to transform the jangling discords of our nation into a beautiful symphony of brotherhood. With this faith we will be able to work together, to pray together, to struggle together, to go to jail together, to stand up for freedom together, knowing that we will be free one day.

Item 10

From *A Man on the Moon* by Andrew Chalkin.

Sunday April 23

On the Cayley Plains

Like most astronauts, Charlie Duke would tell you that he rarely dreams at night, and remembers his dreams even less often. But Duke had a dream, six months before the flight, that he had no trouble remembering. In Hawaii on a geology trip, Duke came down with the flu and ran a high fever; at times he was almost delirious. Some of the wives had come along, and Duke's wife, Dotty, took care of him while his colleagues were out in the field. In a fever sleep, Duke saw himself and John Young on the moon, driving their Rover toward North Ray crater. They came up over a ridge and suddenly Duke spotted something that made his heart race. A set of tracks crossed the ground ahead. Young stopped the Rover and they got off to investigate. The imprints in the dust looked like those from the Rover, but they were definitely different. Duke asked mission control, 'Can we follow the tracks?'

'Go ahead,' was the reply from earth. The twin trails stretched eastward, and Young and Duke turned to follow them. They drove onward for miles, over hills and across craters, until finally, topping another rise, they saw it: a vehicle, looking amazingly like the Rover, stopped on the surface. Aboard were two figures in space suits. After calling

Houston to announce their incredible discovery, Young and Duke climbed off the Rover and approached the two figures, motionless in their seats. When Duke reached the one in the right seat, he could not see into its helmet because of its opaque sun visor. He put out his hand and raised the visor and saw his own face. The one in the left seat was John Young's double. After taking pieces of the space suits and Rover at mission control's request, Young and Duke drove back to the LM and blasted off for home. The next thing Duke knew, he was on earth, presenting the samples to the scientists. The test results: The craft was 100,000 years old. Then he woke up. The dream was so vivid – not scary, just *real* – that Duke remembered it from then on, and as he descended to the real moon inside *Orion*, he glanced out to his right at North Ray crater, and scanned the ground not only for boulders – 'Looks like we're gonna make it, John; there's not too many blocks up there' – but for a set of tracks.

Item 11

From *Your Dreams*, in *The Weekend Guardian*, 17 February 2001.

Aristotle reckoned that dreams are nothing more than memories and sensory impressions, colliding and distorting as they pass through our brains. And now sleep theorists are coming around to his way of thinking. But for thousands of years, prophets and priests, doctors and magicians have scoured the contents of our dreams for meaning. And today, the fruits of their research are accessible as never before – on the internet.

For a few dollars, a dream interpreter will explain what your unconscious mind has been trying to tell you. Just key in your credit-card number, type the relevant details on to the form, and all will be revealed, 'usually within 24 hours'.

For those who dream in digital, there are software packages that turn a PC into an interpretation engine. ProDream 'allows you to enter, store and interpret one or multiple dreams' and 'to retrieve previously saved dreams, or analyse those dreams'. And all for just $29.

If this sounds a little steep, you can work it out for yourself. In the online dream dictionary, the meanings of your dreams is never more than a couple of clicks away. Just pick a word from the alphabetical list of key words and press that button. Dream Dictionary (diverseworld.com/fate/dreams/dream1.html) describes itself as the 'new presentation of an ancient wisdom'. . .

Here are some of the most common dream elements:

Teeth If your teeth fall out in your dreams, it may be that you fear powerlessness, or sexual impotence. You need to assert yourself more, and have a higher regard for your own opinion.

Exams If you find yourself sitting an exam in your dreams, but you don't understand the question, it's likely that you are being somehow judged or tested in your waking life. Your anxiety and frustration in the dream suggest your feeling of inadequacy.

Being ahased Again, the general anxieties in your life are being transferred to a dream. Your pursuer may well represent a part of yourself, or your own feelings of fear, jealousy or anger, which turn on you in your dream and threaten to harm you.

Flying Often, the experience of flying in a dream is exhilarating. Flying with ease suggests that you are on top of things, while having difficulties staying aloft implies that you are struggling to control your life.

Falling Instability, insecurity, anxiety, inferiority – all the usual suspects contribute to the dream sensation of falling, which is common in the early stages of sleep and is frequently accompanied by twitches and jerks. Freud reckoned that such dreams indicate that you are about to give in to a sexual urge.

Nudity Dreaming that you are naked in public may indicate that you have something to hide, that you have made a mistake or are ashamed and insecure. If your nudity goes unnoticed, it may be that your fears are unfounded.

Item 12

From *The Blind Assassin* by Margaret Atwood.

I used to have a daydream about myself – still have it, come to that. A ridiculous-enough daydream though it's often through such images that we shape our destinies. (You'll notice how easily I slip into inflated language like *shape our destinies,* once I wander off in this direction. But never mind.)

In this daydream, Winifred and her friends, wreathes of money on their heads, are gathered around Sabrina's frilly white bed while she sleeps, discussing what they will bestow upon her. She's already been given the engraved silver cup from Birks, the nursery wallpaper with the frieze of domesticated bears, the starter pearls for her single-strand pearl necklace, and all the other golden gifts, perfectly *comme il faut,* that will turn to coal when the sun rises. Now they are planning the orthodontist and the tennis lessons and the piano lessons and the dancing lessons and the exclusive summer camp. What hope has she got?

At this moment I appear in a flash of sulphurous light and a puff of smoke and a flapping of sooty leather wings, the uninvited black-sheep godmother. *I too wish to bestow a gift,* I cry. *I have the right!*

Winifred and her crew laugh and point. You? *You were banished long ago! Have you looked in the mirror lately? You've let yourself go, you look a hundred and two. Go back to your dingy old cave! What can you possibly have to offer?*

I offer the truth, I say. *I'm the last one who can. It's the only thing in this room that will still be here in the morning.*

Commentaries

Activity 1

Statements 1 and 2 imply that literature is good for you and that the study of it makes you a better person. Statement 3 offers a different perspective: literature is any kind of writing, and it gains its status from the reception it gets from the reader. This last point is vital and represents an important dividing line between twenties-century critical theories. On one side of this imaginary line stand the critics who believe that the most important thing in literary study is the text and the way it satisfies the conventions of a particular genre. They offer advice on such matters as form and structure, poetic devices, word choice, descriptive devices and rhetorical techniques. The text is seen as a work of art, something to be examined by those experts who have acquired the skills needed to form qualitative judgements. On the other side are those who believe that the real activity occurs when the text is read. The reader and the methods s/he uses to make sense of the text and the interpretations that arise are what literature and its study are all about. Your role as the reader is central to the activities presented in this section.

Activity 3

The arrangements include planning, assembling a cast, booking and funding a venue, advertising, rehearsals. The list of jobs is huge: cleaners, actors, carpenters, reception staff, director, printers, electricians, musicians, costume makers – and these are only the people directly involved in the production.

Another essential difference rests in the public and performance aspect of drama. People have to gather, co-operate, agree to work to a schedule. The audience buy tickets, arrive on time, remain seated and quiet, and clap at the end.

How much less complicated is obtaining the text of a prose writer. You decide when to buy. It fits in your pocket. It goes where you go. When you are reading it – unless it is in public, say on a bus – you do not need to form part of a co-operating social group, nor to communicate with anyone. If you like a particular passage you can re-read it, and if you want to write comments on the page you can.

Activity 5

It will probably have taken you a very short time to discover that writers invariably use the distinction of males and females. Yet there may be other ways to describe people. What is interesting is the effect such a classification has on the reader, introducing a wide range of assumptions and expectations.

Activity 6

If at any stage in your answers you have used the words 'a man', ' a woman',' he', or 'she', go back to the text and support your assumptions about the gender of the two people. At no stage does the text give the participants a gender – no names, no he/she pronouns. Your cultural assumptions probably lead you to these conclusions. Reverse the roles: a woman can control a boat – after all, in February 2001 Ellen McArthur sailed around the world single handed and was second in the Globe Vendee race! A man can wait to be visited. Two women can carry out the same activities identified in the poem, and so can two men.

If you visualised the people as a man crossing the sea and land to meet a woman waiting in a house, your assumptions could be based on traditional assumptions about the 'active male' – out in the world, in the dark, using strength and expertise to move by sea and land, daring to enter someone else's space (owned by another male?) to be received by a passive and female. If you knew that Browning was a Victorian writer, you could have use a historical context in your reading of the poem – women at that time did not (unless they were Grace Darling!) generally put themselves in charge of boats.

Activity 7

You have had to *select* facts and events – you could not put in everything, even if you had for ever to do it. What you have created is based on personal choice, but also on the aspects you believe make up such a piece of writing. You probably considered what you thought other people would want to read about, and you may have wanted to encourage the reader to form a point of view about you or your flair for writing autobiography. Yet what you chose to write about will have also been influenced by the culture in which you live. You almost certainly did not, for example, write about whether you have attached or detached ear lobes, because these are not seen as an agreed way of regarding people. In other words your culture has led you to select and value certain details over others.

Activity 8

We will concentrate on the second possibility, that your text will be found in 100 years. Although you cannot predict how the language will change, you would certainly need to provide an explanation of important cultural differences. We will assume English survives and is used. The reader may not live in a family; may not consider a person's birth date as significant; may have been educated all her/his life; may not make the distinction between work and leisure . . . such elements are considered contexts.

Activity 9

In the first five sentences the narrative offers a positive and enthusiastic description of the grandmother, and yet this is tempered by the use of the relative pronoun 'which', bringing to the reader's attention the cultural influences that there were upon a young woman at this time in China.

There is the precise selection of details – from the many that could have been described – to emphasise aspects of behaviour which are culturally bound. The development of a narrative viewpoint that is Chang's, yet which at the same time suggests the voice of her grandmother recalling the events, allows the reader space to sympathise. A Western reader may well be horrified by the fact that mothers felt they had to cripple their female children in order to conform to tradition and gain cultural acceptance.

Activity 12

Attitudes: All three reviewers have a critical response to aspects of the film's story line and themes, finding its claims for the power of chocolate unconvincing. James in Extract 1 uses the expressions 'heavy on the schmaltz', 'too emotional', 'bit far-fetched'. The film reviewer in Extract 2 uses the terms 'gobbet of caramelised nothing', 'smug', 'harmless fairy-tale'. Michèle Roberts in Extract 3 feels that the oppositions implicit in the film are too simplistic and so she exaggerates, or parodies, the contrast in this balanced structure: 'the female chocolate maker is Good and the repressive male priest is Bad.' Did you make similar comments on the attitudes and values conveyed?

Contexts: Differences in the way each reviewer expresses his/her reservations reflect aspects of their contexts. Extracts 2 and 3 were written for publication in a national newspaper, whereas Extract 1 is an impromptu conversation. The writers of 2 and 3 can assume a position of authority – they are writers by trade and their audiences expect to read an informed, often critical, opinion. You may have mentioned other relevant aspects of context.

Form, style and vocabulary. As a student talking to his teacher, James may feel less able to state a critical point of view, so he tends to offer some praise as well, making his comments more tentative; he qualifies his judgement with 'I thought' and 'a bit' and 'sort of'. He checks on his listener's response with phrases like 'if you know what I mean' and generously adds 'but er you could see that er some people might like that'. The reviewer in Extract 2 does not qualify his opinions to the same extent, expressing his negative view with entertainingly insulting terms ranging from colloquial to more formal: 'smug . . . flip . . . risque . . . hedonism.' Part of the purpose of a review is to entertain, as well as convince the reader of the knowledgeable status of the writer. He addresses the reader directly with a tone of exasperation: 'Fine, enjoy chocolate – it'll rot your teeth but for heaven's sake, it won't make you a nobler person.' The relationship between speaker and listener in text 1 is more deferential, as is James's attitude to a film star. Whereas he describes Johny Depp as 'good', the reviewer feels able to make the extreme comment 'suave and altogether ludicrous'. As a novelist herself, Michèle Roberts refers to the style of the novel, *Chocolat*, and has the authority to criticise it as 'unremarkable, often loose and unfocused' though she allows some praise for the descriptions of chocolate. Extract 3 is a more personal article than a review, so it begins by describing her own experience as a basis for comment on the storyline of the film. (These remarks reflect one reader's response. You will have focussed on other language features that you feel are significant.)

You may have commented on other aspects of the extracts, for example: the role of the other participant in the conversation; the use of French words in both of the written texts; allusions to shared knowledge of e.g. Flake adverts; the use of alliteration in the review; the ways sex scenes were referred to. Just like the three 'reviewers' of the film, each person will find a slightly different angle on the texts and focus on different examples.

Activity 13

loaded is a magazine that is aimed primarily at young single males. In considering the attitudes and values of the piece, it is useful to list the reasons why others might go to Barcelona. By describing the nightlife, the view from cable cars, the aquarium, the outside of the cathedral, a garden, value for money, bars and eating places, and so on, it is assumed that this is what the readers want to know or should want from a trip to the city.

Notice too that the writer is well aware of the conventions of the official city guide and happy to break them. (Don't worry about the error in the calculation of the number of years Barcelona has been a place to take a holiday.) We are provided with the expected facts about the city: its history, climate, location and architecture. The graphology uses the convention of headings to structure the information and make it easy for the reader to check out essential information at a glance. Guidance and advice are offered. Yet the piece does not simply advise or inform, it persuades and entertains too. The ways it counterbalances an official guide against a **loaded** guide can be seen as quite subversive or challenging to an accepted way of describing a city to tourists. This is partly achieved by the personal anecdotal approach, but there are ways in which the use of language is subversive too. The sentences in the first paragraph use a grammatical pattern of three – a well known rhetorical device – but used here to create bathos.

Founded . . . named . . . has been a *nice* place to go for *your holidays*.

The weather's hot, the sea is Mediterranean (*if slightly pooey*) and everything looks stunning.

The architecture, the women, even *the pigeons* are better looking in Barcelona.

The word choice throughout the article moves between the formal and the casual. Insults appear and exaggeration is used to encourage – to enjoy the humour and therefore side with the writer. The casual forms and self-mockery (he hurt his chin, chose a hotel unwisely and ate awful food) are offset by the educated lexis he chooses: resplendent, be wary, legendary. He makes passing references to famous painters such as Dali and Miro. You may or may not know anything about these people but the word choice and name-dropping encourage you to accept the writer's authority. It is useful to consider the persuasive effect of the choice of activities too. If you are a reader of **loaded**, these are the things you should want to know about. Even if you never go to Barcelona you are having confirmed a set of attitudes and values. This includes the mysterious reference to Dr Mick at the end of the piece. If you are one of those in the know you do not need to ask who he is and if you do not recognise him you would feel foolish asking.

Activity 14

Common elements: both articles choose a particular person to be the subject of an attack: Hunter Davies and Anthea Turner. Both subjects have published – Davies an article about John Lennon, and Anthea Turner has written about herself. Both Burchill and Storr have put forward reasons to justify their views.

Burchill begins by describing irritants. She does not say explicitly that Davies is an irritant, but she precedes references to him with references to everyday irritants – and the reader is left to make the connection. Davies, who is described unflatteringly as 'squeaking', is contrasted with the strongly positive view Burchill has of Marilyn (Manson). She refers to the writing style of Davies as being very dull. She ridicules an aspect of his appearance. She accuses him of criticising her. She surmises that the reason he did this was because he was jealous of her own meteoric rise to fortune.

She categorises him as one of a type and accuses him of hypocrisy.

Coinings: sad-sack, pay-your-dues-laddie penny-a-liners

Storr assumes authority by asserting that he is speaking for many British people. He uses the term 'hatred' to describe his response to Turner. He parodies the style of a showbiz build-up. He gives examples to justify his view: her television programmes, her eyes, and her delivery. He goes on to be rude about her face. Her contribution to the literary world is described as excrement. Anthea Turner is described as having a 'worthless world of light entertainment'. Examples from her autobiography are given to justify this description.

The reader is expected to agree – to cut out a target board depiction of Anthea Turner and to pretend to have access to eight-megatonne warheads.

Coinings: '*Daily Mail*-fantasy vacant eyes'

Activity 15

Both extracts offer examples of attitudes to language and the power. The common element is the use of a term of address and the effect it has on others. The Tarentino exchange with Questioner 2 begins by the member of the audience publicly admonishing the director for using the term 'nigger'. The implication is that it is a deeply offensive racist term and in Britain white people do not use it. Tarentino justifies his use of the term by implying that he is as close to Sam Jackson as one of Sam's Black American friends could be and as such can use the word and not offend. Tarentino wins the argument and the audience (made up of Tarentino fans) sides with him.

In the novel *Riding the Rap*, the narration describes an attempt a white male made to become accepted into a black male group. The account centres upon who has the right to use the word 'nigga'. Bobby may share common experiences with 'the homes' but that does not give him access to their social group, and acceptance.

Activity 16

The two reviewers have different views about the novel. These differences lead one to ask whether there is ever a right answer as to how a text should be read, understood and valued.

Activity 17

You may well have found that you could not agree about anything. Your taste in film or music may be very different from those of others.

Activity 18

The second-person pronoun 'you' is unusual because it does not in change its spelling to show singular and plural versions. When reading the extract, one is torn between picturing an intruder and feeling that the language is describing us personally. Above all, the device preserves the anonymity of the person and adds to the sense of threat that they represent.

Activity 19

When one student did this the group thought she had written about lovers meeting illicitly. She had in fact chosen to create a piece about a child and an adult who had cared for the child in the past, but who did not want to meet the child again. Gender identity is hidden in this poem and this can add to the intrigue. It is usually the case that each response offers a convincing case for the particular genre identified. You listened to the sense each person was making of hearing your piece. None of them may be what you intended. However, you cannot control their responses – they have occurred.

Activity 20

A non-literary form has been changed into a literary form; its written language is best spoken to aid understanding; a medium for private exchanges has become public when it was published as a text-message poem.

The poem's features: it's jokey; it has technical resourcefulness and inventiveness and does have a go at expressing feeling; it uses internal rhyme; and it avoids the usual subjects of love/sex and special moments.

Glossary

adjacency pair: the basic unit of conversation, consisting of an utterance and its response

agenda-setting: the negotiation or control of the subject discussed in conversation

approbation maxim: Leech defined the maxim as 'minimise dispraise of other; maximise praise of other'. Thus, if we need to say something bad about the other person, we should choose an indirect way.

archetype: from the Greek meaning original pattern, this word is often used colloquially to mean typical or the perfect example.

audience: the person or people at whom texts are addressed

back-channel behaviour: words or sounds used by the listener to give feedback to the talker during conversation, e.g. 'Oh?' 'Yeah'

collage: the inclusion of material from various sources

connotation: not so much the surface meaning of the word, as what it implies or suggests, i.e. home = 'warmth'

creole: a pidgin that has become the mother-tongue of a speech community with developed structures

dialogue: a spoken interaction involving more than one person

discourse: this term is used in slightly different ways. Three are summarised below:

1. conversation in general, or dialogue in particular

2. a stretch of language larger than the sentence; the overall structure of texts and genres

3. the ways of seeing and saying; the ideology expressed in texts

ellipsis, (elliptical): the omission of words, usually used for reasons of economy. In spoken discourse it can create a sense of informality, e.g.

exchange: a sequence of turns in a conversation

flout, violate, imply, infer: according to Grice, **flout** means the deliberate departure from a maxim, which therefore **implies** meaning; the listener is encouraged to **infer** some meaning from the flouting of a maxim. He uses the term **violate** to mean the unintentional departure form a maxim.

foregrounding: a concept used by the Russian Formalist group of critics, bringing something to your attention by **deviation**- breaking the usual pattern, or **parallelism**- creating patterns by repetition

form v. function; sentence v. utterance; sense v. force: these three pairs of terms refer to a distinction between a particular sentence in isolation (often written down) and its meaning or effect in the context of a conversation or longer stretch of language. In isolation, the sentence 'You make great coffee.' has the grammatical form of a declarative and might seem to make a positive statement. However as the response to the question 'Do you think I'm a good cook?' its function is to avoid giving a compliment and thus implies an insult.

framing-move: words or phrases used to indicate that the speaker has completed one topic and is moving to another, e.g. 'So, anyway.'

genre: a recognisable form or type of text that is governed by the ways that particular texts are written for particular purposes

(Grice) co-operative principle: the underlying understanding between speakers and their observance of conversational rules which enables talk to take place. (the way in which most conversations are conducted in a coherent manner with particiapants acting towards one another as efficiently and collaboratively as possible) Grice suggests four maxims of Quality, Quantity, Relation and Manner

illocution: see **locution**

implicature: what can be deduced from an utterance

inference: what the speaker deduces from an utterance

interrogative, declarative, imperative:

interrogative refers to a particular sentence structure where the verb precedes the subject, e.g. 'Have you got a light?' Its function is often that of a question or request.

It is contrasted with a declarative structure: 'I have got a light.' The function of declaratives is often to make a statement which may be either true or false.

Imperative structures begin with the verb in its base form: 'Give me a light.' Or its negative form: 'Don't give a light.' Its function is often to direct action in a way stronger than a request.

locution, illocution, perlocution: the three terms distinguish between the sense of the utterance, the intended meaning and the perceived meaning

maxim: a general principle, that can serve as a rule or guide

monologue: a composition intended to be spoken by one person

move: each turn in an exchange can be termed a move

overlaps: one participant speaks before the previous participant has finished their turn

parody: an imitation of the style of a text, often including exaggeration and for satirical purposes

performative: there is a small group of verbs, called **performatives**, that *do* something, e.g. 'I promise'; 'I hereby pronounce you man and wife.'

perlocution: see **locution**

perspective: the position and distance from which events are viewed (1st person: the character to whom the event is occurring) (3rd person: an outsider, or one of the other characters involved in the situation)

phatic: phatic talk is the small talk, which frequently opens and closes conversations, whose primary function is social rather than informative

positive face, negative face, positive politeness, negative politeness: Brown and Levinson (1987) developed a framework around the concept of **face**, which refers to our public self-image. There are two aspects to this concept: **positive face** refers to our need to be liked and accepted; **negative face** refers to our right not to be imposed on. Thus politeness involves the speakers showing an awareness of other's face needs. Speakers use **positive politeness** strategies with friends to emphasise solidarity. **Negative politeness** strategies, on the other hand, emphasise respect when there is a social distance between speakers, so more formal lexis and grammar and indirect requests would be used.

pragmatics: not so much what the speaker *says*, as what the speaker *means*

presupposition: the information that a speaker assumes to be already known

purpose: the function of the text, what it is trying to do.

self-selection: in a conversation, one speaker takes a turn by such strategies as 'Can I say something?'

semantic field: a grouping of words with related meanings

soliloquy: in drama, a speech uttered by a character for the ears of the audience, rather than other characters

speech act: refers to what is done when something is said, for example 'I declare this meeting open.' does what it says. In other cases, the force of the utterance depends on the context, e.g. 'I'm in the bath.' as a response to 'The phone's ringing.' means that the speaker is unable to answer the phone.

taboo: words or expressions felt to be shocking or unacceptable in polite situations

tact maxim: Leech defined the maxim as 'minimise the cost to other; maximise the benefit to other.' For example, if we request some action that would inconvenience the other, we should use a politely indirect form of the imperative

turn-taking: a study of the ways that speakers in a conversation alternate turns to speak

vernacular: the native language of a country or nation, in particular its colloquial form

Further Reading

English Language and Literature, An Integrated Approach, Ron Norman, Stanley Thornes, 1998

A Glossary of Literary Terms, M. H. Abrams, Thomson, 1998

A Practical Glossary of Literary Terms, NATE

Talk on the Box, NATE

Language and Gender, A. Goddard and L. Patterson, Routledge, 1999

Women, Men and Language, J. Coates, Longman, 1986

Conversational Style: Analyzing Talk Among Friends, D. Tannen, Ablex, 1984

You Just Don't Understand: Men and Women in Conversation, D. Tannen, Ballantine Books, 1990

Analyzing Casual Conversation, S. Eggins and D. Slade, Continuum International Publishing Group, 1997

Directions in Sociolinguistics, J. Grumperz and D. Hymes (eds), Holt, Rhinehart and Winston, 1972

Forms of Talk, E. Goffman, University of Pennsylvania Press, 1981

Lectures on Conversation, vols 1 & 2, H. Sacks, Blackwell, 1992

Grice
Syntax and Semantics Volume 3: Speech Acts, P. Cole and J. Morgan (eds), Academic Press

Leech
Principles of Pragmatics, G. Leech, Longman, 1984

Brown and Levinson
'Universals in Language usage: politeness phenomena', P. Brown and S. Levinson, 1978, in *Questions and Politeness*, E. Goody (ed.), CUP

Lakoff
Language and Women's Place, R. Lakoff, Harper and Row, 1975

Tannen
Conversational Style: Analyzing Talk Among Friends, D. Tannen, Ablex, 1984

You Just Don't Understand: Men and Women in Conversation, D. Tannen, Ballantine Books, 1990

Edelsky

'Acquisition of an aspect of communicative competence: learning what it means to talk like a lady', C. Edelsky, 1977 in *Child Discourse*, S. Ervin-Tripp & C. Mitchell-Kernan (eds)

O'Barr & Atkins

'Women's language' or 'powerless language', W. O'Barr & B. Atkins, 1980 in *Women and Language in Literature and Society*, McConnell-Ginet et al (eds), Praeger, 1980

Goddard

Language and Gender, A. Goddard & L. Patterson, Routledge, 1999

Coates

Women, Men and Language, J. Coates, Longman, 1986

Austin

How to do things with words, J. Austin, OUP, 1976

Searle

Speech Acts: an essay in the Philosophy of Language, J. Searle, CUP, 1969